Contents

List of figures

List of tables

Acknowledgements

Few authors ever write without the aid of others and I am no exception. First, I must express my gratitude to Dr Carlton S. Van Doren, Texas A & M University. Van, in more ways than one, made it possible for me to write this book.

Special thanks go to Barbara Brown, University of Waterloo, and Bryan Smale, University of Western Ontario. Barbara, a close friend and a sports sociologist, was a constant source of criticism – whether or not I wanted it – and of ideas – which I always needed. Bryan, a close friend and one of the new breed of recreation geographers, gave encouragement and advice on concepts, content, and organization of the entire book. Patty Winterbottom and Chris Thomas, University of Waterloo, also gave welcome help on difficult sections.

Dr Bruce Mitchell, University of Waterloo, deserves singular recognition for assisting me with this book from its very inception. The Longman Group, publishers of the book, have a most valuable editor in Bruce.

This is too public a place to express my debt to my family – Carol, Kristin, and Stephanie. They lost a husband and a father and gained, temporarily, an impatient, ill-tempered writer. Private apologies and gratitudes have been expressed.

Finally, I dedicate this book

> To my Teacher:
> *m' insegnavate come l'uom s'etterna*
> *e quant'io l' abbia in grado, mentr'io vivo*
> *convien che ne la mia lingua si scerna.*
> Dante
> *Inferno*, XV 83–85

Acknowledgements

We are grateful to the following for permission to reproduce copyright material:

American Geographical Society for our Fig. 6.1 from Fig 1 (Wolfe 1964); Association of American Geographers for an extract from p 358 (Symanski 1974); Contact for our Fig 1.1 from Fig 1 (Smith & Smale 1980); Economic Geography for our Tables 4.3–4.6 from Tables 2, 3, 5 & 6 (Adams 1973); Journal of Leisure Research for extracts by F. J. Cesario and our Table 6.3 from Table 1 (van Lier 1978); Journal of Travel Research for our Table 4.1 from Table 5 (Schewe & Calantone 1978); Michigan Academy of Science, Arts and Letters for our Table 6.1 from Table 1 (Ullman & Volk 1962); Ontario Ministry of Transportation and Communication for our Fig 2.1 from Fig 10 (Wolfe 1963) and our Fig 2.9 from Fig 15 (Wolfe 1967); United States Army Engineer Institute for Water Resources for our Table 6.2 (United States Army Corps of Engineers 1974).

Foreword

The Themes in Resource Management Series has several objectives. One is to identify and to examine substantive and enduring resource management and development problems. A second is to assess responses to these problems by researchers and policy makers. This book on *Recreation Geography* by Stephen Smith addresses both of these objectives.

Understanding patterns and processes associated with recreation behaviour will be an important issue in the 1980s as both public and private decision makers attempt to provide an appropriate mix of facilities to satisfy demands. With rapidly increasing energy costs and other changes in society, decision makers cannot assume that previous trends will be the key to understanding the future. In such a situation, a book which stresses the 'methods of problem solving' is a welcome addition to the literature on recreation geography.

Indeed, the approach underlying this book reflects a belief held by many that if we are to resolve resource management problems it is essential for us to recognize the strengths and weaknesses of the evidence and analytical tools on which we base decisions. In this sense, Smith's book is highly applied, even though the focus is upon a systematic assessment of the research activity in recreation geography. We have lots of people who are eager to solve society's many problems, but it is important that they have the analytical skills to do the job.

Using examples from around the world, Smith categorizes studies as descriptive, explanatory, predictive or prescriptive. Using this four-fold classification, he examines the progress achieved and problems encountered by investigations associated with locational and travel/movement questions. The approaches to 'problem solving' range from the traditional to the more recent, from the simple to the complex, and from the qualitative to the quantitative. The reader is thus exposed to a wide range of methods and is able to see how they have been applied to a variety of problem-solving situations.

Foreword

By considering the recreation problems of both developed and lesser developed countries, by systematically and explicitly evaluating accomplish-
ments and frustrations in this field, and by suggesting issues and problems
demanding attention from those interested in recreation research, Stephen
Smith has written a book which should appeal to a broad audience.

Bruce Mitchell
University of Waterloo
Waterloo, Ontario

October 1981

Preface

This is a book about recreation geography and about how recreation geographers do the things they do. There are two purposes of this text, one obvious and one less obvious. The subject of the book – its obvious purpose – is to examine the body of methods employed by recreation geographers. *Means* of research, rather than the *ends* of research, are important in this particular book. The less obvious purpose is to create a working definition of the field of recreation geography by systematizing a representative sample (it is to be hoped) of the questions and methods employed by recreation geographers around the world and over the last two generations. Before we pursue either purpose in earnest, however, it is useful to discuss a few terms and to sketch an overview of the organization of the book.

Recreation geography is the systematic study of recreation patterns and processes on the landscape. Three words or phrases in that definition are especially important. The first is 'landscape'. This term should not be interpreted too narrowly. For our purposes, landscape includes not just the surface of the earth, but also the atmosphere (as the source of weather and the 'highway' for air travel) and subsurface environments such as caves and coral reefs. The landscape also includes intangible phenomena. The movement of people, their use of resources, political boundaries, patterns of area differentiation, climate, economic ties among industries, patterns of social organization, and human values are invisible but important aspects of landscape as we shall use the term. The landscape, in the context of recreation geography, can be either active or passive. It is affected by human activities and industrial development, and in turn, affects those activities and developments.

'Recreation' is a basic concept in recreation geography, yet it appears to defy definition. For most of this century social scientists and philosophers have put forward one definition after another, yet none has received the enduring support of a majority of researchers. No single, acceptable definition is yet in sight. A proposition of this book is that everyone has an intuitive

xiii

definition of what recreation is, and that it is not always possible or necessary to put that definition into words. On the other hand, a geographer working with 'recreation' will need to develop a working definition to explain how he selects and measures phenomena to be studied in a particular research project. This definition, though, is only a tool. It is usually not a complete, or even philosophically adequate, statement of everything that is connoted by 'recreation'.

In practice, recreation will often mean a particular set of observable land uses or an itemized list of activities. Recreation, like 'landscape' should not be interpreted too narrowly. It is meant to include phenomena also called 'tourism', 'leisure', 'sport', 'games', and to some degree, 'culture'. At the risk of sounding like Humpty Dumpty in Lewis Carroll's *Through the Looking Glass*, we are free to make these words mean whatever we wish them to mean. Common sense and sensitivity to other perspectives should guide the choice of terms and definitions, of course, and we should be consistent in our use of any particular word; but common sense and sensitivity also tell us there is no single, eternally correct definition for any of them.

The third phrase of special relevance is 'systematic study'. There are several ways in which research in recreation geography may be studied. A book might be organized around a series of social issues. Such an approach allows for a timely and often interesting analysis of important political questions. However, an issues approach can become quickly out-dated and is usually relevant to only one region or country. Alternatively, a book might be written to systematically summarize pertinent facts, such as the total area of national parks in Canada. Again, this can be a useful approach, but such a book is also limited to one time and place. The approach adopted here emphasizes a more timeless and global concept than specific issues or inventories of facts. It emphasizes the methods of problem solving. Our subjects are the techniques and applications of research.

A helpful way to categorize research methods is to begin by describing all the questions researchers ask as falling on a continuum from descriptive to normative research. Descriptive research is the basic level of scientific inquiry. It is the process of answering questions about where, what, who, and when. Description – including identification and classification – forms the basis of virtually every other type of research. Thus the book begins here: a discussion of the foundations of description in recreation geography.

The next level of research is explanation: the answering of questions about how. Some of the most exciting work currently under way is the development and verification of explanatory models. Attempts to analyse the origins of park use problems, of activity conflicts, of the patterns of international travel, and of the development of recreational landscapes are a few of the many topics researchers are currently studying.

One purpose for undertaking explanatory research is to develop models for prediction. Some predictive research is symmetrical to explanatory research. In other words, if a researcher is able to empirically explain how things came to be the way they are, he may be able to use the analysis to forecast how things will be. Another type of predictive research, however, does not rely on explanation. By observing statistical regularities, and by assuming these will hold into the future, a researcher can project the likely outcome of future events.

A long-standing subject of interest among recreation geographers is normative research: research that attempts to say what should be, or that is employed to guide policy decisions. To be able to do normative research a researcher needs to be able to describe what exists, explain how it came to be, predict future trends and consequences, and to apply value judgements to the analysis.

Each of these four types of research will be examined in detail, in the context of actual research. This research is divided, for each type, into two basic topics: travel and location. The body of the book, therefore, consists of eight chapters describing descriptive, explanatory, predictive, and normative research on both travel and locational questions in recreation geography. The text concludes with a review of the methods and topics and with some observations about future directions.

The content of the book is drawn from the work of hundreds of researchers. The interested reader is encouraged to go to the original sources for more information on any topic discussed if he needs more detail. References to all the sources used are found at the end of the book; additional reading is also provided at the end of each chapter. These lists should not be thought of as comprehensive. Nor do they necessarily represent all the best work on any particular subject, and thus by inference, berate the work of authors not on the lists. The materials cited are of high quality, that I had access to, that generally are available to other researchers, and that served my purposes. Their number could be increased two- or three-fold if all possible sources were used. However, to echo a frustration expressed by Mary Stewart at the conclusion of her three-volume fictional biography on the life of Merlin, enchanter of Camelot: if I had read any more widely, I would have never completed this book. If I had known how much there was to read, I would have never had the courage to begin. But I did begin, and I finished. It is now time for you to begin.

CHAPTER 1

Descriptive research on location

The description of location is the study of differences. For recreation, however, relevant locational differences are not easy to identify. A frozen mountain lake and a tropical beach are both recreation resources. Pollution-free air of the Canadian Rockies and the polluted air of some big city theatre districts are both associated with desirable vacations. Historical restorations, ancient ruins, and the most modern architecture interest tourists. The dark depths of karst-region caverns in Yugoslavia attract visitors as do the bright and windy observation decks of the Canadian National Tower in Toronto. People seek the solitude of wilderness as surely as they seek companionship of friends or the crush of the masses.

Recreation is not a single phenomenon with many forms. It is a myriad of different phenomena, each with different resource requirements, enjoyed by different participants who derive different satisfactions in different locations. The problem of naming, describing, and classifying recreation resources and uses is complex and inchoate. Researchers agree on that. They also agree that naming, describing, and classifying are important. They do not agree, however, on a single classification system.

Methods for describing the location of recreation resources and activities are as numerous as the objects to which they are applied. Nevertheless, the methods can be grouped into three major categories: (1) description of facility and activity location; (2) inventory of resources; and (3) description of images of regions and resources.

The ordering of these three subjects reflects their historical development. Recreational land use was the first aspect of the field to attract geographers. Tourism and recreation were recognized as important contributors to local economies as early as the 1920s. This early interest soon prompted the identification of resources that could support future growth. Finally, realizing that the connection between resource and use is subject to a filter of human values, researchers turned to analysing the role of images and perceptions in resource exploitation. Today, distinctions among these subjects in the liter-

1

ature are not as neat as this chapter might seem to suggest, but the structure does help to order a complex history of one aspect of recreation geography.

Facility and activity location

Facility location

Naming and counting existing facilities provides some of the most useful information a geographer can have. Because all of us have been naming and counting since childhood, it is difficult to describe the process without utterly confounding a common practice. In general, the task can be divided into four steps:

1. Define the objects to be counted.
2. Explain how the objects will be counted.
3. Count.
4. Summarize and present the results.

Step 1, definition, is fundamental to everything else. A good working definition will avoid unmeasurable or unobservable attributes. Recreation may ultimately be a state of mind, but unless that state has an observable effect on the landscape or on human behaviour, a geographer can do little with it. Facilities are usually defined in terms of the activity that occurs at them. A summer cottage is a seasonally occupied dwelling. Recreation clubs are places where people do things previously defined as recreation. These things may be any of a list of activities commonly agreed to be 'recreation' in a particular social setting, or they may be more broadly defined as any activity engaged in for non-economic reasons.

Whetten and Rapport (1934), to use an example from the early years of recreation research, defined a recreation development to be a combination of locale, facility, and activity: hunting and fishing on private lands; golf on designated courses; visits to a summer camp; overnight stays at a seasonally occupied dwelling. Their definition excluded some forms of recreation common in urban areas, such as attending motion pictures, and some forms of rural recreation, such as picnicking along roadsides. On the other hand, they did include some activities that might not 'really' be recreation. Someone who moved for the season into a summer house and continued the daily routine of work was considered to be the same as someone who rented a summer cottage for a one-week vacation.

There are always limits to objective, working definitions, but there is no acceptable alternative to their use. Only objective definitions allow for independent verification of findings. Ironically, it is difficult to give a good working definition of 'objective'. Here, and elsewhere in this book, 'objective' is meant to describe that which is systematic, explicit, and generally verifiable by others. Research can never be totally value-free or devoid of subjective judgements. One must strive to find a balance between the unacceptable

2

extremes of total bias and untested subjectivity on one hand, and unattainable, totally value-free objectivity on the other. In practice, objectivity is an ideal rather than a reality.

Step 2, explanation, establishes the units of measurement and the scale of description. Because any single unit of measurement emphasizes only one aspect of facility development, geographers often use several units in the same study. Whetten and Rapport used four. On a county-by-county basis they tabulated the number of individual facilities, the total land area for each type, the percentage of county area for each type, and the assessed value of associated real estate.

Per capita measures are also common. Dividing a total figure by the population (or some other measure of size) yields a measure of relative size or participation. A special version of this is the locational quotient. Rooney (1974) provides an example. To describe the distribution of the production of professional football players in the United States, Rooney first divided the number produced in each state by the population of the state to obtain a *per capita* measure. He then calculated the national *per capita* average. By dividing the state rate by the national average, he obtained a measure of the relative productivity of each state. A quotient of 1.0 indicates a state produces players at a rate comparable to the national average. Rates above or below 1.0 indicate above or below productivity, respectively.

Another ratio that has been found useful for tourism research is Defert's (1960) tourist function, *Tf*. *Tf* is the ratio between the capacity of a region for receiving visitors (measured by the number of tourist beds, *N*) and the number of 'hosts' to receive them (measured by the resident population, *P*):

$$Tf = \frac{N \times 100}{P} \qquad [1.1]$$

Defert's *Tf* has been measured for Colorado (Thompson 1971), Provence (Atlas de Provence 1976), selected Pacific islands (Rajotte 1977), and New Zealand (Pearce 1979). The function is useful for comparing the relative importance of tourism among comparable regions, but it does have a limitation. World cities, such as New York, London, Paris, and Tokyo, have *Tf*s that are relatively small compared to resort towns such as Las Vegas, Puerto Vallarta, or Brighton, yet the world cities may account for more than half of all tourist income in their countries. *Tf* indicates only the relative importance of tourism within a regional economy; it does not indicate how important that region is as a tourist destination within the context of a national economy.

The units of measurement presented have been applied at scales ranging from individual cities to entire countries. Choice of scale depends on a study's objectives, on available data, and on the scale of other studies that are to be used for comparison. As a rule, a scale of aggregation that produces 10 to 100 regions is useful. Fewer regions can result in generalizations too broad to be meaningful; more regions can produce undecipherable complexity.

Steps 3 and 4, counting and summarizing, conclude the description. Data for descriptive studies come from two general sources – information collected expressly for a particular project (primary data) and information collected by other researchers for other purposes (secondary data). Primary data, whether from questionnaires, field observations, or the laboratory, can give a researcher information available nowhere else. A researcher can also be sure of consistency in definitions and counting. If any judgements have to be made about a particular case or observation, they can be made so as to not jeopardize the ultimate purpose of the project. Primary data collection, however, is usually expensive, time-consuming, and administratively demanding. Description of the specific techniques used in geographic sampling are beyond this book. Interested readers can find a useful overview in Berry and Baker (1968). Hendee, *et al.* (1976) describe a method for inventorying dispersed recreation sites in primitive areas.

Secondary sources, such as data files of surveys, maps, statistical reports, and national censuses, avoid the expense and administrative problems of original surveys for the user. For this benefit, a geographer must accept the methods, definitions, purposes, and abilities of the original data collectors. Information may have been miscoded; definitions may have been inconsistently applied; potential cases may have been missed through ignorance, misinterpretation, or carelessness. Of course, these problems are not avoided just because you collect your own data. If the original researchers are reputable, well-trained, and well-funded, and if the information adequately suits the purpose of a project, one should consider using a secondary data source.

The actual enumeration methods are influenced by the purpose of the study. Frequency tables and maps are traditional. In addition to providing useful summaries, these can be easily compared with those from other studies to formulate or test possible explanations. Pattern descriptions can highlight areas of relative deprivation or surplus, such as Piperoglou's (1966) 'vacation regions', Ouma's (1970) identification of facility shortages for East African tourism, and Taylor's (Taylor, V. 1975) 'recreation business districts'. Maps of recreation developments can also be used to identify regions of relatively uniform character to serve as planning districts (Moeller and Beazley, n.d.).

The previous studies describe the location of single facilities at one point in time. They usually indicate nothing about the total distribution, nor do they easily adapt to describing pattern changes. One method available for summarizing complex patterns in a single statistic that can be charted over time is nearest-neighbour analysis.

Nearest-neighbour analysis (Clark and Evans 1955; Morisita 1957; Pielo 1959) was developed to describe vegetation distributions. The nearest-neighbour statistic, R, equals 1.0 if the distribution of individual plants (or other units) is random. An aggregated pattern or a pattern more regular than random, produces a value less than or greater than 1.0, respectively. Grieg-Smith (1964) has reviewed applications of nearest-neighbour analysis for a number of different problems. Dacey (1967), Dacey and Tung (1962), and Pinder, *et al*. (1979) have described some of the problems and methods of correcting for these in nearest-neighbour analysis.

R is a ratio between the observed average distance to each point's nearest neighbour ($\bar{r}_0$) and the average distance expected ($\bar{r}_e$) if the pattern were random:

$$R = \frac{\bar{r}_0}{\bar{r}_e}$$ [1.2]

where: $\bar{r}_e = \dfrac{1}{2\sqrt{\lambda}}$

λ = density of points

Rolfe (1964) applied this measure to test his belief that the pattern of urban parks tends to become more regular over time. The degree of regularity is measured by the degree to which the pattern of parks approximates to the ideal hexagonal distribution of central place theory. Under this condition, $R = 2.1419$. Rolfe tested the hypothesis that R approaches 2.1419 over time in the Lansing, Michigan (USA) park system. He represented each park by a point, and plotted distributions for 1920, 1930, 1940, 1950, and 1960. After calculating R for each year, he compared them and concluded that, although the pattern of parks was random before the Second World War, it became significantly more regular after the war. Lovingood and Mitchell (1978) compared the distributions of public and private recreational facilities in Columbia, South Carolina (USA) by means of nearest-neighbour analysis. They observed that public facilities had a ratio significantly less than 1.0, indicating a tendency for these facilities to agglomerate. Private facilities showed a more complex pattern – some highly clustered and some approaching a uniform distribution.

Activity location

Counting people is not as simple as counting facilities. People move. Numbers and patterns of users change with weather, time of day, day of week, season of year, and in response to the crowd's perception of itself. Because of the difficulty in describing this ebb and flow, much work has been devoted to refining methods of counting users. Manned gates and doors, mandatory and voluntary registration systems, records of ticket sales, photo-electric counters, mechanical counters, pressure-sensitive counters, aerial photography with both visible and infra-red film, and cordons of field surveyors hidden in strategic locations have all been tried. Some of the literature discussing these methods includes James and Henley (1968), Cordell, James, and Griffith (1970), James and Schreuder (1972), James, Wingle, and Griggs (1971), James and Quinkert (1972), Burton (1974), Lime and Lorence (1974), and Sidaway (1972).

As always, the first step is to choose appropriate units of measurement. In addition to individual bodies, one might count groups or vehicles. Cheek

5

and Burdge (1974) have discussed the rationale for considering the social group of an activity as part of its description. Several other units of measurement are employed to summarize user counts. In addition to simple totals, counts can include percentages, average lengths of stay, frequencies of different lengths of stay, or a combination of several variables such as 'tourist-nights' or 'patron time per acre' (Foster 1964). Numbers of visitors can be compared to a resident population, to the number of people doing something else, or to the number of people who do nothing at all. The choice, again, depends on the purpose of study.

Burton (1974) mapped the number of pedestrians and cars per acre in her study of Cannock Chase, Staffordshire (UK) to obtain better information on the effects of access, parking, weather, and the location of washrooms on the distribution of visitors. White, *et al.* (1978) obtained records of Ontario provincial park camping attendance and compared these to the number of complaints about rowdyism and crime in the camp-grounds. A 'rowdyism quotient' was calculated for each park by dividing the number of complaints by the total number of campers in one season. Any park with more than 0.01 complaints per camper was arbitrarily described as a problem park. These were then studied in greater detail to learn possible causes and cures.

Inventory of resources

Arithmetic methods

The simplest method of inventorying resources – whether one is interested in the simple physical presence of resources or in the potential of a region to support some form of recreation – is to define those resources considered important and then to count them. Resource inventorying can be done through simple enumeration or by developing relatively complex 'systems' models for arithmetically combining descriptive variables.

A study typical of dozens of simple inventories is the US Outdoor Recreation Resources Review Commission's examination of shoreline recreation resources (Campbell, *et al.* 1962). Along the coasts of the Great Lakes, the Atlantic, the Gulf of Mexico, and the Pacific Ocean, Campbell calculated the total length of shoreline, bluff shore, marsh shore, beach shore, the number and size of designated public recreation areas, and the number and extent of restricted areas. These data were then tabulated and mapped by state.

Killion (1969) proposed a slightly more complex method for inventorying recreation resources. He examined a region, the North Coast of Australia, and divided it into four broad geographical zones: I coastal; II estuarine; III riverine; and IV inland. Each zone was then divided into five 'themes' representing potential uses: (a) general recreation; (b) natural landscape appreciation; (c) unique natural area use; (d) wilderness area use; (e) historical or cultural appreciation. A zone code and a theme code were combined for specific sites to form a descriptive index. Kingscliffe, for example, is a coastal resort area that supports both general recreation and has some exceptional landscape scenery, so it is indexed as I/a,b/.

The value of, and capacity for, tourism in each region were described with other indices by Killion. He defined a tourist value index as the product of mean accommodation costs; the number of parties using commercial accommodation, and the proportion of all regional expenditures devoted to recreation. Capacity was defined as the ratio between the resident population and the number of available beds – essentially the inverse of Defert's *Tf*.

An index describing the potential user-satisfaction from visiting a nature preserve to view wildlife, based on a census of wildlife populations, has been developed by Chanter and Owen (1976). Because animal and plant diversity is one of the major attractions of preserves (Duffey 1974), Chanter and Owen combined two measures of wildlife populations into a single index:

$$\theta = \log(\beta N) \qquad\qquad [1.3]$$

where: N = total number of animals seen

β = the complement of Simpson's index of species diversity:

$$1 - \left[\frac{\displaystyle\sum_{j=1}^{k} n_j(n_j - 1)}{N(N-1)} \right]$$

n_j = number of individuals of jth species seen
k = total number of species seen

These types of classification and indices are useful, but they have certain limitations. Definitions of geographical zones, activity themes, or user satisfaction are not often based on any theory. Nor is there usually an adequate explanation of how different classifications are to be distinguished from each other. While the existence of numerous regional and resource classifications attests to the inherent value of the ideas represented by Killion's and Chanter and Owen's work, a truly useful system should be capable of adaptation to a wide variety of environments and setting, and should be based on some tested concepts.

Planners and decision-makers often desire information about intangible (non-physical) aspects of resources and regions. Financial characteristics, such as real estate values, are an example. Other intangible variables include user fees, hours of operation, name and type of operating agency, and type of programmes available. Many planners spend as much time, effort, and money obtaining these data as they do to compile physical inventories.

An example of this type of work is that of the New York State Comprehensive Outdoor Recreation Plan (State of New York 1970). This plan is notable not only for its incorporation of intangible data, but also for the development of a method to estimate missing physical data. If a local agency failed to report the number of campsites, for example, state planners employed a regression equation to estimate the number of sites. The campsite model, calibrated from existing inventory data, was of the form:

Number of campsites = 12.8 × (total park acreage + 0.308) [1.4]

Other equations were estimated for picnic facilities, shoreline developments, and pools.

Another aspect of the New York state plan provides an illustration of other methods used to identify recreation resources. An information retrieval system known as LUNAR (Land Use and Natural Resources) was developed from an examination of statewide aerial photographs of 1 square kilometre sections. Existing land uses, geological and human features, and vegetative cover were identified and computer-coded. Maps showing the distribution of selected features in any combination could then be produced.

Regional information systems such as LUNAR are based on a scale too broad for site-specific studies, but they do reduce field work by eliminating areas that are unlikely to have any potential for development or that might be environmentally sensitive.

The listing and mapping of resources is made more sophisticated when one bases the lists and maps on a theoretical typology of resource types and uses. Rather than developing a single list of resource variables, such methods utilize several lists related to each other in a systems or ecological context. One example is Parks Canada's proposal for a system of wild rivers. This particular system was based on a four-part inventory: (1) land and aquatic biotic and abiotic features; (2) scenic quality; (3) human presence along the river; and (4) potential for future recreational activities.

The first and most lengthy step was to produce a complete inventory of biotic and abiotic features and to assess the scenic quality of sites along likely rivers. Rivers most representative of previously defined natural regions were then selected and further assessed to determine water quality and human encroachment. The result of this description was to produce a short list of rivers that might be considered for protection as wild river recreation. An important part of the debate about protection was the delineation of the 'zone of influence' around each river. On-site surveys conducted early in the initial evaluation were consulted to provide more information about boundary-related variables. These variables included how far away from the river recreationists could see and hear. This was influenced by the noise of the river and the height of both the riverbank and streamside vegetation. Distribution of possible pollution sources was also mapped. The extent of the drainage basin and the presence of privately owned land were given special consideration because these would influence both the natural and political future of the river.

One criticism of the resource description used in the wild rivers proposal was that the description was not tied to specific recreation activities. This may not be a relevant objection if the intent is to identify a resource that ought to be protected because of some inherent wild quality, but it is a serious weakness if that quality depends on recreational use. An early approach that ties resource description to use was developed by Fisher (1962) and modified by Taylor (1965).

The Fisher–Taylor method applies to intensive outdoor recreation, such as camping. Five site criteria were identified to summarize the resources needed for these activities: (1) presence of a site attraction; (2) adequate vegetation coverage; (3) suitable slope; (4) sufficient size; and (5) good drinking water. An on-site survey is made to assess the presence/absence or suitability/unsuitability of each criterion. A site with all five criteria present is highly suitable; a site with an attraction but lacking one other requirement is considered good. The absence of two qualities lowers the site to fair, while the absence of three or more qualities disqualifies the site from development. Definitions and assessments are made by experienced planners. The system can be modified to describe winter sports areas, extensive recreation areas, or other types of use areas.

Criticisms of Fisher–Taylor include the problem of defining the criteria so that independent verification of ratings can be made. Further, there is no theoretical basis for defining what is included in the concept of intensive outdoor recreation. Finally, their method requires on-site evaluation, and thus it is not always practical for regional reconnaissance studies. The need for broad regional studies of land capabilities was recognized by Taylor and led to a revision of his method (Taylor and Thompson, 1966). In this revision, they added a preliminary analysis to select possible sites and to eliminate unlikely ones. After this had been done the analysis could proceed as before. This study is especially significant because it formed part of the basis for the massive Canada Land Inventory, which is discussed later in this chapter.

Other criticisms of Fisher–Taylor can be overcome by adding more precision to the definition of activities. This precision, of course, leads to greater costs in collecting data. A method that adds a limited degree of precision at modest costs is that of Coppock, Duffield, and Sewell (1974). Their analysis included three classes of activities and one limiting environmental factor: general land-based recreation; water-based recreation; scenic area recreation; and the presence of environmentally sensitive areas. The scale of analysis is regional, which allows the use of aerial photographs and maps.

To use their method, one begins by dividing a region into squares, 2 kilometres on a side. From secondary sources and regional resource inventories, a number of judgements about the ability of each square to support each type of recreation, or the presence of sensitive areas which detracts from recreation potential, are made. Each activity group is defined in terms of specific activities. Land-based recreation, for example, means (1) camping, caravanning, and picnicking, (2) pony-trekking, (3) walking and hiking, (4) game shooting, (5) rock-climbing, and (6) skiing. Squares are given one point for each specific activity they can support.

Scores for each group are combined and expressed as a percentage of the total possible. These percentages are summed and multiplied by 100. Activity scores are added; the sensitive area score is subtracted. A total of 250 or more usually indicates a site with good potential for development.

The Canada Land Inventory may be one of the most ambitious resource inventories ever undertaken. The purpose of the project was to measure and describe the potential of every part of Canada (except for incorporated areas) for producing user days of recreation, for supporting wildlife, for growing timber, and for agriculture. The recreation classification system was based on existing resource characteristics rather than on manmade potentials. Current preferences for rural outdoor recreation activities were considered, with a distinction made between land-intensive and land-extensive activities. Water bodies were not classified, although adjacent shorelands were.

Altogether seven classes of recreation productivity were established, ranging from 1 (very high) to 7 (very low). Twenty-five subclasses were identified to indicate positive features associated with the more general land-use classes. These tended to be described in terms of activities that could be supported. Each land-use class was limited to a maximum of three subclasses. To implement this system, field researchers were hired to collect local information and to interpret it using uniform, national guidelines and standards. The results were finally published in a series of recreation-potential maps showing the distribution of land-use classes and capabilities at a scale of 1 : 250,000.

The Canada Land Inventory provides an example of both the scope of projects that might be undertaken and of the difficulties some descriptive projects can run into. Because more than one person collected data, there is some concern over the consistency of data interpretation in the field. And if one can accept that the data are consistent at the national level, then the criticism can be raised that the interpretations should be based on local values and preferences rather than on some national average. For example, the recreational value of 1,000 hectares of trees in the Canadian prairies would be quite high because of the lack of forest cover, but it would be assigned only an average productivity rating because of the predominance of forest cover in the nation as a whole.

Similarly, the dominant values used to select activities and to evaluate resources were also based on national averages – that is, on the tastes of the dominant social groups in Canada in the 1960s. Some value system must be used, of course, but its choice and the point in time it is assessed is a matter for careful consideration.

We have already noted that the Inventory ignored water bodies. The reason for this was the problem of obtaining reliable information for the biological distribution of fishing resources across large bodies of water. Finally, the Inventory might be criticized for its emphasis on productivity and the use of user-days as relevant measures. Some wilderness areas may be very important national resources, but they could have low carrying capacities, even for land extensive activities, and as a result, would receive a low evaluation.

Table 1.1 is a summary of the land use capability classes and subclasses.

Table 1.1 The land use classes of the Canada Land Inventory

Classes

1 Very high capability –	These lands have natural capability to engender very high total annual use of one or more intensive activities. These lands should be able to generate and sustain a level of use comparable to that evident at an outstanding and large bathing beach or a nationally known ski slope.
2 High capability –	These lands have natural capability to engender and sustain high total annual use based on one or more intensive activities.
3 Moderately high capability –	These lands have natural ability to engender and sustain moderately high total annual use based on moderate-intensive or intensive activities.
4 Moderate capability –	These lands have natural capability to engender and sustain moderate total annual use based on dispersed activities.
5 Moderately low capability –	These lands have natural capability to engender and sustain moderately low total annual use based on dispersed activities.
6 Low capability –	These lands lack the natural quality and significant features to rate higher, but have the natural capability to engender and sustain low total annual use based on dispersed activities.
7 Very low capability –	These lands have practically no capability for any popular type of recreation activity, but there may be some opportunity for very specialized activities with recreation aspects, or they may simply provide open space.

Subclasses

A – land providing access to water for angling or viewing of sports fishing
B – shoreland capable of supporting family beach activities; in high class unit this may include family bathing; in classes 4 and 5 this may include dry land use due to cold water
C – land fronting on and providing access to waterways with significant capability for canoe tripping
D – shoreland with deeper inshore water suitable for swimming and boat mooring
E – land with vegetation possessing recreational value
F – waterfall or rapids
G – significant glacier viewing or experience
H – historic or pre-historic site
J – area offering opportunities for gathering items of popular interest
K – shoreland or upland suited to organized camping

11

L – interesting landform features other than rock formations

M – frequent small water-bodies or continuous streams in upland areas

N – land, usually shoreland, suited for lodging use

O – land affording opportunity for viewing upland wildlife

P – area exhibiting cultural landscape patterns of agricultural, industrial, or social interest

Q – areas exhibiting variety in topography or land and water relationships that afford or enhance opportunities for general outdoor recreation and aesthetic appreciation

R – interesting rock formations

S – a combination of slopes, snow conditions, and climate, providing downhill skiing opportunities

T – thermal springs

U – shoreland fronting water suitable for yachting and deep-water boat tripping

V – a vantage point that offers a superior view

W – land affording opportunity for viewing wetland wildlife

X – miscellaneous features with recreational capability

Y – shoreland providing access to water suitable for general family boating

Z – areas exhibiting major, permanent, non-urban manmade structures of recreational interest

---

Source: Canada Land Inventory

Chubb and Bauman's (1977) RIVERS model is another method developed to assess recreation potential. RIVERS is actually a computer program to describe and compare resources of entire river basins against a previously defined set of resource needs of each of sixteen activities. The first step is to select one of the sixteen activities and to inventory a pre-set list of river variables. These variables are divided into eight categories: basic physical features; special physical features; water quality; bank soil limitations; biological features; adjoining land uses; aesthetics; and accessibility. Inventory information, from primary and secondary sources, is coded on a five-point ordinal scale, summarized by 1 mile (1.6 km) segments, and is stored in a machine-readable format. Chubb and Bauman wrote a program to select those variables previously designated by them as potentially relevant to a particular activity in a specific environment. Once selected, the program assigns a positive or negative weight to reflect the nature and importance of each variable. All signs and weights are expressed as a percentage of the total possible for each activity. These scores then allow for comparisons among various rivers.

Limitations to Chubb–Bauman include the need to assign subjectively determined weights to each variable, and the availability and reliability of secondary data sources. RIVERS also fails to adjust for potential conflicts among uses. Most limiting, though, is the fact that this specific technique requires access to the program the authors have written. However, other researchers can follow the general logic and compile their own systems for combining weighted variables for activities of interest to them.

Nefedova (1974) and a team of researchers studying the Moscow Oblast used a 'qualitative systems analysis' (their term), logically similar to RIVERS, to combine 'internal' landscape characteristics (landforms) and 'external' landscape characteristics (connections among landscapes and human activity). Analysis began with the compilation of three maps for the region: a general landscape map, a land-use map, and a map of constraints. All elements of each map were classified as 'active', 'limiting', or 'compensatory'. Active factors are those that encourage an activity, such as the presence of scenic attractions for hikers. Compensatory factors affect the quality of the activity, such as the steepness of the trail for hikers. Limiting factors include the presence of environmentally sensitive areas, developed areas, and areas with undesirable characteristics, such as swamps or high noise levels.

After classifying the resources on each map, Nefedova identified ('from previous experience') activities the resources could support. The mix of activities can then be adjusted to reflect proposed zoning or development changes in the landscape. Finally, the mix of resources, their evaluations, the distribution of potential activities, and the distribution of current and potential land uses are compared to develop a plan for future growth.

A resource whose importance to outdoor recreation and tourism is so apparent that it is often taken for granted, is climate. One of the better descriptive studies of the relationship between climate and recreation is the work by Crowe, McKay, and Baker (1977) on the recreational climates of Ontario (Canada). Their goal was to produce a standardized, quantitative summary of Ontario climatic conditions, summer and winter, in terms of their effects on selected outdoor activity groups. The activities they chose were automobile touring, passive recreation, land sports and hunting, beach activities, swimming and water sports, skiing, and snow-mobiling. Separate variables were examined for summer and winter. Seasonal conditions were described by:

Summer	Winter
Air temperature	Duration of daylight
Humidity (directly and in combination with temperature)	Air temperature (directly and in combination with wind)
Precipitation	Precipitation
Cloud cover	Cloud cover
Visibility	Visibility
Wind speed	Snow and ice cover
Water temperature	Length of season
Length of season	

Appropriate definitions for each variable were established and then the spatial and temporal patterns mapped and summarized. Similar studies have been completed for the Canadian Northwest Territories (Crowe 1970) and for Western Europe and the Mediterranean area (Heurtier 1968).

A different approach to the study of weather and its effects on recreation is illustrated by the work of Danilova (1973). Her approach was to concentrate more directly on the physiological effects of weather conditions than on general climatic patterns. She defined optimal climatic conditions for a norm of healthy individuals, eighteen to forty years old, engaged in light physical labour. These conditions were measured in terms of their effects on skin temperature, perspiration, and the load placed on the heat regulatory system of the body. The relationship between climate and these variables was established and the relevant variables mapped for the Baltic region with isolines showing the number of days during a given period with weather conditions producing the optimal conditions for recreation.

Other work in the relationship between climate or weather and recreation is often anecdotal (e.g. Pigram and Hobbs 1975; Perry 1972). Considering the potentially large effects of weather on the recreational economy of an area, or of the effects of a reputation (good or bad) of a region created by weather, more systematic studies are needed. Analysis of the perceptions of climate and weather, and of relative benefits and costs of obtaining better climatic and meteorological information is especially important.

Deglomerative methods

More advanced methods for resource inventories include deglomerative and agglomerative classifications. Deglomeration is the process of dividing a region or a set of resources into increasingly specific subgroups. Agglomeration is the reverse – resources are grouped into increasingly general categories.

Deglomeration is useful when one has a reasonably good understanding of a general pattern and wishes to add precision to the understanding by identifying sub-units within that whole. Deglomeration requires a theoretical structure or set of rules that allows a phenomenon to be divided and subdivided into mutually exclusive categories. The rules identify how the categories relate to each other within a given level and between levels, and indicate when to stop the process of deglomeration.

A deglomerative classification has two aspects, form and structure. Structure is the conceptual relationship of different divisions within the entire hierarchy. Form, on the other hand, is the expression of that hierarchy in reality. In other words, a deglomerative hierarchy must have a conceptual basis for its organization and it must have a practical application to the landscape or resource base it describes.

Deglomeration is often used to describe biotic regions in parks. The biophysical inventory of Pukaskwa National Park in Ontario (Canada) (Gimbarzevsky, Lopovkhine, and Addison 1978) is typical. Using data from secondary sources, the researchers divided the resources base into three classes: land, vegetation, and water. Each was subdivided, and a brief description made of the resources at each level. Land areas were first classified as part of an overall land region, based on geological landforms and climate. Pukaskwa is located in the Abitibi Uplands of the North American James Bay Physiographic Region. Climatically, it is located in the Lake Timagami Humid Eastern Ontario Region. Definitions of these regions were based on previous, independent work.

On this basis, four land districts were delineated. These smaller units are characterized by distinctive patterns of relief, geology, and vegetation. Each land district was divided into several land systems, that were in turn divided into land types characterized by relatively homogeneous topography, soils, drainage, and origin of surface materials.

Park vegetation classes were subdivided from the most general – the vegetative region. This region is an expression of a complex stand of climax species in a distinct climatic region. A vegetative region can be divided into vegetation sections, stands, types, and finally, subtypes on the basis of increasingly precise distinctions between vegetation characteristics.

Water resources were simplest to classify. They were divided into rivers and streams, lakes and ponds, and coastal features.

Another example of deglomeration is Filippovich's (1979) description of recreation resource development around Moscow. Although he did not use as many levels as the Pukaskwa study, he considered more variables. The Moscow Oblast was first divided into transportation corridors to form a matrix for describing the location of users on the landscape on an average summer day. The oblast was then divided into recreational and non-recreational land uses. Location of recreational land uses were described relative to the location of other land uses, transportation corridors, and distance from the Moscow ring road. Finally, the oblast was subdivided into natural feature zones: forests, lakes, hills, and so forth. These zones also provided a rubric for describing the distribution of users and resources. A similar approach, with more detail and precision in subdivisions, was used by Niewiarowski (1976) to describe the recreation and tourism potentials of the Bydogszcz Voivodship in Poland.

Smith and Smale (1980) developed a deglomerative hierarchy of park users and facilities for the Canadian national park system (Fig. 1.1). At the most general level (Level A), all people entering a national park were divided into: (1) visitors; (2) traffic passing through the park; and (3) all others, such as park residents and local commercial traffic. Visitors were then subdivided on the basis of how they entered the park (Level B), where they came from (Level C), what they did while in the park (Level D), and where they did what they did (Level E). The five levels take a researcher, planner, or manager from the context of policy decisions through progressively more specific user-related issues, to detailed concerns about the type of development and management at specific sites. The hierarchy provides a flexible way of describing users and associated resources in terms that allow a researcher, planner, or manager to focus on specific problems at any level of complexity.

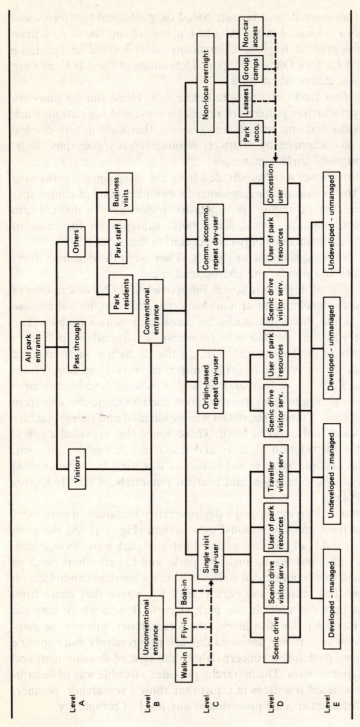

Figure 1.1 An example of a deglomerative hierarchy: the classification of users of Canadian national parks and related areas (after Smith and Smale 1980)

Agglomerative methods

Requirements for agglomeration are generally the same as those for deglomeration except for the need of the researcher to have some theoretical understanding of the final 'total' description that is the end-product. This is more difficult to achieve in practice and, as a consequence, relatively few agglomerative studies have been done.

One of the few examples is Dorney's (1976) classification of urban land for recreation planning. The method agglomerates maps (at a scale of 1:5,000 to 1:15,000) to produce a generalized description of the urban landscape in a recreational context.

Burial grounds, pictographs, village sites, and other features associated with pre-Caucasian settlement were identified from secondary sources and field surveys to produce the first map. Existing parks, churches, libraries, theatres, and other modern cultural and recreational landscape features are plotted on two maps, one for the dominant culture and one for special ethnic groups. Together, these three maps were combined to form a single pattern of historical/cultural land uses.

Variables that describe aspects of the abiotic resource base, such as river valleys and soil slope, were defined, located, and mapped. Dorney grouped these into five categories: air system variables; sub-surface geological variables; superficial geological and soil variables; hydrological variables; and noise levels. These were aggregated to produce an abiotic landscape map.

Next, a series of biotic variables were grouped into aquatic and terrestrial groups. These were located and mapped, with accompanying notations about the capability of each resource to support recreation and about values and problems of each resource. Together, the aquatic and terrestrial biotic maps produced an aggregated picture of the urban biotic community.

Finally, the three patterns – historical/cultural, abiotic, and biotic – were combined to produce an aggregate pattern showing the location of existing recreational features, areas for potential development, and areas that are barriers for development. A similar method has been applied to regional planning by Dubaniewicz (1976) in the Łódź Voivodship of Poland. Because he worked at a regional scale, Dubaniewicz included climatic variables and travel times from population centres as well as human, biotic, and abiotic resource patterns. The logic common to these methods is the hierarchical combination of variables describing different aspects of the total environment. Once combined, the pattern is subjectively evaluated to identify any relationships of interest.

An approach that represents an alternative to this type of agglomeration is the incorporation of objective resource evaluations as part of the agglomeration. An example of this is Isachenko's (1973) work on the recreation potential of the region around Leningrad (USSR). Isachenko began with a map of a combination of current land uses, vegetation, and *urochishcha* (landscape units composed of geomorphological forms, soils, and drainage

17

patterns). His next step was to examine this initial inventory map and to group combinations of natural features into areas of relatively homogeneous 'recreation potentials'. Isachenko emphasized this was not a simple arithmetic weighting of descriptive variables – such as that used by Chubb and Bauman – but rather a complex analysis involving all relevant variables. Unfortunately, he did not explain how this 'complex analysis' was actually done.

Once he obtained the 'evaluative map' that was the result of the first stage of analysis, he prepared a 'predictive' map to show likely patterns of land use and landscape features, based on the assumption that current trends will continue uninterrupted. This is both the key link and the weakest link in the analysis. Isachenko believed that no reliable examples of landscape forecasting had been accomplished in a form that could be applied to his method of agglomeration. Lacking these maps, he assumed no change. In the final step, the evaluative map was compared to the predictive map, and with objectives and policies of relevant land managing agencies, to produce a 'recommendatory' map showing future development and preservation zones.

Images of regions and resources

Descriptions of images may be naïve, preferential, or evaluative. Naïve descriptions report only the facts of images as perceived by recreationists, with no inquiries into the likes or dislikes of the recreationist. Preferential description, on the other hand, records likes and dislikes, as well as the images. Finally, evaluative description compares a resource assessment to some neutral standard.

Naïve description

Naïve description of the images of resources and regions is often used in tourism research. The purpose is to identify how potential tourists perceive vacation regions, which then allows a marketing professional to either build on a favourable image or to improve a negative one. Given this purpose, image studies often culminate in a predictable model of preferences, but this is subsequent to the description of the actual image. We will focus on the descriptive task only.

Typical among image studies is Scott, Schewe, and Frederick's (1978) analysis of the images of car travellers in the US New England states. Tourists who stopped at information centres were asked questions about their perceptions of New England states with special emphasis on predominant scenery, highway conditions, history, culture, water quality, climate, accommodation, and the friendliness of the residents. Ratings were compared on each characteristic for all states to identify the images that set one state apart from its neighbours. Similar image studies have been undertaken by

Hunt (1974) for the western states and by Goodrich (1978) for Florida, California, Hawaii, Mexico, and some Caribbean islands.

Other geographers have described how historical migrations, both short-term (such as vacations) and long-term (such as settlement changes) are influenced by images rather than reality. Among these are Zaring's (1977) work on literary accounts of Wales during the Romantic era, Blouet and Lawson (1975) on railroad promotion of the American Great Plains, and Gould and White (1974) on location decisions of Tanzanian bureaucrats. The nature of all this work suggests, of course, that there are significant differences between the image and the reality. Some of the effects of this disparity in the context of tourism is described in Britton (1979) and in Chapter 8 of this book.

Preferential description

Preferential descriptions, also known as aesthetic measurement studies, formed an important group of studies during the late 1960s and early 1970s. Much of this research stemmed from a concern over the need to objectively describe the effects of landscape alterations on scenery in terms of human preferences. Because of this policy-based origin, many of these studies resulted in models to predict the effects of specified changes. As before, however, our focus here is only on the descriptive phase of this research.

The basic technique to evaluate landscape aesthetics is to assign a certain number of points to a particular scene to represent its relative beauty to a particular group or society. One of the most influential studies has been Fines's (1968) work on landscapes in East Sussex. Fines asked a group of people skilled in design work to assign a point value to each of a series of landscape photographs in comparison to a reference photograph of an indifferent landscape whose value was set at 1.0. The respondents were given a geometrical scale for a guide:

16.0 – 32.0 Spectacular
 8.0 – 15.9 Superb
 4.0 – 7.9 Distinguished
 2.0 – 3.9 Pleasant
 1.0 – 1.9 Undistinguished
   0 – 0.9 Unsightly

Most landscapes would not be ranked above 'distinguished'. The best scenery in Great Britain, such as the views of the Cuillin across Loch Coruisk, would approach 18. Views of the Himalayan peaks from their foothills might approach 24. Once the judges had become familiar with the photographs, they were asked to use them and the consensus point value assigned to them as a scale to rank landscapes viewed on-site around East Sussex. The judges were sent into different parts of the county, evaluated as many views as pos-

19

sible from all angles, and noted their ratings on a map. The individual maps were combined to form a scenic evaluation map of East Sussex for use in planning the location of power line rights of way and the location of road extensions.

Several criticisms have been made of Fines's work, especially by Linton (1968). Linton was uncomfortable with both the nomenclature and the geometrical progression of Fines's scale. A more pragmatic criticism was that this method is expensive and time-consuming. Fines's survey of about 2,000 square kilometres required four years of part-time work. At best, this could have been reduced to five months. A five-month project is reasonable, but if anyone wished to replicate the method in a larger region, the time would increase dramatically. Moreover, the cost of supporting trained judges in the field for months, or even years, can become prohibitive.

To avoid these difficulties, one might attempt to map the elements of the landscape that contribute to scenic beauty, and then evaluate the map in a laboratory. Linton suggested that there were two such elements: land use and landforms. Both could be mapped at a variety of scales from secondary sources, once specific categories were set. If one assigned points to each type of landform and use, a composite score could be obtained that summarized the beauty of the landscape. Linton proposed the following system for Scotland:

Landforms	Points	Land uses	Points
Mountains	8	Wild landscapes	6
Bold hills	6	Richly varied farming	5
Hill country	5	Varied forest with moors and farms	4
Plateau uplands	3	Moors	3
Low uplands	2	Treeless farms	1
Lowlands	0	Continuous forest	−2
		Urban and industrial land	−5

Certain criticisms can be made of Linton's method. Landscape beauty may be a 'whole', that is more than the sum of its parts. A component approach that merely sums up two or more scores is therefore theoretically unsound. Although Linton's system adds a measure of objectivity in that everyone should apply the same points to the same landform, the basis of the point system is arbitrary; certainly many urban geographers would disagree that all urban landscapes are equal and ugly.

Other criticisms include the potential for misinterpreting secondary data sources, especially aerial photographs. Linton did not adequately explain what scales his method applies to, nor over what distances the effects of certain landforms should be evaluated. For example, the aesthetic impact of mountains can easily extend to 20 kilometres away, but the aesthetic impact of a treeless farm may reach only a few hundred metres. Finally, Linton's method emphasized permanent natural features rather than features that are susceptible to relatively easy manipulation or control. The intrusions of roads, clearcutting, and dams is not accounted for or measured by Linton's method. Despite these limitations, Linton's technique has been shown to produce relatively consistent and valid results (Gilg, 1974 and 1976).

In North America, landscape preference studies were often associated with the name of Shafer. Shafer (1969, 1970) used preferences for landscape photographs to estimate preferences for actual landscapes. The method used in his 1970 Utah study illustrates the basic approach. Each of fifty respondents were given two sets of seven photographs each. The photographs in each set were ranked from most preferred (1) to least preferred (7). The ranks assigned by each respondent to a given photograph were summed to a total. This total, ranging from 50 to 350, was used as a dependent variable in a multiple regression model to predict preferences for different groups of respondents, representative of different types of users. Other researchers have used the same method with black and white photographs, coloured photographs, or colour slides. Each attempt has been plagued by two related problems: the doubtful generalization from a photograph to a real landscape, and the possible biases introduced by photographic composition and quality. Shafer's predictive model also has several problems. These include the lack of any theoretical basis for his choice of independent variables measured from the photograph, the use of a linear additive model to simulate complex aesthetic judgements, and the use of independent variables that are not truly independent of each other. In fact, several of his measures are merely the same variable in different forms. This practice might cause serious problems of multi-collinearity, resulting in spuriously high measures of the explanatory power of the model. Useful summaries and critiques of other preferential studies can be found in Veal (1974) and Elsner (1976).

Evaluative techniques

The best-known evaluative technique is that developed by Leopold (1969). He developed an index of uniqueness of river valleys. Uniqueness was a relative concept to Leopold, with no special value other than his belief that unique rivers tend to cause society greater concern. That concern may be either positive or negative. In other words, unusually beautiful rivers or unusually dirty rivers are those that require special attention, whether for preservation or rehabilitation.

Leopold's method was based on an analysis of an inventory with forty-six variables representing the physical, biological, water quality, and human use aspects of each river. Variables were measured on a five-point ordinal scale. Values were determined by noting how many other rivers shared the same quality as a given river on a particular variable. For example, width was classified into the following categories:

21

Category	Width (ft)
1	0– 2 (0–0.6 m)
2	3– 10 (0.7–3.0 m)
3	11– 30 (3.1–10 m)
4	31–100 (10.1–33 m)
5	100+ (33+ m)

The uniqueness ratio for each river for width, as for all other variables, was obtained by dividing 1 by the number of rivers in a given category. Thus, if only one river of a group of ten had a width of more than 100 ft (33 + m), its uniqueness value for this variable was $1/1 = 1.0$. If five rivers had widths between 11 and 30 ft (3.1 and 10 m), their uniqueness values would be $1/5 = 0.2$. Note that the actual width is irrelevant. What is important is the number of rivers of approximately the same width. Values were summed over all forty-six variables to give a total uniqueness score. The higher the score, the more unique the river.

Leopold was almost alone in his attempt to divorce the researcher's task of description from the task of imputing values to a description. This, in part, is why his method has gained both attention and criticism. Most objections concern the difficulty of interpreting the uniqueness score. Other criticism concerns some procedural difficulties in combining certain scores. This literature is summarized in Hamill (1974, 1975). Despite the criticism, Leopold's method appeals to researchers attempting a neutral evaluation of river landscapes. His inventory list has received wide application (e.g. Dearinger and Woolwine 1971; Fabos 1971).

A different method for evaluating landscapes was developed by Litton (1968, 1973). Rather than quantifying landscape aesthetics, Litton proposed guidelines for systematically observing landscapes. As such, his approach is more a description of how to describe, rather than a description of landscapes, *per se*.

Central to Litton's approach is a series of landscape control points – a network of permanent observation sites to provide a basis for evaluating proposed landscape changes. The sites are located along highways and trails, and are used as sampling points for scenic quality. Special attention is given to locating sites at parking lots, trailheads, curves in roads, visitor centres, and other areas of congestion. Litton also described a number of landscape compositional types that attract special visual attention and that should be closely monitored.

Once the observation points have been established, the visible landscape is plotted and sketched to describe existing conditions. Plotting may be done from field observation or from topographic maps to form a series of sectional plots along various lines of site, or by using one of several computer plotting programs. These plots and maps can be used to identify areas that are highly visible or sensitive to alterations. Artists' conceptions can also be employed to simulate various forms of the alteration to provide additional information.

Summary

The description of location covers three major subjects: (1) facility and activity location; (2) resource inventory and location; and (3) images of regions and resources. Fundamental to most of the work in these three subjects is the task of counting. Counting involves four steps. First, the cases or objects to be counted must be defined in precise, workable terms. Once a definition of cases is established, the methods and units of counting must be selected. The choice will be influenced by the purpose of the study and the availability of data. Once this preliminary work has been completed, the actual counting can begin. The results, finally, are tabulated or mapped.

Much past research has been devoted to exploring the usefulness of different definitions and measurement units. Data collection techniques, especially for counting people, also have been the focus of concentrated research. Much more work to improve existing techniques and to develop and test new methods needs to be done.

The concepts that guide the enumeration of developments and activities are relatively straightforward, although the actual work can be difficult. Concepts for describing resources, on the other hand, are numerous and complex. The basic ideas are presented in the body of this chapter; additional material may be found in the articles listed under 'Additional Reading' at the ends of chapters. See especially the research by the Craigheads, by MacConnell and Stoll, and by Olson.

Three methods are used in resource description. Arithmetic techniques cover a wide range of ways to enumerate, weigh, and combine resource variables. Deglomerative techniques begin with an entire resource system or environment and subdivide it to reveal significant patterns of relationships. Agglomerative techniques begin by defining basic elements in a resource system or environment, and then combine these in such a way to produce a complex, descriptive 'whole'. Deglomeration and agglomeration represent the most promising and challenging methods for future resource classifications because they require both a theoretical basis for their structure and an empirical relationship with the reality they purport to describe. The most important advances in these two methods will be the development of theory to guide the formation of new and imaginative systems.

Descriptive image studies can be divided into three types of questions. The first asks, 'What are the images people have of Region (Resource) X?' The goal here is only to identify the existence and nature of an image. The next question concerns the value of that image, whether the image is pleasing or not. Research designed to answer this question is usually motivated by a concern to describe and then predict the effect of landscape alterations on scenic beauty. The third question expresses interest in the quality of a particular resource, but seeks the answer in a neutral framework of 'uniqueness' or some other context that avoids value judgements.

The methods for description presented in this chapter are the most common ones in recreation geography. It is not possible to provide a step-by-step guide to the use of every one of the methods that has been presented. For this information the reader should go to the sources.

Some of the classifications applied to grouping the methods in this chapter are open to revision or debate. Distinctions between development and resource, between resource and use, between use and image, or between image and resource require informed judgement. The distinction between description itself and the uses to which it is put, is often arbitrary. The point of this statement is to remind the reader that descriptive research, despite its apparently elementary character, is complex, challenging, and necessary for virtually every other type of research. Explanation, prediction, or evaluation are rarely possible without description; and once a researcher begins describing, it is difficult not to push on into the research questions we shall examine in subsequent chapters.

Additional reading

Bell, M. (1977) 'The spatial distribution of second homes', *Journal of Leisure Research*, **9**, 225–32

Bonapace, R. (1968) 'Il turismo nella nere in Italia e i suoi aspetti geografici', *Revista Geografica Italiana*, **75**, 157–86 and 322–59

Coppock, J. T. (ed.) (1977) *Second Homes: Blessing or Curse?*, Pergamon Press, London

Cosgrove, I. and Jackson, R. (1972) *The Geography of Recreation and Leisure*, Hutchinson, London

Craighead, F. G. and Craighead, J. (1962) 'River systems: recreational classification, inventory, and evaluation', *Naturalist*, **8**, 2–19

Lavery, P. (1971) 'Resorts and recreation', in Lavery, P. (ed.) *Recreational Geography*, Ch. 8, 167–96, David and Charles, London

MacConnell W. P. and Stoll, G. P. (1969) 'Evaluating recreation resources of the Connecticut River', *Photogrammetric Engineering*, **35**, 666–77

Mercer, D. C. (1972) 'Beach usage in the Melbourne Region', *The Australian Geographer*, **12**, 123–39

Meriaudeau, R. (1963) 'Les stations de sport d'hiver en Suisse, en Autriche et en Allemagne Méridionale, *Revue de Géographie Alpine*, **51**, 675–718

Olson, C. E. (1969) 'Inventory of recreation sites', *Photogrammetric Engineering*, **35**, 561–68

Pigram, J. J. J. (1977) 'Beach resort morphology', *Habitat International*, **2**, 525–41

Preau, P. (1968) 'Essai d'une typologie de stations de sports d'hiver dans les Alpes du Nord', *Revue de Géographie Alpine*, **56**, 127–40

Pryce, R. (1967) 'The location and growth of holiday caravan camps in Wales, 1956–65'. *Transactions of the Institute of British Geographers*, **42**, 127–52

Ragatz, R. L. (1970) 'Vacation housing: a missing component in urban and regional theory', *Land Economics*, **46**, 118–26

Robinson, G. W. S. (1972) 'The recreational geography of South Asia', *Geographical Review*, **62**, 561–72

Sentfleben, W. (1973) 'Some aspects of the Indian hill stations: a contribution towards a geography of tourist traffic', *Philippines Geographical Journal*, **17**, 21–9

Smith, S. L. J. (1975) 'Similarities among urban recreation systems', *Journal of Leisure Research*, **7**, 312–27

Stansfield, C. A. (1969) 'Recreational land use patterns within an American seaside resort', *Revue de Tourisme*, **24**, 128–36

Wolfe, R. I. (1951) 'Summer cottagers in Ontario', *Economic Geography*, **27**, 10–32

Wolfe, R. I. (1978) 'Vacation homes as social indicators: observations from Canadian census data', *Leisure Sciences*, **1**, 327–44

Chapter 2

Descriptive research on travel

Three concepts provide the basis for descriptive research on travel: *nodes* (usually an origin–destination pair); a *route* connecting the nodes; and a *mode* of travel for moving along the route. Nodes are more than just the location of some resource or population; they represent the interaction between supply and demand. Nodes generate movement and thus are the fundamental spatial units for the study of travel. Routes develop as patterns of regular travel between nodes, and are usually characterized by one or two modes of travel specific to them. Overland travel may take the form of paved highways used primarily by cars and buses. Other routes include rails for passenger trains, air routes for airplanes, and shipping lanes for cruise ships.

Another approach to the description of travel, suggested by Van Doren (1975), makes the concept of movement fundamental to any study of recreational travel. Movement, in Van Doren's view, gives rise to a network of routes. The intersections of the segments of the network develop into nodes. This approach (which Van Doren traces back to Haggett 1966) raises an important question: without the existence of nodes, why did the movement begin? The organization of this chapter suggests that nodes, because they are the site of actual or potential interaction between supply and demand, provide the reason for movement, and that the study of recreational travel should be predicated on a description of these locations. The differences between the two approaches, nodes-first or movement-first, should not be overemphasized. The disagreement is largely a matter of perspective or personal interpretation; the results of both approaches are the same.

Nodes

Origins

Nodes can be divided into origins and destinations. Although origins represent about half of all the nodes one might study, the amount of research on origins is meagre. The most common type of origin research is the description of past and intended travel patterns of the residents of a given origin. The Canadian Government Office of Tourism, for example, publishes annual surveys of vacation travel made by Canadians in the immediately preceding season, and of the intentions of Canadians to take vacation trips in the future. These surveys describe the number of people by selected origin (usually a province) and by selected socio-economic characteristics who have taken a trip (or intend to), the mode of transportation used, the destination(s), whether or not the services of a travel agent were used, and so on. Many countries also collect national information on vacation travel as part of either a special survey or a regular transportation census. A major source of international statistics is the World Travel Organization's *World Travel Statistics*, published annually.

An important consideration in describing travel patterns is the definition of a trip and of the traveller. Because most geographers rely on secondary data sources for studying travel behaviour, it is especially important for the geographer to know what the definition is, and whether or not it is comparable to others that might be used. The United States *Census of Transportation*, for example, considers only those trips that take the traveller more than 100 miles (161 km) from origin to destination. The Canadian vacation pattern surveys, on the other hand, consider only those trips that keep the visitor away from home overnight. There will be many trips in both countries that meet both criteria, but the definitions are not synonymous.

Definitions of travellers also vary. A few of the various national definitions used to define international travellers include the following. Note also that some countries distinguish between 'tourist' and 'visitor'.

1. *Tourist*:
   Any non-resident who stays less than twelve months (Australia).
   Any non-resident entering on a tourist visa other than an immigrant, temporary resident, or air passenger in transit. Tourists may stay more than twelve months (Israel).
   Any non-resident visiting the country for purposes of recreation, health, or unremunerated sport or artistic activities for less than six months (Mexico).
   Any non-resident who visits for business or pleasure, study, or transit. Canadian visitors are counted only if they stay more than twenty-four hours (United States).
2. *Visitor*:
   Any non-resident entering the country for any reason, including commuting to work and seasonal labour except diplomatic personnel and the military (Canada).
   Any tourist or cruise ship visitor except citizens resident abroad or residents of the Administered Territories (Israel).

27

Any non-resident entering for any purpose, including diplomats and members of armed forces (Jamaica).

Any non-resident staying at least six months (Mexico).

Still other definitions would apply to domestic tourists in each of these countries.

Variables used to summarize travel patterns away from origins are numerous, but certain ones show up again and again in research reports. The basic measurement, of course, is the number of people who have made a trip. This may be expressed as the number of individual travellers or as the number of travel parties. Sums can be grouped into all trips anywhere for any purpose, or they may be disaggregated by destination or reason for trip. Travel statistics are usually reported for specified time periods: daily, weekly, monthly, quarterly, annually. Other trip data often obtained includes:

Socio-economic characteristics
Mode of travel
Distance travelled
Expenditures during trip
Number in party
Duration of trip
Accommodation used on trip
Number and types of stops
Routes followed

A variable that is sometimes useful is the preferred direction of travel. Such preferences, or directional bias, result from physical or boundary constraints, the distribution of desirable destinations, the pattern of existing transportation networks, historical or cultural ties between nodes, or from other causes. Wolfe (1966) described a directional bias in the travel of Toronto residents to cottages in Ontario that is influenced by the location of the central business district of Toronto in relationship to the cottager's permanent residence. Cottagers tend to own vacation property on the same side of Toronto as their permanent residence, avoiding the necessity of cross-town travel (Fig. 2.1). The strength of this tendency was defined by a directional bias index:

$$D = \frac{10^5 (C_{ij})}{\Sigma C_i \Sigma C_j} \qquad [2.1]$$

where: D = an origin-specific index of the tendency to travel in a certain direction

C_i = number of cottagers from a given origin, i

C_j = number of cottagers at destinations in a given direction, j

i, j = origin and destination zones. i refers to any of six zones in Metropolitan Toronto; j refers to cottage zones to the west, north, and east of Toronto

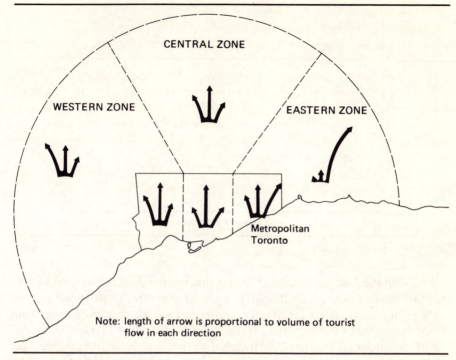

Figure 2.1 Directional bias in the travel of Toronto, Ontario cottagers (after Wolfe 1963)

Destinations

Destination descriptions are based on many of the same variables used for origin description: number of arrivals, socio-economic profiles, lengths of stay, expenditures, times and seasons of arrival, routes travelled, and points of entry (for international trips).

The most widely used variable for destination-specific studies is the distance travelled by arriving visitors. This information can be expressed in the form of a distance decay curve (Fig. 2.2), derived by plotting the distance travelled against the number of trips.

The slope of this curve expresses the drawing power of the destination. The flatter the line, the greater the ability of a destination to draw travellers from a distance. The area under the curve is proportional to the total number of travellers who arrive in a given period of time.

Different facilities have different abilities to draw people, and these can be compared by comparing distance decay curves. Figure 2.3 shows a set of hypothetical distance decay curves that might be found in a study of intra-urban recreational travel. Here the relatively steep slope of the curve asso-

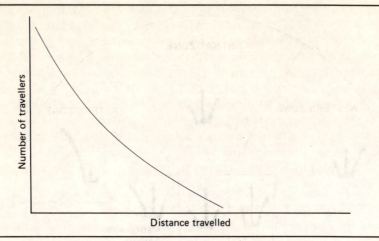

Figure 2.2 A hypothetical distance decay curve

ciated with the fast-food outlet indicates that people tend not to travel as far for fast food as they do for dinner at a good restaurant, or to attend a game at a professional sports facility. The differences in these curves may result from variations in willingness to travel for different types of experiences, or from variations in the need to travel. In other words, a steep slope may indicate a hesitancy to travel very far, or the availability of that particular destination close to most customers.

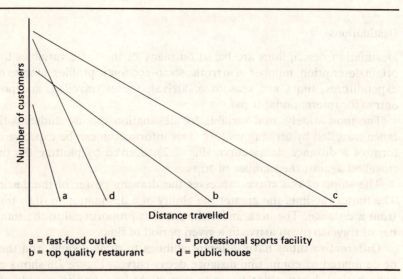

a = fast-food outlet   c = professional sports facility
b = top quality restaurant   d = public house

Figure 2.3 Hypothetical distance decay curves for different urban recreation businesses

Lentnek, Van Doren, and Trail (1969) used a similar approach in their study of Ohio (USA) boaters. However, rather than compare destinations, they compared the willingness of different types of boaters to travel. They discovered significant differences in the population of boaters. Sailors and water-skiers showed the greatest resistance to travel, while pleasure cruisers and fishermen showed less resistance.

An imaginative use of distance decay curves has been suggested by Ross (1973). Noting that different facilities of the same type in the same region will often exhibit different distance decay curves, Ross speculated that the cause of these differences is variation in the attractiveness of the facilities. To put this idea to work, he defined an attractivity index of competing facilities to be:

$$A_{jk} = T_{jk}/(T_{jk} + T_{kj}) \qquad [2.2]$$

where: A_{jk} = the relative attractiveness of the site actually visited (j) to all other sites (k)

T_{jk} = number of times travellers chose j over k

T_{kj} = number of times travellers chose k over j

A problem with this formulation is that if the region being studied has several centres with greatly different populations, biased estimates of the attractivity of one or more destinations can be produced. The problem is due to the fact that the attractivity index fails to account for the total number of trips from all origins to any given destination. To adjust for this, Ewing and Kulka (1979) added a weighting component to the equations:

$$A_{jk} = \{T_{jk}/N_{jk}\}/\{(T_{jk}/N_{jk}) + (T_{kj}/N_{kj})\} \text{ for } N_{jk} \text{ and } N_{kj} > 0 \qquad [2.3]$$

where: N_{jk} = number of travellers for whom j is a more distant alternative than k

N_{kj} = number of travellers for whom k is a more distant alternative than j

and other variables are as defined before.

Distance decay curves need not be based only on a coordinate system with the number of travellers along the vertical axis. Another measure that is often used is *per capita* travel rate. This variable corrects for the fact that if data are collected by concentric zones surrounding a destination, the more distant zones, being larger, tend to have larger populations. This, in turn, would cause an overestimation of the willingness to travel in these distant communities.

Filippovich (1979) used 'persons per square kilometre' in his analysis of the distribution of travellers around Moscow. In this case, the distance decay curve is origin-specific. The reason for using density of users was to adjust for the biasing effect of the larger zones at greater distances from the central node.

Filippovich's curve, unlike most distance decay curves, resembles a Maxwell–Boltzman distribution: steeply increasing from a local minimum to a maximum, followed by a gradual decrease (see Fig. 2.4). Smith (1981) found a similar pattern in the travel of Dallas, Texas (USA) residents to urban recreation centres; Wall and Greer (1980) also observed this type of distribution for day-use facilities, cottages, camp grounds, and resorts in Ontario (Canada). This type of curve reflects the interplay between the increase in the supply of centres as one moves further away from an origin, and the increasing costs of travel with greater distance.

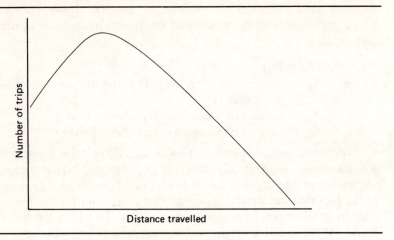

Figure 2.4 A generalized Boltzman curve for trip distributions

Crowding

Crowding, in the context of recreational travel, refers to the concentration of arrivals at a destination within a short period of time. Several measures for describing variations in arrivals over time are available. Building on the work of Van Lier (1973) and Beaman and Smith (1976), Stynes (1978) summarized the most important of these.

The simplest measure of the temporal concentration of users is the ratio between the number of arrivals in a given period of time to the total number of arrivals over a longer period of time. The concentration of use of a sports facility, for example, over the year might be studied by dividing the attendance in each of the four seasons by the annual total.

If visitation levels are plotted so that the visitor curve begins and ends at local minima, with a maximum somewhere in the middle of the curve, such as plotting daily use from midnight to midnight, or annual use from January to December (in the Northern Hemisphere), the resulting curve can be interpreted as a probability curve describing the expected rates of arrival at various times (see Fig. 2.5a). Given this interpretation, the kurtosis of the curve, a statistic describing the peakedness of a distribution curve, can be calculated.

This measure is more useful than the ratio described previously because it compares many periods at once. Kurtosis is calculated as:

$$K = \sum_{i=1}^{n} \frac{n\,(X_i - X)^4}{n(\sigma^4)}$$ [2.4]

where: K = kurtosis
X_i = number of users at time i
X = mean of all X_i
σ = standard deviation of X_i
n = number of time periods

A value of 3.0 is obtained for a normal distribution (mesokurtic). Values less than or more than 3.0 indicate curves that are relatively flat (platykurtic) or relatively peaked (leptokurtic), respectively. The more peaked, the heavier the concentration of users in one time.

Calculation of kurtosis is more meaningful when the time periods selected are at a scale that produces a relatively smooth curve. Detailed scales can produce very spiked use curves. Figure 2.5b, for example, is a plot of the number of camp-ground users at a typical provincial park in Canada. The series of peaks are produced by heavy use on weekends. This peaking pattern can be eliminated in graphing (if it is so desired) by aggregating the data on a weekly basis rather than on a daily basis.

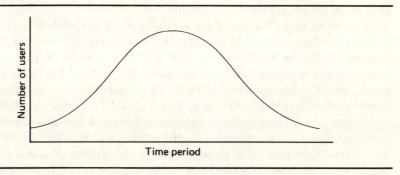

Figure 2.5a A generalized use curve for an entire season

Beaman and Smith (1976b) discussed other aspects of modelling these spiked use curves plus some of the potential applications of annual use curves. One important application is that an annual use curve calculated from several years of daily rates can provide estimates of expected use levels at any point throughout the year. In other words, the descriptive model can be used, with limitations, as a type of predictive model. Moreover, these curves can be used to obtain estimates of probable use levels to supplement missing data. Finally, departures from an average annual use curve can serve as an indicator of the

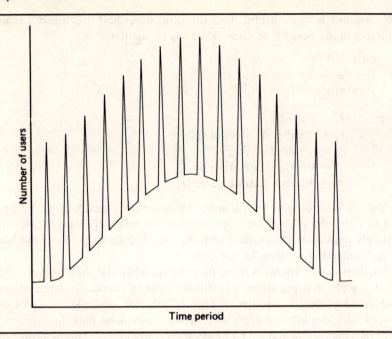

Figure 2.5b A detailed use curve for an entire season

effects of weather, changes in scheduling, a promotional campaign, or other changes in the management of a facility.

Another measure for describing the distribution of visitation over the year is the exceedance curve. If one first orders the days of the year from the highest use day to the lowest use day, it is then possible to plot use levels over time in a monotonic, decreasing curve. The slope of the line at different points indicates the tendency of visitors to concentrate in one time period. A curve relatively steep in the upper end (Fig. 2.6a.), is produced when many users come on a few days, and most days have few visitors. On the other hand, a relatively flat curve (Fig. 2.6b) reflects a more even distribution of use. It should be noted that these curves, by themselves, do not describe the capacity of a destination node. They can be used, however, to guide decisions about desirable levels of capacity (Van Lier 1973).

To measure the slope of the exceedance curve, several issues need to be considered. Because the slope of the line changes along the curve, the slope must be measured at a specific point or it must be an average. But because the changes in the slope are meaningful, an average slope, such as might be produced from least squares estimation, would miss significant information. The most informative part of the curve is its upper end, so a slope measurement is needed that can be applied to any of several points in that portion of the curve. Stynes suggested the following:

34

$$M_n = \frac{U_1 - U_n}{(n-1)U_1}$$ [2.5]

where: M_n = the peaking index
U_1 = the number of arrivals on the highest use day
U_n = the number of arrivals on the nth use day
n = rank of the nth use day (1 = highest use day)

This index can thus be calculated for any of several different points along the curve. In general, the higher value of M_n, the greater the peaking of use at that point in time.

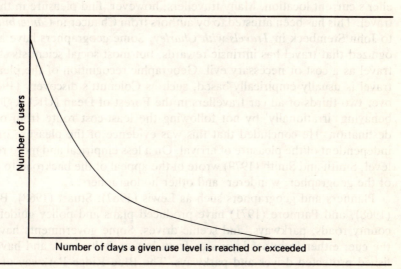

Figure 2.6a An exceedance curve for a facility with substantial peaking

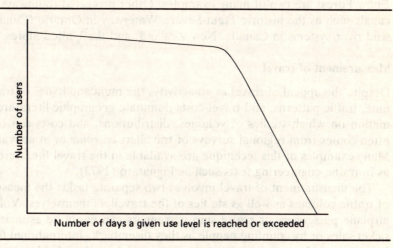

Figure 2.6b An exceedance curve for a facility with relatively uniform use

Routes

Pleasure of travel

Movement between nodes follows, and sometimes produces, regular and identifiable corridors of travel. The most visible of these is the network of paved highways that supports countless cars, trucks, buses, motorcycles, and even bicycles. Routes also include the humbler footpath and the invisible but vitally important shipping lanes of the oceans and corridors of air travel.

Routes are usually thought of only as a means of connecting nodes, as a tool to facilitate the enjoyment of recreation somewhere other than the traveller's current location. Many travellers, however, find pleasure in the act of travel. This has been attested to by authors from Chaucer in *Canterbury Tales* to John Steinbeck in *Travels with Charley*. Some geographers have also recognized that travel has intrinsic rewards, but most social scientists still treat travel as a cost or necessary evil. Geographic recognition of the pleasure of travel is usually empirically-based, such as Colenutt's discovery (1969) that over two-thirds of all car travellers in the Forest of Dean (UK) region were behaving 'irrationally' by not following the least-cost route from origin to destination. He concluded that this was evidence of the pleasure of travel, independent of the pleasure of arrival. On a less empirical and more romantic level, Smith and Smith (1979) wrote of the appeal of the backroad to the soul of the geographer, wanderer, and other hodographers.

Planners and geographers such as Lewis (1967), Stuart (1968), Brancher (1968), and Patmore (1971) have produced plans and policy guidelines for county roads, parkways, and scenic drives. Some governments have taken the cue, either from academics or from human behaviour, and have established protected drives and parkways. The Blue Ridge Parkway of the US Appalachian Region and the Cwmcarn Scenic Forest Drive in the Welsh Ebbw Forest are two of many examples. Other protected routeways include canals such as the historic Trent-Severn Waterway in Ontario (Canada) and wild river systems in Canada, New Zealand, and the United States.

Measurement of travel

Despite the appeal of travel as an activity, the mundane issues of traffic volume, traffic patterns, and travel costs dominate geographic literature. Information on which studies of volumes, distributions, and costs can be based often comes from regional surveys of travellers *en route* or at arrival points. Many examples of this technique are available in the travel literature as well as in traffic engineering texts such as Pignataro (1973).

The measurement of travel involves two separate tasks: the measurement of traffic volumes as well as studies of the travellers themselves. Volumes of airplane passengers or cruise ship passengers can easily be estimated from ticket sales or by counting people as they disembark. International flows can be monitored by customs agents or other officials stationed at border crossing points. Vehicular counts, usually of cars, are slightly more difficult when no international border is being crossed. The most common method is the use of mechanical or electrical counting devices.

Such counters, both portable and permanent, include the following. Electric contract counters rely on a subsurface detector consisting of a charged plate and a strip of spring steel which form a closed circuit when depressed by passing traffic. Photo-electric devices consist of a light source and a light sensitive cell on either side of a traffic lane. Any object passing between the light source and the cell interrupts the beam, registering a count. The idea of an interrupted beam is also used in radar counters, ultra-sonic counters and infra-red counters. Magnetic counters monitor a disturbance in a mild magnetic field by the passing of a vehicle.

These devices are relatively inexpensive ways of obtaining information on an hourly basis and they can be used to provide long-term coverage of traffic patterns. They cannot, however, classify vehicles, count passengers, or determine the purpose of trips. There is also the danger of malfunction, vandalism, and car accidents damaging the equipment. Some detectors count sets of wheels and thus vehicles with three or more axles, such as a car pulling a trailer, can bias the results.

To obtain information about the passengers inside the cars, it is necessary to contact a sample of those making trips. The traditional method for doing this is to stop drivers at roadside locations and to conduct a brief interview. While this interview is under way, another researcher counts and classifies vehicles to obtain an estimate of the total vehicle population.

Although this method provides data not otherwise available, it has several disadvantages. Personnel costs and administrative arrangements can be substantial. Stopping traffic can create congestion and antagonize travellers. Accurate measurement of the travelling population and of the sampling frame is very difficult. This makes the generation of weights for extrapolating from the sample to the population very doubtful. If interview teams are working at several locations in a region, a certain amount of double counting can occur. This can be avoided by 'marking' previously interviewed vehicles with some distinctive device such as a card under the windshield wipers, or by asking the drivers to leave their lights on while in the area.

An alternative to roadside interviews within a region are cordon surveys along routes crossing a real or imaginary boundary marking the limits of a region. Bridges, railroad crossings, and underpasses are useful because they form a visual boundary and the number of points crossing them are few. If every access and exit route to a region is covered, it is possible to obtain a reliable measure of the total number of travellers entering and leaving a region, which permits more trustworthy generalizations to be made from sample data. To avoid congestion at the cordon, surveyors often provide the driver with a postpaid mail questionnaire to return and a brief explanation of the purpose and importance of the survey.

One example of a cordon survey is Carter's (1971) assessment of the travel patterns of tourists in the Highlands and Islands Region of Scotland. Carter placed survey teams along every major vehicle artery and ferry dock at the border of the vacation region. The delineation of the region and the sampling procedures are detailed in Carter's report. His data base illustrates many of the travel flow variables used to describe travel patterns. Because he was able to count the total number of cars leaving the region, and because he was further able to determine what percentage of these contained tourists heading for home, he estimated the total number of travellers, tourists, and cars that could be expected in the region at any given time. From his questionnaire, distributed to departing motorists, he also estimated the total number of tourist-nights in the region for a given time period. This total was disaggregated by origin, destination within the region, income, number of previous visits, length of trip, and other characteristics. The mean number of nights per destination stop and the location of each stop were also determined from the questionnaire. Finally, Carter identified the distribution of trips and travellers over all segments of the highway network, preferred routes, and preferred directions of travel. The information was summarized in both maps and tables.

The cordon survey, like most other methods, has some disadvantages. It is limited to road traffic, frequently private cars only. Commercial modes such as buses and trains theoretically could be included, but the logistics are often too great to overcome. Travellers who live and recreate within the region are also missed. In the case of the Highlands and Islands, the native population is small, so this was not a serious problem. If the cordon survey uses a mail return questionnaire, non-response can be a problem. If it is possible to obtain the name and address of the driver, a follow-up for non-response could be made. Travellers, though, are understandably reluctant to give names and addresses to strangers while away from home. Costs of a cordon survey are substantial. One way to reduce costs is to staff the cordon stations only during peak driving hours, but this may reduce the generalizability of the sample returns. Cordon surveys, like all other roadside surveys, require cooperation from local police if cars are to be hailed to the side of the road for an interview. Finally, it is not usually possible to identify the cars of tourists as opposed to those of other travellers, so it is necessary to sample all cars, and to ask a few brief questions to determine the nature of the occupants.

A graphic method for summarizing some of the information that can be obtained from traffic studies is the Lorenz curve. The Lorenz curve compares the distribution of travellers to the distribution of a network of routes. Figure 2.7 illustrates a hypothetical example.

The important features of this diagram are its square form with the left side and bottom representing the cumulative percentage of two transportation variables, plotted at the same scale, a 45° diagonal extending from the lower left-hand corner to the upper right-hand corner, and a curve (AB'C) that typically falls some distance away from the diagonal over most of its

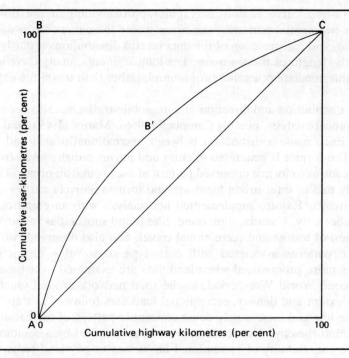

Figure 2.7 A hypothetical Lorenz curve for recreational travel

length. This curve provides a measure of the degree of congruence between the distributions of travellers and routes. The greater the separation between the curve and the diagonal, the greater the concentration of travellers on a few routes. To obtain a Lorenz curve, follow these steps:

1. Divide the network into segments, usually the sections of roads between intersections. Determine the length of each section in kilometres.
2. Obtain the number of travellers over each segment during a given time period. Assume a traveller uses the entire segment if he uses any portion of it.
3. Multiply the distance of each segment by the number of travellers to obtain user-kilometres for each segment. Total these.
4. Rank the segments in order of decreasing user-kilometres.
5. Convert the user-kilometre ratings of each segment into percentages of the total from step 3.
6. Calculate the corresponding percentages of total road distance for each of the road segments.
7. Plot each segment of the Lorenz curve, AB'C.
8. Calculate the area under the curve AB'C and divide by the area under ABC. This ratio is the index of concentration. The higher the number, the more spatially concentrated the use.

39

The Lorenz curve is only a graphic approximation of the divergence between two spatial patterns. The areas under the curves are usually only estimated, and the precision of the data on trip distributions is partly a function of the length of the segments. For long segments, many travellers may find an intermediate point and turn around, rather than travel the entire segment.

Flow distribution and direction of automobile traffic has also been subject to theoretical analysis, notably Campbell (1966), Mariot (1969), and Rajotte (1975). Each made a distinction between 'recreational' travel and 'tourist' travel. The former is generated in cities and moves radially away from population centres to form a dispersed pattern of use around an origin. The latter is closely tied to inter-urban highways and forms relatively narrow vacation travel circuits. Rajotte supplemented her analysis with an empirica. test in the Quebec City, Canada, hinterland. She found substantial support for the separation of tourist and recreational travel. She also observed two distinct land use patterns associated with each type of travel – distinction that becomes more pronounced when land uses are examined over time. In the post-Second World War period, as the road network around Quebec City grew in extent and density, recreational land uses followed in step, forming an expanding and increasingly dense concentric pattern of recreational facilities around the city. The concentric zones are created by a combination of the differential ability of recreational businesses to pay land rents, and the differences in the willingness of different recreationists to travel.

Concomitant with the intensification of recreational travel, Rajotte observed a decline in the aesthetic appeal of the landscape, a loss of fish and wildlife resources, and increased weekend traffic congestion. Tourist development and travel, on the other hand, has grown more slowly. What few changes have occurred are located mostly in the central part of Quebec City in the form of improved accommodation, and newer tours and accommodation packages.

Cost of travel

Travel cost is often estimated by the physical distance between nodes, but other methods are used, too. If physical distance is the choice, two alternatives are available: actual road distance and straight-line distance. The advantage of the latter is that it can be calculated quickly from a map. However, it can result in significant error if the travel follows winding country roads or a maze of one-way city streets. Before making a choice between road distance and straight-line distance, one might first calculate the distance between a few randomly selected nodes with both techniques and compare the two with simple regression. If the correlation is 0.90 or higher, the simpler method of straight-line distance can be safely used.

The question of road versus straight-line distance has received special attention by geographers studying marriage patterns in under-developed regions. Crumpacker, *el al.* (1976) discuss the theoretical and practical aspects of this question and provide a brief review of the relevant literature.

Distance costs are also measured in time units. Time–distance automatically adjusts for the added costs or frustrations of travel in heavy traffic, through densely populated areas, and for variations in speed limits. Time as a distance measure also allows for comparison between the effort put into travel (measured by its duration) with the rewards of the activity at the end of the trip (measured by its duration).

Dee and Liebman (1970) suggested using the number of street crossings to measure the distance children walk to playgrounds. Travel agents sometimes 'measure' distance to vacation destinations by the number of airplane changes. International tours are occasionally described by the number of international boundaries crossed or the number of days' duration (e.g., '22 countries in 21' days) .

Financial measures of travel costs can be used when data are available. One reason why distance and time measures are as common as they are is that they are available and acceptable surrogates for the more difficult economic measures (see Dwyer, Kelly, and Bowes, 1977, for a summary of the literature using surrogates to estimate travel cost and value). Financial variables are most easily obtained for commercial transportation, such as air travel. For car travel, out-of-pocket costs might be estimated by determining the number of litres of fuel consumed by the average car to make a trip of a specified distance. Multiplying this average fuel consumption by the average cost of fuel will give an estimate of one component of travel cost.

Because travel takes time, it may be desirable to estimate the opportunity cost of the time consumed in travel. The most common method for this is to determine, usually from a survey, the income of the people making a particular trip of known duration. The income of every party member is converted to an hourly figure, and this is multiplied by the duration of the trip. Either the total product or some specified fraction may be used. Individual travellers not gainfully employed may either be ignored or be assigned a devalued estimate of the wage-earner's time. Examples of this method can be found in Brown, Singh, and Castle (1965) and Edwards and Dennis (1976).

Directional bias

Travel flows are often summarized by the gravity model:

$$T_{ij} = \frac{G\,P_i P_j}{D_{ij}^a}$$

[2.6]

where: T_{ij} = number of trips from i to j
                   $P_{i,j}$ = population of either i or j
                   D_{ij} = distance between i and j
                   G, a = empirically estimated parameters

A problem with this formulation is that it implies that flows from j to i are the same as those from i to j. This, of course, is usually not true for recreational travel. To correct for asymmetrical flow, one might explicitly design a 'one-way' gravity model. This 'correction' is more of an avoidance of the problem than a real solution. A more basic change to accommodate for situations where $T_{ij} \neq T_{ji}$ in travel flows is to add a directional bias component:

$$T_{ij} = \frac{G P_i P_j (r + \vec{w}_{ij})}{D_{ij}^a} \qquad [2.7]$$

where: r = a basic rate of travel, possibly set to unity
$\vec{w}_{ij}$ = a force biasing the direction of travel
and other variables are as defined before.

The component $(r + \vec{w}_{ij})$ might be best explained through an analogy. Consider a pilot in a light airplane, travelling at an air speed of r. His ground speed or net rate of travel will be augmented if he has a tail wind, or retarded if he has a head wind. The amount of change is equal to the wind speed, $\vec{w}_{ij}$. An algebraic definition of directional bias has been suggested by Borejko (1968), Schwind (1971), Tobler (1976/77), and Smith and Brown (1981):

$$\vec{w}_{ij} = \frac{T_{ij} - T_{ji}}{T_{ij} + T_{ji}} \qquad [2.8]$$

$\vec{w}_{ij}$ is calculated for every origin–destination pair. For a region with ten origins and destinations, each node has $(10 - 1) = 9$ $\vec{w}_{ij}$s; travel from a node to itself is not considered. These individual observations are plotted as arrows with the tail at the origin, the length proportional to the value of $\vec{w}_{ij}$, and the head pointing either toward the destination if there is a net flow from i to j, or away from the destination if the net flow is from j to i. If the individual arrows at each node are combined , the resultant vector represents the overall directional bias of travel at that node. Figure 2.8 is a map of the directional biases associated with the 1976 pattern of Canadian vacation trips. The overall pattern shows a clear preference for westward travel. In the case of British Columbia, the westward arrow indicates that more people travel into British Columbia than British Columbians travel eastward.

Wolfe's R

The plotting of the number of arrivals at a destination node, as described in a previous section, has a counterpart in research on routes – the plotting of traffic volumes along a stretch of highway for a given period of time. Wolfe (1967) has taken data from traffic counts and has shown how the proportion of summer weekend travel on non-limited access highways that is recreational may be estimated from other variables. This relationship is important for a couple of reasons. Summer recreational weekend travel is sometimes ignored in traffic counts, even though weekends are the most important period for recreational trips, and this travel may be the dominant road use in some

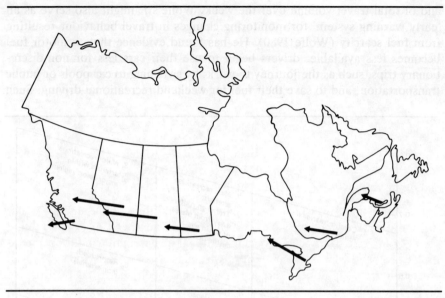

Figure 2.8 Resultant vectors showing directional bias for 1976 Canadian vacation
travel

areas. Wolfe's equation for the proportion of summer weekend recreational
travel is:

$$R = 0.84\frac{W_R}{W_T} + 3.41\frac{D_T}{W_T} - 3.056 + 0.118 \left[\frac{W_R}{W_T}\right]\log^{-1}\left[\frac{W_R}{W_T}\right] \log\left[\frac{3.5D_T}{W_T} - 2.5\right] [2.9]$$

where: R = ratio between weekend summer recreational travel and the
             average daily summer traffic
W_R = average weekday recreational summer traffic
W_T = average total weekday summer traffic
D_T = average total daily summer traffic

This equation predicts an ideal traffic pattern for rural highways: total
traffic on the average Saturday or Sunday that is three times greater than the
recreational traffic during the rest of the week. Deviations from this ideal
occur in predictable ways that are related to the land uses surrounding the
highway. Thus, Wolfe's R is more than just a way of comparing two types
of traffic volumes; it is an indicator of land uses in highway corridors. A
nomograph that summarizes these relationships is presented in Fig. 2.9. For
example, if one observes that the ratio between total weekend summer traffic
and total weekday summer traffic is about 1.5 along a particular stretch of
highway, and that the ratio between weekday recreational traffic and total
weekday traffic is about 0.7, one can reliably hypothesize that this particular
highway serves as a major recreational arterial within a major resort region.

Because it summarizes both the relative importance of recreational travel

43

and of total travel volume over the week, Wolfe's *R* might also serve as an 'early warning system' for monitoring changes in travel behaviour resulting from fuel scarcity (Wolfe 1980). He has found evidence that as motor fuel becomes less available, drivers begin to use their cars less for non-discretionary trips, such as the journey to work, by switching to car pools or public transportation, and to save their fuel for weekend recreational driving. Such

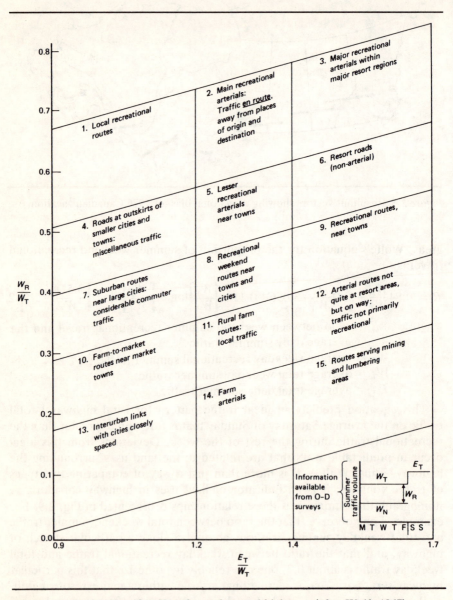

Figure 2.9 Wolfe's classification scheme for rural highways (after Wolfe 1967)

a change, if it were to become long-term, would cause a general increase in R for many highways. This change could be a harbinger of stress induced by fuel scarcity and of major shifts in travel behaviour that should be of concern to policy-makers.

Accessibility

The existence of a route increases the accessibility of the land along the route. Accessibility, by itself, may be either good or bad. If the land made accessible has a basic attraction for recreation and is not environmentally sensitive, protected, or needed for some other purpose, the greater the accessibility, the better. On the other hand, if a region has a fragile environment, is already used to capacity, or has competing demands on it, increasing accessibility to recreationists may only increase problems. In any event, it is often desirable to be able to measure the accessibility of any point or site. Three measures are useful for most recreation problems.

The simplest is highway accessibility, usually measured by the physical distance between some point and the road. This measure can be obtained by plotting the road network on a map, and then plotting parallel boundaries on either side of the road at some appropriate distance, such as 0.5 km (see Patmore 1971, for an example). A somewhat more sophisticated version of this method is to classify existing roads by some measure of capacity, such as the number of lanes or speed limits. A grid at an appropriate scale can then be superimposed on the network and every cell that touches a road of a particular class can be tabulated. If the cells have an identification code, the information can be computer-stored to produce maps.

An alternative measure of highway accessibility is to plot lines of equal travel time (isochrones) around an origin. This is a temporal version of the concentric zones used to construct distance decay curves. Isochrones graphically represent the 'shrinkage' of distance caused by the presence of a highway. Figure 2.10 is a simple map of isochrones surrounding a hypothetical origin. Note how the distance one can travel in a given time extends outward along the major highways.

The second measure of accessibility is regional accessibility. This measure is also known as the potential of a point, and it has been used widely by transportation and marketing geographers. It reflects the interaction of demand and supply for a particular resource at any point in a region. Ross and Ewing (1976) calculated the potential for outdoor recreational facilities in the Windsor to Quebec City, Canada, corridor with the equation:

$$OR_i = \frac{\sum\limits_{j=1}^{m} \dfrac{lnS_j}{D_{ij}}}{\sum\limits_{k=1}^{n} \dfrac{P_k}{D_{ik}}}$$

[2.10]

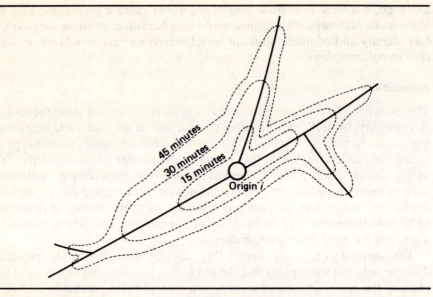

Figure 2.10 Hypothetical patterns of isochrones around an origin

where: OR_i = outdoor recreational potential for point i
S_j = area of facility j; there are m such facilities
D_{ij} = distance between i and j
P_k = population of centre k; there are n such centres
D_{ik} = distance between i and population centre k

The higher the ratio, the more accessible is a particular point, and the higher its potential. A high potential is associated with either an above average supply of facilities, a below average demand, or a combination of the two.

The third measure of accessibility, point accessibility, has been proposed by Lineberry (1975) as a measure of the availability of urban services. A city is divided into census tracts and five points in each are randomly selected. The distance from each point to the nearest facility is measured, and the average is obtained for each tract. This average is interpreted as a measure of the accessibility of discrete public facilities to the population of each tract. Mladenka and Hill (1977) calculated Lineberry's point accessibility for public parks and libraries in Houston, Texas (USA) and correlated the level of accessibility with various tract demographic characteristics. They found there was a slight tendency for parks to be more accessible to lower income groups and racial minorities while libraries were slightly more accessible to upper income groups and the majority culture in Houston.

All three measures of accessibility (highway, regional, and point) require several assumptions, especially regarding human perception. In the case of highway accessibility, the most important assumption is the lack of any restrictions on movement other than the lack of highway access. Regional potential, as defined by Ross and Ewing (1976), not only assumes straight line distance to be the most meaningful measure of travel ease, but also is based on a definition of supply and demand as simple ratios between area or population and distance. Point accessibility also assumes that straight line distance is an adequate measure of accessibility and that five points are sufficient to derive an average accessibility index.

Different definitions, different relationships among variables, and selection of different variables can change the measured accessibility without a single change in reality. This problem is not unique to accessibility measures, of course. As we have discussed before, a working definition has to be established for anything to be done, but every working definition has weaknesses.

Modal choice

Choice of mode of transportation (type of vehicle) has received scant attention in recreation geography. The primary reason may be the predominance of the private car for pleasure travel. Cars account for over 80 per cent of all recreational travel in most regions. The flexibility, freedom, and privacy of the private car makes it ideal for personal travel. The time may be coming when fuel availability and price force people to use more efficient forms of transportation such as buses, railroads, and wide-bodied jets more than they do now, but that time is probably far off. People have shown remarkable resistance to giving up pleasure travel in cars once they have obtained it. During the Great Depression of the 1930s gasoline consumption and distances travelled by car in North America continued to rise even though unemployment reached 33 per cent. During the Arab oil embargo against the United States in 1973, and in the years immediately following the embargo which saw dramatic price increases in fuel, vacation travel by car and the purchase of recreational vehicles continued unabated.

The choices of transportation modes are influenced in the first place by technology. Improvements in transportation technology have increased the modes available, and have improved the quality of travel. The most dramatic effect of technological change is the 'shrinking world'. Janelle (1968) described this phenomenon as time–space convergence, and illustrated it with the reduction in travel time between London and Edinburgh over the years 1658 to 1966. Three hundred years ago, the two cities were separated by 20,000 minutes of travel time. As technology provided faster modes of travel, the two converged at an average annual rate of 30 minutes per year (see Fig. 2.11). The reduction in travel time, of course, has not proceeded uniformly; the history is one of a series of dramatic improvements such as that caused by the introduction of commercial jet travel.

At a local level, technological improvements, primarily the automobile's invention and improvement, have done more than just bring the countryside 'closer' to the city. Cracknell (1967), Mercer (1970), and Wall (1971) have

47

suggested the car is used more to add flexibility and choice to day and week-end travel than to extend the range of travel. Geographers writing at the time the automobile was becoming established as a major social resource (Wehrwein and Parson, 1932; Carlson, 1938; Deasy, 1949) also described a pattern of travel that indicated the car was used to add novelty and flexibility to recreational outings. They observed, too, some of its unexpected effects on the rise and fall of certain types of attractions and changes in tastes for accommodation and services.

Besides consideration of historical changes and related land use effects, the study of transportation modes in recreation geography has been limited largely to providing supplemental information for studies with purposes other than the analysis of modal choices. In these, vehicle use is just one of several variables cross-tabulated with socio-economic and other independent trip-related variables to cast new light on the standard questions of who goes where, how, and why. The Upper Great Lakes study of regional travel patterns in midwestern United States (Recreation Resources Center 1975), Edwards and Dennis's (1976) study of long distance day tripping in Great Britain, and Glushkova and Shepelev's (1977) description of travel in the Moscow Oblast are examples of this approach.

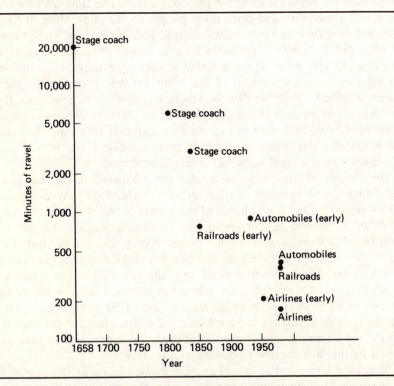

Figure 2.11 Time–space convergence of Edinburgh and London: 1658–1966 (after Janelle 1968)

Summary

Three concepts are basic to the description of recreational travel: nodes, roads, and modes. Nodes are more than just the location of the traveller's origin or destination. They represent the spatial effects of supply–demand interaction. Roads, or more generally, routes, are both cause and effect of regularities in movement between nodes. They may be tangible, such as a paved road, or intangible, such as a flight corridor. Modes are the types of vehicles chosen to move between nodes.

Nodes can be divided into origins and destinations. The variables used to describe travel characteristics associated with either origins or destinations are similar. The most important of these are distances and directions of travel, the characteristics of travellers, and measures of the concentrations of travellers in time and space.

Descriptive studies focusing on travel routes usually emphasize the costs and volumes of travel, although a few geographers have recognized that travel can be a pleasure and not just a means to an end. More work needs to be done on empirically describing and measuring the patterns and processes of pleasure travel as distinct from other forms of travel, including recreational travel undertaken only to get to a destination as quickly as possible.

Measurement of travel along routes is based on the number and distribution of vehicles as well as on the characteristics of travellers. Data required for volume measurements can come from mechanical or electrical counters; data to describe travellers require a survey. These data are collected to answer questions about numbers, purposes, locations, distances, directions, and purposes of trips. Accessibility indices for describing the effects of a route on local land uses are also helpful. Accessibility indices take three forms: highway accessibility that measures distance between a site and a route; regional accessibility that compares supply and demand variations in space; and point accessibility that measures access to discrete facilities in the context of population centres.

Variations in transportation modes occupy only a small portion of the recreation geography literature. Most of this research is either historical or is a minor part of a larger study. The reason for the relative lack of interest by geographers is that one mode of transportation, the private car, dominates recreational travel. This fact may change in the future, but the change will probably be slower than many believe.

Additional reading

Heggie. I. G. (ed.) (1976) *Modal Choice and the Value of Time*, Clarendon Press, Oxford

Lowe, J. C. and Moryadas, S. (1975) *The Geography of Movement*, Houghton Mifflin Company, Boston

Matley, I. M. (1976) *The Geography of International Tourism*, Resource Paper 76–1, Association of American Geographers, Washington, DC

Pazic, M. (1976) *A Short Survey of the Danish Tourist Market and Travel Trade*, Scandinavian Media, Ltd, Copenhagen

Wall, G. (1972) 'Socio-economic variations in pleasure trip patterns: the case of Hull car owners', *Transactions of the Institute of British Geographers*, **57**, 447–55

CHAPTER 3

Explanatory research on location

The basic reason for the location of any recreational facility, from wilderness preserves to sports stadia, is that someone wanted to use that location and successfully competed with other potential users. As Drury (1957) once put it, 'Parks are like gold; where they are is where you find them.' This answer, though, does not adequately explain the forces that affect the preference for a particular site or those that influence the outcome of competing demands for the same site. These forces can be divided into two groups: those affecting public location decisions and those affecting private location decisions. Each of these decisions can, in turn, be divided in two: decisions about the location of a facility and decisions about the location of activity.

This chapter is organized along the lines of this four-fold division: (1) use of public facilities; (2) location of public facilities; (3) use of private facilities; and (4) location of private facilities.

The definitions of and the distinctions between these subjects are imprecise. Because the nature of many facilities completely determines the use found at them, a model explaining the location (i.e., development) of tennis courts, for example, would be virtually indistinguishable from a model explaining the location (i.e., use) of where tennis is played.

The distinction between public and private, superficially simple, is also difficult in practice. Locational models have long existed for locating purely private economic goods – those goods whose production or ownership is controlled by an individual or business. More recently, models have been developed for locating purely public goods – those that are theoretically available to an unlimited number of consumers. Many recreational facilities fall between these two ideals. These facilities cater to a limited number of people who have joined together to jointly acquire a good or service. They are willing to share ownership or consumption with a limited number of other consumers. In other words, they have formed a 'club' – not in the sense of a group joined for camaraderie, but in the sense of sharing a desired service with a limited number of others (Buchanan, 1965). However, because most

51

work in recreation geography, indeed in all of economic geography, is still limited to purely public and purely private ideals, this chapter will continue this distinction.

Use of public facilities

Explanations about the locational patterns of public facility use are obtained primarily by (1) observation of existing activity and resource patterns and (2) by noting statistical correlations between socio-economic characteristics and locational choices for given activities. For the first type of analysis, a researcher might observe that campers along a stretch of coastline cluster in a few well-defined areas, even though there are no formally designated campsites. To explain such clustering, he identifies land ownership patterns and observes that most of the shoreline is privately held, and that only the limited number of public areas have campers. A conclusion is that one variable affecting the location of beach camping is the availability of public land.

From this conclusion, the researcher goes on to search for areas of public land that might not be used for camping to see if other variables might have other effects. Ritchie and Mather (1976) did just this in a study of beach recreation in the Highlands and Islands of Scotland. They found that while recreation was concentrated on public beaches, not all public beaches were used, nor was use uniformly distributed on public beaches. Unused or lightly used beaches tended to be obscured from the road by vegetation or an embankment. The authors thus reasoned that perceived access was as important as 'actual' access.

On the beaches themselves, regular footpaths radiating from entry points were observed. Levels of use were highest near access points and at certain natural features. Shelter from wind and a sense of privacy afforded by headlands, and the recreational opportunities provided by tidal pools and low cliffs tended to draw groups of beach users. These patterns, in turn, suggested accessibility and 'local interest features' as additional influences.

Knowledge of these patterns and the forces that create them can be used to guide both future research and the policy conclusions that might result from them. If ferry access were provided to an island, what would be the likely distribution of beach users, and what effect would they have on the beach environment? Are signs and parking space effective in redirecting use? Are there actual or potential conflicts between users, for example, between people playing sports on a beach and bird-watchers observing waterfowl? Can these conflicts be eased by altering access? These are just a few examples of the types of questions to which geographic analysis of locational forces can lead.

Examination of socio-economic characteristics of users to identify possible causes of user patterns is an approach often taken by sociologists. A rich literature describing the social characteristics of different recreationists and

a preserve are complex technical and political issues. National parks are located at the sites of significant mammal populations (Serengeti NP), wildfowl populations (Point Pelee NP), geological features (Grand Canyon NP), archaeological sites (Humayun's Tomb NP), or other resources of national significance.

The location of a protected area requires more than just pinpointing a resource to be set aside. Boundaries that enhance and ensure the successful protection of the resource must be decided upon and defended. Zentilli (1975) suggested five criteria that influenced the location of boundaries for Chile's Rapu Nui National Park on Easter Island, and which have relevance to other parks. Boundaries were set to encompass:

1. the resources that justified the establishment of the park;
2. natural areas that exerted a major influence on the protection of the national park's resources;
3. sufficient buffer zones to protect the future integrity of the park against incompatible land uses;
4. sufficient area for administrative, visitor, and maintenance services;
5. any areas whose alteration might have deleterious effects on the aesthetic values of the park.

Explanation of park location is not limited to the contemporary landscape. Some types of historical park developments leave traces on the landscape that allow historical geographers to apply their tools to the analysis of recreation landscapes. An example of this type of study is the work of Cantor and Hatherly (1979) on the distribution of medieval parks in England. They combined physical evidence marking the location of former parks (see Crawford 1960, Hoskins 1965, and Beresford 1971, for a review of field methods) with documentary evidence, especially records from various king's household and administrative records including the Pipe Rolls; the Close, Charter, and Patent Rolls; and the *Inquisitiones Post Mortem*.

Public service

One of the first theoretical attempts to explain the location of public recreation facilities was Mitchell's (1969) application of central place theory to urban parks. He began by hypothesizing an ideal city with residential, educational, and recreational land uses only, circular in shape, with an average and uniform population density of 14,000 people per square mile (5,400 people per square km) equal accessibility in all directions, equal distributions of free time among all neighbourhoods and individuals, citizens who seek to minimize distance travelled, and a system of recreation facilities hierarchically arranged from playgrounds, through playfields, parks to large parks. Each higher order facility would provide all the services of lower-order facilities plus a new service.

Under these conditions, the distribution of facilities would be hexagonal

55

and uniformly spaced. Standards in use in the US at the time suggest that playgrounds should be about 0.5 miles (0.8 km) apart, playfields 0.85 miles (1.37 km) apart, and large parks 2.6 miles (4.19 km) apart. Because each park is surrounded by a hexagonal hinterland and because the facilities are uniformly spaced, the hinterlands will also be uniform in size. The spacing of playgrounds, for example, produces a hexagonal of 0.16 square miles (0.414 sq. km) in size. With this area known, the populaton served by each facility can be estimated by multiplying the area of the hinterland by the population density. A playground is thus supported by 14,000 people/sq. mile × 0.16 sq. mile = 2,240 people (5,411 × 0.414 sq. km = 2,240 people).

Mitchell then relaxed some of his assumptions by allowing the presence of industrial and commercial land uses and variations in the distribution of population density within the city. The result is still a hexagonal pattern, but one that expands or contracts to reflect the effects of different population densities.

The central place theory adopted by Mitchell had several strengths and weaknesses. Of the strengths, and the most important, is the simplification of the complex process of facility location decisions to a small number of easily understood forces. This simplification allows a researcher to focus on selected parts of reality to understand how some of the most important forces shape the reality of the landscape. Exact adherence to a theoretically ideal pattern is not really expected. Rather, certain long-term tendencies are identified that can be tested for. Unfortunately, this points to a shortcoming in Mitchell's analysis – he did not verify his theory empirically.

The other side of Mitchell's simplification was the deliberate ignoring of potentially important variables: land prices; land availability; political influence; land donations; budget limitations; the possibility of substituting intensive developments or programming for land; user conflicts; and public/private joint use of facilities. The omission of variables is regrettable but the total number of influences on the final pattern of park development defies complete analysis. One is left with the unwelcome choice between an unrealistic simplification allowing a limited analysis, or elaborating the model to the point where it may approach 'reality' but becomes too complicated to work with.

A final limitation in this model concerns the estimation of the threshold population needed to justify the provision of a service. In the market place, the threshold population is that size market that allows a business sufficient sales to make a profit and keep in operation. Mitchell extends the concept to public service, and, indeed, it seems appropriate. Whether the service is a hospital, a school, a landfill or a park, the expenditure of public funds demands that some minimum level of need must exist before that expenditure is socially justifiable. Mitchell's formulation, however, fails to provide any basis for assessing just what that threshold might be, or how it might be determined, or how 'need,' as the basis for threshold, might be defined. Given an initial population density, and the presence of a system of parks, a 'threshold' is mathematically determined. This is quite different, though, from a threshold determined by a market. Either the concept of threshold needs to be reconsidered for public facilities, or more theoretical and empirical work should be directed to measuring thresholds for specific services in different social settings.

An empirical approach to explaining the location of public facilities is similar to that employed by Hecock: map the location of facilities and look for socio-economic correlates. Mitchell and Lovingood (1976) used this approach in a study of public park locations in Columbia, South Carolina (USA). Distribution was measured by the park density per census tract. This is a debatable choice, as the two authors admit, but they argue that the US public recreation profession (Butler, 1972) found this to be the most useful and understandable indicator of public facility distribution.

Correlating park density with the geographic distribution of population characteristics resulted in a strong inverse correlation betweeen income and socio-economic status, on one hand, and the density of parks, on the other. Parks were found in greatest concentration in poorer neighbourhoods. Middle and upper-middle class neighbourhoods had relatively few parks, and the affluent suburbs were almost devoid of public parks. A similar pattern has been verified in other cities by Haley (1979). The explanation for this may be that parks were located to meet the demand of the dominant social classes in a previous generation. With time, these classes moved to new neighbourhoods, leaving the old neighbourhood and its parks for the less privileged classes. Such as explanation, however, is not backed by a rigorous analysis of historical evidence or of the forces affecting park location when the existing facilities were designated. This remains a topic in need of further testing.

Mitchell and Lovingood also speculated on some political and social reasons why the suburbs remain 'recreational deserts'. In these communities, there was no legal requirement or financial incentive for land developers to build or designate land for parks. Furthermore, there is the belief on the part of some homeowners and developers that public parks attract 'undesirables' and that local residents would be happier without the potential nuisance. Park and recreation development also depends on a minimum level of political organization. The authors suggested that many Columbia suburbs are politically unorganized and thus cannot make their demand for service heard. Moreover, many features of suburban life tend to minimize the desire for parks: the preference for low taxes over social services; big yards; low-density development; private recreation facilities; and the ability to travel to recreation sites outside the city, all discourage public expenditures for suburban parks.

One limitation in the 1976 study was the omission of private recreation facilities from consideration. Lovingood and Mitchell added this element and considered a different measure of park location in their 1978 examination of the same area. After defining groups of facilities and then mapping the location of 172 public facilities and 112 private facilities, they examined the spatial patterns of each group using nearest-neighbour analysis. Each of the five types of public facilities had nearest-neighbour ratios significantly less than 1.0 indicating a tendency to cluster. On the other hand, three types of private facilities (camp-grounds, country clubs, and miscellaneous) had ratios significantly greater than 1.0, indicating a distribution more regular than random. Water-based facilities and hunting/fishing clubs, however, were highly clustered.

A consideration of the needs of each type of facility and of the clientele, suggested the following explanations for these patterns. Public facilities depend on good accessibility, and are therefore concentrated in areas of high population density. Moreover, most public facilities provide general services and do not have any special resource requirements, nor do they compete for a limited market, which could lead to dispersion. Private facilities tend to be located on one of two basic types of sites. Camp-grounds and country clubs are located in or near open space. Their clientele is not especially sensitive to distance, at least at the scale examined, and thus they tend to uniformly spread themselves around the region. Water-based facilities and hunting/fishing clubs are closely tied to a water or land habitat and thus cluster around the available concentrations of these resources.

Use of private facilities

Existing methods for research into the explanation of the location of activities concentrate on two general activities: tourism and vacation-home use. Methods for the study of tourism include qualitative approaches (historical, social, anecdotal), quantitative methods, and theoretical models. Vacation-home use analysis relies primarily on quantitative methods.

Qualitative analysis of tourism activity

Qualitative methods used for the geographic analysis of tourism rely primarily on observations of cultural differences, although some researchers (such as Pearce, 1979) have made occasional references to historical accidents, such as Broughham's unintended sojourn at Cannes, as the triggering event for the rise of some tourist destinations. Ritter's (1975) examination of tourism in Islamic countries is an example of how geographers employ qualitative methods. He combines field study to identify the presence, absence, and relative distribution of tourist developments with a study of the history, social structure, and religion of his selected countries.

Ritter observed that there are very few seaside resorts throughout the Islamic world. Assuming that seaside resorts are practically synonymous with swimming, he looked to the history and social forces affecting the sport and 'discovered' a strong religious taboo in Islam against men and women swimming in the same body of water. There was also a strong age bias in swimming. Young men and boys were the predominant group in the water. Older men, women and girls tended to stay on the shore and watch. Even this level of acceptance took eighty years to develop from the time that the English introduced swimming as a recreational and health activity into Egypt. In marked contrast, skiing was introduced into the Middle East by Scandinavians around 1910 and by 1930 it was well-established in Turkey and Lebanon.

Interest in historical sites and monuments also showed a marked difference between Western Europe and the Middle East. While Europeans have tended to regard themselves as the heirs of all intellectual traditions from Sumeria onwards, Ritter argued that citizens of Middle Eastern countries, whether Muslim or Christian, prefer those sites that pertain directly to local traditions or a sense of nationalism, such as Iran's Achemenian monuments. The result has been a slow decline in many valuable historical and archaeological sites in the Middle East.

Middle Eastern attitudes toward nature seemed to show some variations from European attitudes as well. The spiritual and intellectual traditions of the European Renaissance, the Romantic movement in art and literature, and Darwinism have produced a taste for wild, untamed nature. Middle Eastern tastes, according to Ritter, ran more toward nature 'tamed and trimmed'. This preference carried over into a lack of interest in wilderness recreation. The tourists found in the wilder parts of Sinai, Turkey, or Morocco were usually European or North American. Ritter hypothesized that this is also why no Islamic country, except Turkey and Iran (under the former Shah), had established national parks or nature preserves.

Preferences in sites for resorts and travel are also linked to religious and social traditions. Pilgrimages to shrines are still a major motivation for travel in the Middle East. The scarcity of running water results in a concentration of activity around any pool, stream, or waterfall. Considering the arid or semi-arid climate, this is hardly surprising. But Ritter suggested an added significance to the appeal of water. The symbolism of flowing waters runs deep in the Koran and Talmud, springing perhaps from the Sumerian belief in two seas – the ocean and an underground sea with the promise of eternal life.

Finally, Ritter suggested that the preference for hill stations and mountainside resorts might have some roots in the history of transhumance in the Middle East. Just as tribes once took flocks up to the mountains in spring or summer, many families – in some cases, whole villages – still move to the mountains for seasonal residence during the hottest part of the year.

Quantitative analysis of tourism activity

The basic quantitative approach to understanding why tourist activity occurs in the location it does, is to survey the people doing it to learn what they believed influenced their decision. The survey is done either on-site or through some form of household interview. Each has advantages and dis-

Table 3.1 Comparison of on-site and household surveys

On-site	Household
Advantages:	*Advantages:*
1 Little problem with recall	1 Sampling design simpler
2 Smaller sample size sometimes possible	2 Non-users and potential users can be contacted
3 Only users are contacted	3. Can be done through mail, drop-off, or personal interview
Disadvantages:	*Disadvantages:*
1. Expectations before arriving might be distorted by experience	1. Large sample sizes needed
2. Administration and sample selection can be difficult	2. Response rates for mail questionnaires may be low
3. Non-users are missed	3. Recall is often limited to about three months for many activities
4. Requires respondents to give up some leisure to answer	
5. Small sample size may limit generalizability	

advantages, and each might be used in different circumstances. Table 3.1 is a summary of the relative merits of each approach.

A compromise between an on-site survey and a household survey is the use of a selected group of people most likely to be of concern to the researcher. Examples of this would be the use of a list of people who hold a travel credit card, who subscribe to certain types of magazines, who are members of special interest clubs, or who have a record of doing a particular activity or using a particular type of facility. Fortin, Ritchie, and Arsenault (1978) used this technique in their study of the decision-making process of North American associations planning the choice of a convention site. By contacting convention centres, hotels, inns, and other establishments which cater to conventions, they were able to obtain the names and addresses of all associations holding conventions in Canada in the previous five years. Questionnaires were sent to a sample of the paid staff, elected officers, and members of the associations to identify the factors influencing site location and the decision to attend. The relative roles of each group in each stage of the site selection process and the influence of personal and association characteristics were also examined.

A different approach to understanding the locational decision-making of people seeking a place for recreation or vacations is to identify the steps involved in making a decision and then to examine how they evaluate the potential locations. Work by Rosenberg (1965), Fishbein (1963), and Dulaney (1968) has produced a two-stage decision process for consumer behaviour, and by implication, for the decision to select a particular site for recreation.

Each consumer decides on a set of qualities desired in a product. For a vacation region, this might include attractive scenery, low prices, friendly people, and good weather. Once this set of qualities has been formulated for a decision, and the relative importance assessed, each brand (or destination) is evaluated on the degree to which it possesses these qualities.

Woodside and Clokey (1974) noted that this model implicitly assumes that decisions about a brand are made independently of all other brands – an assumption that is usually not true. A more realistic model would be to suggest that each brand is assessed on the basis of the degree to which it possesses previously determined attributes in comparison to all other brands.

Even this formulation is oversimplified. It assumes that a consumer has equal knowledge of every choice. Scott, Schewe, and Frederick (1978) accepted Woodside and Clokey's basic formulation and added another variable representing the relative knowledge a consumer has about each brand. Thus, a brand which might possess many preferred characteristics, but which is not familiar to a consumer, might be bypassed in favour of a more familiar but lower quality brand.

Scott, Schewe, and Frederick applied this theoretical framework to an assessment of the relative attractiveness of a region as a vacation destination. They distributed questionnaires to a sample of out-of-state motorists entering Massachusetts (USA) on vacation. Each driver was given a questionnaire and asked to mail it back. Respondents were requested to indicate on a semantic differential scale the degree to which Massachusetts and three neighbouring states possessed eighteen different qualities. Following this task, the respondents then indicated which of the four states they most preferred to visit. Once the data were collected and tabulated, two hypotheses were tested: (1) tourists who prefer to visit a particular state evaluate that state differently, in terms of the attributes examined, from tourists who prefer to visit other states; (2) tourists who live closer to a given state evaluate that state on different attributes from those used by tourists who live far away.

The results supported the usefulness of the two-state decision model, and they led to the identification of certain images Massachusetts would need to upgrade. The authors, however, did not extend the model to use it as a predictive tool. Specifically, they did not predict the changes in the volume of tourist travel that might be expected if the image of Massachusetts changed on the attributes considered. Moreover, because they used a close-ended list of attributes, they may have missed some of the more important qualities or factors that influence a locational choice. Among the omissions are previous visits to the state, the presence of friends or relatives, the availability of specific facilities or activities (such as conventions, sporting events, and specific types of resorts). Such refinements represent a possible area for future research and development.

An alternative to the analysis of decision-making (usually focusing on the individual) is the search for group or population correlations between activity and place. The logic of this approach is relatively straightforward and has been used before in the study of public facility location and use. Two examples of this approach are the work of Cribier (1969) and Goldsmith (1973).

Goldsmith, in comparing the locations of vacation destinations of the residents of Dunedin (New Zealand) with incomes, found a strong spatial pattern. Families with modest incomes vacationed farther away from home than those with higher incomes – but they stayed with relatives. Families with higher incomes travelled less far, but preferred staying at commercial resorts. Cribier's analysis of French summer recreation patterns revealed the reverse pattern. After mapping the destinations of various types of vacation and holiday trips, and delineating the hinterlands around each urban centre, she found that travellers staying close to home tended to stay with relatives and friends. More distant destinations were usually commercial accommodation and resorts.

Theoretical models of tourism activity

Theoretical models of tourism activity have been only weakly developed by geographers. Contributions to the solution of the problem of location tend to be made by generalizing from observed patterns or by reference to previously established theory in other industries. Christaller (1964), the father of central place theory, offered an analysis of tourism location based not on the tenets of central place theory, but on their antithesis. His analysis was empirical and behavioural, and involved examination of destination patterns, and the locations of tourist nights, inns, resorts, and other establishments. This provided him with material from which he attempted to deduce possible motivations. His conclusion was that tourism is an avoidance of central places. Tourists – to which Christaller added artists, authors, and pensioners – seek 'places favoured by climate and landscape . . . high mountain chains, barren, rocky landscapes, heather, unproductive dunes.' Cities were to Christaller unimportant tourist destinations in Europe. 'To be sure, towns are also frequented by foreigners. But such visits are mostly business and education journeys.' These conclusions were supported by a series of maps compiled from secondary sources for France, the Bergstrasse and Odenwald, Jutland, Wallis (Switzerland), and Sicily.

Two other elaborate theoretical models of tourism location have been developed by Yokeno (1974) and Miossec (1977). Their models are similar to each other because they are based on the land use model of von Thünen. Both hypothesized a decline in the volume of tourist trade away from a population centre. The basic pattern is a series of concentric rings around a city with successively less tourism development as one moves further afield, because of the increasing costs of travel. Gunn (1972) also conceptualized the tourism landscape around a population centre as a series of concentric zones, but he emphasized variations in the quality and type of activity more than the intensity of travel.

Yokeno and Miossec hypothesized that certain forces distort this ideal pattern. On a regional level, the presence of other cities with their own hinterlands, variations in the accessibility of different parts of the hinterland due to variations in the highway network, and historical or cultural links between a city and certain parts of the hinterland complicate the concentric pattern. On a still broader scale, climatic variations, variations in the distributions of resources (especially coasts and mountains), and political disputes or international tensions also cause variations. The relative isolation of Cuba, for example, from the rest of the world since the take-over by the Castro regime in the early 1960s, has not only hurt the Cuban tourist trade, but improved it for Puerto Rico and other Caribbean islands.

Vacation-home use

Certain explanations for the use of vacation homes are 'common sense.' These explanations are based on simplistic psychological analyses of the motivation to seek vacation property and on casual observations of recreational behaviour, and they persist because many examples seem to support them. As Wolfe (1978) argued, though, these common-sense answers are more common than they are sensible.

Vacation-home owners claim to seek the isolation and freedom of the countryside, freedom from city traffic and the congestion of large resorts. And yet they place themselves in traffic jams on Friday night and Sunday night in the periphery of cottage country that are bigger and denser than most city traffic snarls. Other vacation-home owners say they have the property for their children. Yet anyone who has spent a long weekend with children in a small cottage knows how easily they can become bored when away from television, friends, and their usual recreation haunts. Others report that they want a place for fishing or skiing. But they frequently tie themselves to a locale with mediocre conditions, and cannot afford to travel to a variety of high quality sites.

The need to own land has been offered as another explanation. Yet renters, who apparently are denied the privilege of owning land, are less likely to own vacation property. Of course, an economic selection may be operating here – if one cannot afford a permanent home, one cannot afford vacation property. Yet most vacation lots are substantially cheaper than residential lots in bigger cities.

Avoiding the difficulties of hypothesizing and testing individual choice behaviour, many geographers prefer to explore aggregate socio-economic regularities in specific destination regions. Such was the approach of Tombaugh's (1970) study of vacation-home location choices in Michigan (USA). His study focused on correlates of the demand for vacation homes, rather than on individual preferences or factors affecting supply.

A survey of vacation-home owners (whose homes were located in Michigan) provided the age, income, and occupation of the head of the household, the size of the community of residence, number of children, plans to convert the vacation home to a retirement home, number of alternative sites considered before making the purchase, and type of primary residence. All were

63

put in the context of the time when the purchase was made. Previous ownership and activity preferences were not considered.

Vacation-home sites were classified as: (1) location on a Great Lake (one of the Laurentian Lakes between the USA and Canada); (2) location on an 'inland' lake; and (3) other locations. Each independent variable was divided into a number of exclusive categories: income, for example, was divided into eight levels. Knowing the percentages of homeowners in each location, it was possible to compare the percentages of homeowners in each income category across all locations to see if any locations had a concentration or a shortage of a particular income level. Thus, the adjusted deviations from the overall average distribution (and therefore, the expected distribution) for homeowners in the $30,000 + income class was: Great Lakes: 0.18; inland lakes: –0.14; other locations: –0.04. This indicates a relative concentration of higher incomes on Great Lake locations and thus a relatively greater demand for Great Lake locations by upper income groups.

Location can be defined in many different ways. Tombaugh's definition was a reference to a landscape feature (lakes). This is fairly common.. Urban/rural distinctions are also used in recreation research. A less common approach is to describe location in terms of distance from the permanent address. Here the focus is not on the demand for a vacation home in a particular region, but rather on the influences on the decision to choose a location for a second home at a particular distance range from the primary residence. In other words, the point of interest is the willingness to travel a certain distance. Murphy (1977) used this approach in an examination of vacation-home distribution in New South Wales (Australia). His problem was to explain the pattern of second home development, defined by the distances between primary and vacation residences, in terms of socio-economic variables.

Data for analysis came from a mail survey of owners of second homes in the coastal area north of Newcastle. Distance was measured by actual road distance. Although Clout (1969) suggested time is the most appropriate measure for studying vacation-home location, the correlation between time and the more easily obtained road distance was so high, Murphy opted for the latter.

Variables chosen to explain location as distance travelled were similar to those used by Tombaugh: age of buyer; occupation; income; reason for purchase; past renting patterns; price and number of rooms in second home; buyer's perception of the size of the community the second home is located in; length of ownership; and frequency of use. These independent variables were related to the dependent variable by a multivariate analysis technique called automatic interaction detection (AID) (Sonquist and Morgan, 1970). AID classified, in this case, second-home owners into groups that are similar to each other, but quite different from other groups on the basis of the independent variables. Similarity was measured in terms of distance travelled. AID allows for non-linear combinations of variables, and helps to identify interactions between pairs of variables.

Murphy identified nine basic groups of second-home owners. The most important variable distinguishing relative location were the reasons for purchase and the frequency of use. People who bought homes for speculation or eventual retirement tended to own homes much farther away than people who purchased for recreation only. People who were more frequent users owned homes closer to their primary residence than those who used them less frequently.

Location of private facilities

Explanations of private facility or recreation business developments are based on whether or not a location allows the developer or owner to make a profit. Economic and marketing conditions change, and some businesses can operate at break-even or even in the 'red' for several years, but eventually the location of a private business must be such that long-term profits outweigh long-term costs. The important question then is, what are the location characteristics that influence profitability.

An adage in retail marketing goes, 'The three most important factors for success are: location, location, and location.' Although the quotation is support for the geographic study of recreation businesses, it is an oversimplification. The advantages of a good location can be lost through poor management, ineffective marketing, or improper capitalization. A bad location, on the other hand, does not doom a business to failure. Bevins, *et al.* (1974) observed that many private camp grounds in the north-eastern USA are located on sites which objective feasibility studies would have recommended against. Aggressive and imaginative marketing combined with outstanding managerial ability can sometimes defeat a gloomy feasibility study. And if the development is built on land which the developer already owns, the need for smaller capital outlay, lower mortgage interest rates, and possibly lower taxes, will give the developer an additional advantage.

Recreation geography has had little to contribute to the analysis of forces affecting the successful location of private businesses and facilities beyond the development of a few use-forecasting models. Existing approaches consider consumer preferences (primarily the willingness to travel and the perceptions of site or facility attractiveness) and a loose set of forces that might be called 'situational' that include regional economic forces related to central place hierarchies, and the influences of legislation.

Consumer preferences

Variations in location imply variations in the distance a customer must travel. It is customary to observe that the further someone must travel to a business, the less likely he is to patronize it. However, the influence of distance on business levels may be slight enough, within certain distance ranges, that other considerations, such as the cost of land, can 'move' a business to a peripheral but still successful location. In order to make this decision, it is helpful to estimate the willingness of people to travel for a particular service. Arbel and Pizam (1977) illustrate one method of doing this. They interviewed 300 foreign, English-speaking tourists in the Ben Gurion Airport in Tel Aviv who had spent at least one night in the Tel Aviv area.

Their interest stemmed from the observation that the increased numbers of hotels in urban centres in many large cities, responding to the desire of tourists to be in the centre of urban attractions, created serious social costs. Hotel development can increase land rents in the urban core, which in turn, encourages developers to put up luxury hotels capable of obtaining high room rates, depriving a majority of travellers of accommodation in the urban core. The influx of large numbers of tourists eventually puts a strain on the urban infrastructure: streets, parking, water, telephones, sanitation. This either reduces the attractiveness of the city or raises local tax rates.

To estimate the potential for moving hotels and their clients away from the main business area, the authors asked travellers about their willingness to accept accommodation at successively farther distances (measured by time) from urban centres. This willingness was compared to the availability of private and public transportation, the actual distances people travelled, and any reduction in hotel prices required before the traveller would be willing to stay in a less central location. By cross-tabulating these variables, the authors concluded that the availability of a private car did not significantly influence the choice of a hotel site as long as public transportation was adequate. A relatively small decrease in hotel rates created a significantly larger shift in the willingness to travel.

Numerous measures of site attractiveness have been proposed by recreation geographers, and the important ones are discussed throughout this text. One method to measure and explain the relative attractiveness of a particular tourist region for development has been proposed by Gearing, Swart, and Var (1974). Although the procedure was developed for Turkey, it can be used in other geographic regions. In fact, Var, Beck, and Loftus (1977) used it later in British Columbia, Canada.

One begins with a list of seventeen locational criteria which the authors believed adequately describes the attractiveness of a tourism region. These are grouped into five general categories: (1) natural factors; (2) social factors; (3) historical factors; (4) recreation and shopping opportunities; and (5) infrastructure, food, and shelter. A panel of tourism experts such as researchers, travel agents, and business managers are asked to rank all the criteria located in one category in order of decreasing importance. Points (0 to 10) are assigned to reflect the relative importance; these scores are then normalized so they range from 0 to 1. After repeating this for each category, the categories themselves are ranked, points assigned and the values normalized.

The normalized value for each criterion is multiplied by the normalized value for its category so that seventeen weights are produced. Finally, all weights for each criterion are added over all experts and an average obtained.

To compare tourist regions, a panel of experts (the same panel or another one) familiar with all regions is asked to rate each region on each criterion using a scale of 0 to 1. That evaluation is multiplied by the weights obtained previously, and a total score calculated by adding all criterion scores for a given region. The higher the score, the more attractive the region.

Several assumptions are hidden in this approach. One of the most important is that the panel of experts rating the regions are uniformly and expertly familiar with all regions. Moreover, they must have the same understanding of each criterion and each category. This is especially problematic when some of the attractions are of a seasonal or temporary nature – such as festivals or climate-related activities (winter sports, viewing fall-colour). Each criterion is independent of each other, and their combined effect on the attractiveness of a region is linear and additive, rather than multiplicative or curvilinear.

The authors also assumed that the weights are constant from region to region. This may be unrealistic. For example, 'natural beauty' was given a relatively high weight of 0.132 compared to 'festivals', which were given a weight of 0.029. For two regions, comparable in everything but natural beauty and festivals, one of which is ranked 1.0 for beauty and 0.0 for festivals, and the other 0.0 for beauty and 1.0 for festivals, the former will always be assessed as more than four times (0.132/0.029) more attractive. Considering the ability of festivals such as the Stratford, Ontario, Shakespeare Festival, the Cannes Film Festival, or the USA 'Super Bowl' football game to pull in tens of thousands of tourists in a short period of time, the assumption of unchanging weights is questionable at best.

One final issue connected with this method is the fact that the authors did not explore the relationship between their measure of attractiveness and levels of development, numbers of visitors, accommodation rates, or any other measure of tourist activity. The assumption that there is a close connection is there, but it remains unexplored.

One method that does relate an attractiveness model to a measure of development is Burby, Donnelly, and Weiss's (1972) analysis of the factors influencing vacation-home development around reservoir shorelines. Their interest was to eventually build a simulation model for vacation-home growth using a technique originally formulated by Chapin and Weiss (1968).

Aerial photographs of privately owned land around two reservoirs in the south-eastern USA were partitioned into cells, each 1,000 feet (305 m) on a side, containing about 23 acres (9.3 hectares). Each cell was divided into nine equal parts. The total number of these ninths showing vacation-home development in each cell represented the level of development for that cell, and became the dependent variable for a multiple regression equation. Interviews with landowners and developers identified thirty variables that affected the site's attractiveness for development. Each of these was measurable from the photographs or from other secondary data sources.

Multiple regression of the thirty independent variables against the development variable for each cell produced a model that explained about 20 per cent of the total variance. This relatively poor performance may be due to the omission of important variables, the erroneous assumption that all private land was available for development, or the use of linear regression (which assumes no variable interaction and an additive relationship between variables). Despite the relatively weak performance of the Burby approach, the authors felt the results were sufficiently strong to allow the use of the multiple regression equation in the construction of a more elaborate simulation model. Additional work should be undertaken to strengthen the relationship, however, between development and site qualities

Situational forces

Mitchell's work on developing a theory of urban park location used the concept of threshold population. The idea comes directly from the geographic analysis of retail location. Some businesses, such as public houses, fast-food franchises, and betting houses, provide a service that is relatively inexpensive, usually requires only a modest amount of capitalization, and frequently generates a high repeat business. Thus, they do not need a large population to make them profitable, and they may be found in both large and small population centres. Other businesses require a high level of investment, have high operating costs, and do not always draw a steady, high level of repeat business. Operas, theatre companies, zoos, luxury hotels, and 'five-star' restaurants are examples. These businesses are found in limited numbers in or near large cities.

A concept related to the threshold population is the catchment area or hinterland of a facility. A facility with a high threshold population will usually have a large hinterland. The larger hinterland is necessary to support the business, and is possible because customers are willing to travel farther distances to obtain a high quality or highly desired specialized service or good. This effect may be seen most clearly in the variations of the willingness to travel to a given facility such as a motion picture theatre or a sports facility, as the quality of the attraction varies. Toyne (1974) has mapped the distances people were willing to travel to watch an Exeter (UK) football team play a top-ranked competitor, versus a game in which they played a bottom-ranked competitor. The stronger opponent, offering the spectacle of a hotly contested game, drew fans from more than twice the distance. Toyne observed a similar shift when an 'ordinary' movie (*I Was A Teenage Werewolf*) was compared to a 'good' film (James Bond in *Live and Let Die*). Another way of expressing the differences between high threshold and low threshold facilities is to compare the amount of time spent, on the average, travelling to a facility with the amount of time spent at the facility. In the case of the two football games observed by Toyne: if the average travel time for the weaker game was twenty minutes, and for the better game, forty minutes, and if the time spent at the game was about two hours, the ratios would be 1:6 for the poorer game and 1:3 for the better game. In other words, people were willing to spend more time travelling (accepting a higher travel-time ratio) if the quality of the time spent on-site increased. Law (1967) suggested that recreational facilities can be grouped in a hierarchy of local, subregional, regional, and national facilities with acceptable time ratios rising from 1:3, 1:1.5, 1:1, to 1.07:1, respectively.

The close relationship between travel time and the attraction at the end of the trip can also be seen in the amusement business. In mid-nineteenth-century America, traction (streetcar) companies built the first amusement parks at the end of their lines to attract people on to their cars at weekends (Crompton and Van Doren, 1976). Today, the feeling of fantasy and escape offered by theme parks is often enhanced by locating the parks 1 to 1.5 hours' drive away from the primary market.

A different set of situational forces operates in the development and morphology of the recreation business district (RBD) in resort towns. Stansfield and Rickert (1970) defined the RBD as that section of a city that is an aggregation of restaurants, amusement businesses, and novelty and souvenir shops catering to a seasonal influx of tourists. Mapping those businesses in three study cities (two New Jersey, USA, seacoast towns, and Niagara Falls, Canada) produced a pattern the authors interpreted as being a result of the combination of major access route location and the relative location of the central tourist feature (beach or falls). The RBD took the shape of an elongated district centring on the point of convergence of incoming visitors and the attraction (these two points closely coincided in these three cities). The districts were 'eccentric' in that they interposed themselves between the central tourist attraction and the central business district (CBD) patronized by the permanent inhabitants of the towns. The authors also observed some local variations in local 'colour' and the types and qualities of stores oriented around the peak value intersection in the RBD.

Taylor (Taylor, V. 1975) examined the East London, South Africa, RBD as defined by the distribution of hotels and other tourist accommodation, cafés, curio-shops, theatres, service stations, amusement parks, restaurants, public bath houses, and the public aquarium. Taylor mapped those city blocks that had at least 50 per cent of designated floor space involved in these enterprises. The pattern he observed was also an elongated district, with a concentration of activity near the beach and a rear fringe area of tourist accommodation, primarily boarding houses. The linearity of the RBD compared to that of the CBD, and the lack of a peak land value intersection (an artifact of competition for central locations) supported Taylor's belief that recreation attractions such as beaches are the most important force affecting the location of an RBD. Further evidence for this conclusion comes from the fact that hotels in East London on the beach or with a good view of the ocean were able to charge higher room rates than those in less-favoured positions.

69

Situational forces also include the effects of legislation on recreation business location. An examination of zoning ordinances and other legislation may be necessary before a geographer can fully understand the locational patterns of certain businesses. Spatafora (1973) described how the spatial pattern and marketing strategies of winery-owned retail stores in Ontario from 1927 to the 1970s has changed in response to changes in liquor legislation. Symanski's (1974) examination of the geography of prostitution in Nevada is another example of the study of legislative influences on recreation businesses. In the earliest years of white settlement in Nevada, brothels were openly tolerated and controlled by informal but effective social sanctions. (Symanski 1974: 358).

> In the 1860s the prostitutes of Virginia City had D Street to themselves. There were two rows of white-washed cottages at the head of the street, the cheaper women in cribs down below, farther down the Chinese, and at the bottom of the slope the Indian mahalies.... At the lowest end of the scale were 'hog ranches,' the cheapest houses on the frontier. The Army permitted these to operate at a distance of five miles from a post.

Eventually civilization, genteelity, or prudishness brought legal restrictions on the location of brothels. Current law forbids any county with a population of 200,000 or more at the last census to license a brothel. In practice, this eliminates only Clarke County, which includes Las Vegas. At a site-specific level, brothels are prohibited by state law from operating within 400 yards (366 m) of a school, religious building, or on a principal business street.

Summary

Numerous techniques exist for explaining the location of recreational activities and facilities. This diversity reflects the variety of questions about the use and development of recreation places. The body of methods described in this chapter come from four analysis traditions: (1) correlation methods; (2) empirical models; (3) theoretical models; and (4) qualitative explanations.

Correlational methods are used to compare levels of participation with site or facility characteristics, or to compare socio-economic characteristics with choice of location. The major disadvantage with these methods is that they are used frequently without any theoretical foundation. They merely describe a statistical relationship between variables for which the researcher has found data. As a result, these methods usually produce inconclusive results. Hecock's study of beach use, and Burby, Donnelly, and Weiss's work on vacation-home development are two examples. Reasons for this include missing variables, the usual assumption of a linear relationship when a curvilinear one may be the case, or the failure to understand the phenomenon adequately with the result that unimportant variables are used. On the other hand, correlational methods can be used to test hypothetical relationships once these have been formulated from a theory. Their use may also suggest possible relationships that could be explored further, in an attempt to develop new theory. Most correlational methods are easy to use and the results are often easy to interpret. In sum, they are useful techniques, but they usually are not sufficient in themselves to explain locational patterns.

Empirical models differ from correlational methods in that they are based on some objectivity specified (or hypothesized) relationship. Gearing, Swart, and Var developed an empirical model to assess regional attractiveness. Scott, Schewe, and Frederick did the same for vacation choice. Their models are conceptually more sophisticated than simple correlation, and as a result, their models tend to be more realistic and accurate. Ironically, though, as a model is designed to do more, it is capable of doing worse. The regional assessment model is based on the opinions of 'experts' and on several assumptions that can be challenged. The model also describes the implicit forces that influence tourism development better than it tests for cause and effect. The same types of observations were made in the text about the vacation choice model. These models accomplish more than other, simpler methods, and they draw attention to how much remains to be done.

Other empirical models include the interplay of accessibility and resources on the development of recreation business districts (Stansfield and Rickert, and Taylor) and the economic forces implicit in hinterland and threshold populations supporting recreation businesses (Toyne). These models are simplifications of reality – a choice that is both a strength and a weakness. Simplification allows one to analyse a few relationships in great detail, but only by ignoring many others.

Abstract models are an even greater simplification of reality. These models are developed to explain general recreational or landscape systems, usually without reference to any real landscape. Yokeno's tourism model and Klausner's activity/location typology are of this type. Their generality and broad applicability are obtained at the expense of being difficult to empirically test or apply to specific circumstances. This is due to their focus on a few essential forces and the overlooking of local or temporary special conditions. The result is that abstract models are not very useful in fully understanding particular problems, but they do suggest regularities or laws that can give insight into a great many different problems. Ideally, these models are used to generate hypotheses that can be tested for local problems with the correlational techniques described earlier.

Qualitative methods emphasize cultural traditions and social policies. Ritter employed this method in his look at tourism in Islamic countries, as did Symanski in his study of prostitution. Qualitative methods often require a strong 'sense of place.' The researcher must understand customs, laws and values in the context of a geographically-bounded region. Qualitative methods frequently lead to unique answers in the sense that they cannot be generalized. Zentilli's study of national park boundaries, or Cantor and Hatherly's explanation of medieval park location are exceptions, however, and show that non-quantitative methods can lead to a better understanding

71

of patterns in many different locales. Quantitative methods can be combined with qualitative ones to enrich the understanding one gains from each other.

Future research in the explanation of location needs to proceed on two fronts. The methods that exist now should be refined and applied to more and different recreation problems. Current understanding of the locational factors that influence the profitability of recreation businesses, especially within cities, is very weak. But before this work can proceed much further, geographers will need to develop better theories about how decisions to locate and to travel are made. The result will probably be the development of two sub-specialties: general, macro-level models that explain the behaviour of groups of people, or the locational patterns of facility types; and micro-level models that explain the behaviour of individuals, or the locatic nal patterns of specific facilities.

Additional reading

Alderson, F. (1973) *The Inland Resorts and Spas of Britain*, David and Charles, Newton Abbot

Aldskogius, H. (1967) 'Vacation house settlement in the Siljan Region', *Geografiska Annaler*, **49B**, 69–95

Alpert, M. I. (1967) 'Identification of determinant attributes: a comparison of methods', *Journal of Marketing Research*, **8**, 84–91

Applebaum, W. (1968) *Store Location Strategy Cases*, Addison-Wesley, Don Mills, Ontario

Freeland, J. M. (1966)*The Australian Pub*, Melbourne University Press, Melbourne

Hern, A. (1967) *The Seaside Holiday: The History of the English Seaside Resort*, The Cresset Press, London

Hodgen, M. T. (1942) 'Fairs of Elizabethan England', *Economic Geography*, **18**, 389–400

Prime, T. S. S. (1976) *Caribbean Tourism*, Key Caribbean Publications, Port of Spain, Trinidad

Pryce, R. (1967) 'The location and growth of holiday caravan camps in Wales: 1956–65', *Transactions of the Institute of British Geographers*, **42**, 127–52

Robinson, G. W. S. (1972) 'The recreational geography of South Asia', *Geographical Review*, **62**, 561–72

Vuoristo, K. V. (1969) 'On the geographical features of tourism in Finland', *Fennia*, **99**, 127–39

CHAPTER 4

Explanatory research on travel

Travel is the result of push and pull forces. Push forces include psychological motivations as well as the influences of sex, income, education, and other personal variables that enable and shape the pattern of travel. Pull forces refer to those features of the destination or route that attract a traveller. These features may be either tangible resources or the perceptions and expectations of the traveller.

The explanation of travel patterns is not complete without considering the effect of push and pull forces on the choice of route and specific modes of transportation. To understand better how these forces combine to produce an actual travel pattern, and to understand better pleasure travel when there is no particular destination, geographers have developed the perceptual concepts of mental maps and spatial search models. Perceptions of space, distance, and the distribution of resources are especially important in the context of explaining supply-induced travel – which includes much recreational travel.

This chapter examines methods used to study each of the above subjects: the push forces at the origin; the pull forces of the destination; and the actual travel resulting from their combination.

Push forces

Psychological motivations

A common method used to explain pleasure travel is reflective thinking. On the basis of personal experience, conversations with travellers, and review of the literature, a researcher develops a 'theory' of travel motivations. One example is the psycho-analytical speculations of Grinstein (1955) who suggested vacation travel 'serves to enhance the feeling of mastery over reality, either directly or symbolically', thus allowing some people to 'extend their ego boundaries'. Lundberg (1972), on the other hand, suggested that travel motivations are based on the need for: change; the exotic; education; feelings of power, beauty, and wonder; ego enhancement and sensual indulgence; or rest, relaxation, and/or excitement. Gray (1970) saw only two reasons for travel: wanderlust (the desire to see new and different things); and sunlust (the desire to go somewhere nicer than home). The meanings of the terms used by such authors are usually vague and overly-general. Further, like most fruits of speculation, they are rarely based on empirical analysis. However, conjecture and reflective thinking are often good starting points for developing questions and ideas for further research and can help focus a new research project.

A more objective approach to understanding travel motivations is to ask people why they go. Their answers are then grouped by the researcher either arbitrarily or through some objective clustering analysis to identify major reasons for taking a trip. An example of this is Tapia's (1967) survey of the expressed travel motivations of Mexican tourists. After obtaining a lengthy list of reasons from travellers, he subjectively grouped the responses into four categories of 'motivators': (1) physical motivators, e.g., the search for a mild climate; (2) cultural motivators, e.g., curiosity about other countries or an interest in cultural activities; (3) interpersonal motivators, e.g., the desire to meet new people; and (4) status and prestige motivators, e.g., the desire for attention from the folks at home.

Tapia noted that these motivators do not operate in isolation. They are modified by experience and by the satisfaction they lead to. The most important set of modifiers are 'reinforcers'. If a person is motivated by cultural interests to choose and chooses a destination to fulfil these interests, the availability of cultural attractions will have a strong effect on the probability of ever travelling to that destination again. Reinforcers can also operate, in a certain sense, through advertising. The traveller with cultural interests will be unlikely to choose a destination if the advertising for that destination emphasizes physical attributes to the exclusion of cultural attractions – thus failing to 'reinforce' his basic interest in making a trip.

Assuming reinforcers can be classified into the same categories as motivators, Tapia asked his respondents to identify the degree to which different destinations met their expectations. A correlation of the strength of each type of motivator with each type of reinforcer, by destination, showed a strongly positive relationship between the same types of motivators and reinforcers. For example, the correlation between the strength of physical motivations and the presence of physical reinforcers was 0.52. On the other hand, the correlation between physical reinforcers and cultural motivators (as an example of disparate motivators and reinforcers) was −0.38. This supports the expectation that someone with cultural interests is not especially attracted by an emphasis on the presence of non-cultural attractions.

A more sophisticated approach than directly asking travellers about their motivations is the use of psychographics. Psychographics are 'personality profiles' designed to provide an insight into the psychology of potential travellers through a detailed examination of their activities, interests and opinions (AIOs). This information is usually obtained by asking respondents to indicate their level of agreement with a series of statements such as 'I like to get away from crowds when I am on vacation' or 'People should not borrow money to take a vacation.'

Once a number of individual personality profiles has been developed, groups of similar personalities are combined to form relatively homogeneous market segments. The intent behind psychographics is the identification and description of potential markets so that advertising campaigns can be more effectively designed. As a result, the technique also provides information about some of the motivations of different personalities that is of use to a social scientist interested in why people decide to make certain trips. Wells (1975) provides a critical review of the use and limitations of psychographics in research.

Schewe and Calantone (1978) employed psychographics to analyse the market for Massachusetts (USA) tourism. Car travellers entering the state in vehicles bearing out-of-state licence plates were randomly selected at an entrance station on the Massachusetts Turnpike. The drivers were given a questionnaire, a brief explanation of the purpose of the study, and a request that the questionnaire be returned through the mail upon completion of their trip. The questionnaire contained over 100 statements about general recreation activities, lifestyle interests and opinions, and travel preferences. Each respondent indicated the level of agreement on a six-point scale. Purpose of the trip and intended destination were also identified.

When the questionnaires were returned, they were grouped by purpose of trip (business, visit friends and relatives, recreation and tourism). Questionnaires from people indicating 'recreation and tourism' were then disaggregated by intended destination (cities, ocean beaches, mountains). Patterns

Table 4.1 Percentage agreement by type of destination of recreationists

	Mountains	*Cities*	*Beaches*
Cape Cod is over-rated	63	73	42
Inland lakes are more enjoyable than the ocean	76	61	46
There is too much emphasis on sex today	56	55	73
I would rather live in the city than in the suburbs	56	32	33
I am more independent than most people	53	41	60
Our family is too heavily in debt	19	26	21

Source: Summarized from Schewe and Calantone

of agreement with various statements were identified to define different market segments and to determine what AIOs characterized these segments. (A few of these results are presented in Table 4.1.)

From these and other statements, the authors developed guidelines for the marketing of each destination region in Massachusetts. For example, tourists likely to go to Cape Cod would probably be turned off by advertisements emphasizing sex as an attraction at the Cape. Still other responses (not included in Table 4.1) indicated that visitors to all three areas were not worried about borrowing for a vacation and that Cape Cod visitors were more likely to read news magazines than were visitors to other destinations.

As useful as psychographics are, they cannot tell the full story about the decision to travel. Information about the economic, social and demographic characteristics of travellers is also needed. Income, age, previous experience, education and other socio-economic variables play a role as important as that of AIOs.

Socio-economic variables

Correlation and cross-tabulation of socio-economic variables with travel variables is one of the most common methods employed to explain individual travel. Although aggregate measures such as median income of a population are sometimes used to explain patterns of travel in national populations (for example, Burkart and Medlik 1974), most analyses focus on individuals or small groups.

Socio-economic analysis of travel begins with the selection of variables that can be objectively measured and that are theoretically or statistically related to travel behaviour. Age, sex, occupation, marital status, income, and years of education are frequently used. Some measure of travel behaviour is also necessary, of course. This might be the incidence of travel (whether or not a trip is made), the frequency of trips, the distance travelled, the purpose of a trip, or other measures. Socio-economic characteristics are then cross-tabulated against one or more travel variables to identify any significant regularities. Typical of this method are Dent's (1974) work on the pattern of Canberra (Australia) residents' trips to the beach and Hill's (1974) examination of snow-mobiling in New York (USA). Hanson (1977) provides an example of a detailed study of the travel patterns of two different population subgroups. In this case, Hanson examined the relative patterns of travel and socio-economic characteristics of elderly and non-elderly residents of Uppsala (Sweden). Travel patterns were defined as the purpose of the trip, the mode of transportation, distance travelled, number of trips per time period, and the number of stops per trip.

Variations in travel behaviour by origin or destination are sometimes of special interest. Two methods can be used to study these. One might simply cross-tabulate socio-economic and travel variables by origin or destination. For example, a geographer may wish to compare the frequency of trips made by males alone with the frequency of trips made by females alone in Western versus Islamic countries. To do this, separate tables showing sex versus number of trips for each set of countries could be constructed (Table 4.2). Differences between sexes within one type of country and differences between countries are then examined with chi-squared or other statistical methods.

Table 4.2 Format of table comparing sex with frequency of trips made alone

	Frequency of trips				
	0	1–3	4–6	7–9	10+
Male	n_1	n_2	n_3	n_4	n_5
Female	n_6	n_7	n_8	n_9	n_{10}

where: n_i is the number of individuals reporting a particular trip frequency within a given period of time.

Another, less common method for describing variations, either by region or by groups of individuals, is to employ ternary graphs. These were developed in physical geography to graphically describe the composition of soil types (Strahler 1969, 297). Campbell (1967) and Lentnek, Van Doren, and Trail (1969) have extended their use to recreational travel. Campbell used ternary graphs to cluster individuals travelling to particular destinations while Lentnek, Van Doren, and Trail classified lakes on the basis of boating done on them.

Ternary graphs are appropriate when the phenomenon being studied can be described as a mix of three different qualities. The mix is expressed in percentages and these must total exactly 100 per cent. In Fig. 4.1, for example, trips for several different purposes have been plotted on a triangle whose sides represent different levels of education. To read the diagram, refer to any one side. The lines of the triangle that define the scale for that side begin at that side and move away to the left. The line that intersects a point on the diagram gives the percentage mix of that particular quality. The same step is repeated for the other sides. Thus, at point A (all those who reported travelling to visit friends or relatives), 20 per cent have a university degree, 50 per cent have grade school or some high school, and 30 per cent have a high school diploma or some university education. One advantage of this method is that it allows for the quick visual determination of possible clusters. For example, on the basis of education, educational and business trips are relatively similar types of trips. Both are engaged in predominantly by people with university education. Family recreation amd shopping trips are also similar to each other, and are engaged in by approximately equal percentages of all three educational groups.

Another aspect of travel behaviour on which socio-economic variables are

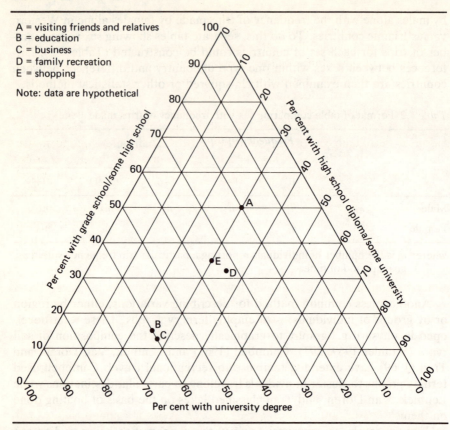

A = visiting friends and relatives
B = education
C = business
D = family recreation
E = shopping

Note: data are hypothetical

Per cent with grade school/some high school

Per cent with high school diploma/some university

Per cent with university degree

Figure 4.1 Example of a ternary diagram: educational variations by purpose of trip

frequently brought to bear are the patterns of multi-purpose, multi-staged trips. These trips are those during which a traveller makes two or more stops with different purposes at each stop. Hemmens (1966, 1970), Gilbert, Peterson, and Schafer (1972), and Jones (1974) have argued for the importance of understanding interactions among time, space, and activities in explanations of intra-urban travel patterns. More recently, Bentley, Bruce, and Jones (1977) undertook an empirical analysis of intra-urban trips and activity linkages in a study of Watford (England) residents. In the Watford study, travel diaries were filled out by a random sample of adults. Data were then aggregated by day of week and by 'housewives' versus 'other adults' and then the number of trips by purpose and number of stops were tabulated. The most common sequences of purposes were noted. More shopping, and then leisure, were the two most frequent reasons for a stop after an initial stop for shopping. The number of single-destination and multiple-destination trips were also calculated for different socio-economic groupings (age, sex, social class, number of cars, number of children). The authors then drew conclusions from these patterns about the forces that influenced the decision to make a multi-purpose, multi-staged trip.

Fuel price and availability, while not traditional socio-economic variables, have grown in importance both as research variables and as policy issues in developed countries. This is due, in large part, to a series of 'fuel crises'. A direct approach to understanding the effects of a fuel crisis is to examine it from an historical perspective. The characteristics of travellers before, during, and after a crisis such as the 1973 oil embargo imposed by the Organization of Petroleum Exporting Countries (OPEC) can be compared to see what effect, if any, the event had on different groups. The number of trips, the distance and duration of trips, the switch to multi-purpose, multi-staged trips, and changes in attitudes can also be included in such a study as possible effects to be looked for. Solomon and George (1976) provide an example.

A slightly different method, one that avoids emphasizing real or imagined crises, is to ask travellers to forecast their likely responses to another round of fuel price increases or to rationing if it were imposed. This approach has been taken by Kamp, Crompton, and Hensarling (1979) in their study of motorists stopping at a Texas (USA) highway welcoming station. Drivers were asked to speculate about changes in travel behaviour (cancellation of trip, change of mode of travel, change of length of trip) in response to different hypothetical price increases and to different levels of fuel availability. Responses were grouped by type of vehicle, purpose of trip, and whether or not they considered their travel essential. Corsi and Harvey (1980) applied a similar research design in a nationwide study of USA travel behaviour and reactions to fuel availability.

The answers in both studies were based on personal opinion rather than on actual behaviour. Thus, while some insight may be gained into possible effects on individual behaviour, there are problems with this approach. In the Texas study, for example, 40 per cent of the respondents said they would forego a vacation trip if the price of petrol reached $1.00 (USA) for a USA gallon. Within a year and a half of the time of the survey, prices had gone that high but there was no significant decline in car travel. There are two reasons for the failure of this prediction.

People do not always know how they will respond to any given situation until it actually develops. When travel decisions have to be made, many people find that so-called discretionary travel may be more important than ever. As the restraints on pleasure travel grow, the desire for pleasure travel may also grow. This may also be the explanation for the pattern Wolfe (1980) observed in France and Czechoslovakia. Under conditions of higher prices and scarcer fuel than North America has yet known, many motorists were finding substitutes for driving private cars on mandatory trips to work and school, and saved their fuel for pleasure trips.

The other reason for the failure of these studies to accurately predict what drivers will do in times of increased fuel costs is that most fail to specify the time period over which the increases are to occur. A 22 per cent increase in petrol prices imposed by the government of Canada in 1979, with only a few days notice, led to the defeat of that government in parliament. If the same percentage increase had occurred over three or four years, it would scarcely cause comment. Rather than actual price levels, a more relevant measure might be an annual percentage increase. Alternatively, some time period might be added to the scenario presented to the respondent. Instead of asking, 'Would you cancel your trip if fuel costs reached $3.00 per gallon?', one could ask, 'Would you cancel your trip if fuel costs reached $3.00 within the next month?'

To be even more realistic, fuel costs have to be placed in the context of other increases in wages and prices. The importance of this can be seen in the light of what happened to American travel after the 7¢ per gallon increase in gasoline between 1974 and 1978. Although this increase, brought about by the OPEC embargo, was a relatively large increase, it was less than the overall inflation rate. In effect, the relative cost of gasoline in the USA actually declined, and the boom in recreational vehicle sales and in pleasure travel over this period was not irrational.

This whole subject is a part of a broader concept often used in recreation research: willingness-to-pay. A common problem in the analysis of consumption of recreation is the fact that many recreation resources and activities are partially subsidized, and some are virtually free. Analysis of decisions regarding the consumption of such resources, therefore, is not possible with traditional market-place economics. Actual prices do not reflect either the true cost of providing subsidized resources, nor do they necessarily reflect the true value of them to the consumer. In order to approach the conditions necessary to allow a traditional market-place analysis, researchers sometimes choose to ask potential consumers their willingness to pay for different resources, rather than to observe actual but distorted payments patterns.

There are problems, however, with the willingness-to-pay concept applied in this form. Because no money actually changes hands, the respondent in a survey may attempt to guess the purpose behind the question about payment and will give a biased answer, reflecting what he believes the researcher's true intentions to be. For example, if the respondent suspects a willingness-to-pay question is being used to determine actual prices, he will tend to answer on the low side, hoping to keep future prices down. On the other hand, if the respondent suspects that the question is designed to reflect the value of the resource – and thus possibly determine whether a resource will continue to be available (at a subsidized price) – the respondent will tend to exaggerate the price he is 'willing' to pay.

An alternative approach is to ask consumers how much they would have to be paid to be willing to forego consuming a particular resource or to stop using a particular facility. But because no money changes hands in this imaginary situation either, there is a tendency for respondents to exaggerate by unknown amounts the size of the 'bribe' they would accept. Dwyer, Kelly, and Bowes (1977) discuss the concept of willingness-to-pay at greater length.

Seckler (1966) illustrates some of the potential abuses of willingness-to-pay concepts in public outdoor recreation planning.

Another class of variables not usually considered 'socio-economic' are physical and mental disabilities. One of the few studies that have addressed the effects of disabilities on pleasure travel is a survey by Woodside and Etzel (1980) of travel patterns among South Carolina (USA) residents. Although numerous case studies have been completed of individuals or facilities, no general survey of the travel patterns of handicapped people had been completed at the time the authors began their work. Their approach was simple and did not represent a methodological contribution to recreation geography. Rather, the significance in their study was in its limited substantive contribution.

Physical and mental handicaps were self-defined, and included temporary conditions such as pregnancy as well as permanent conditions such as the absence of limbs. Limitations on mobility such as being confined to a wheel chair, as well as limitations on effort, such as heart conditions, were also included. Given this broad compass, it should not be surprising that 10 per cent of the respondents reported a member of their travelling party on their most recent trip away from home had a disability that affected travel. Analysis was limited to tabulating types and frequencies of disabilities as well as the reported changes in travel plans compared to what might have been if the condition did not exist. Comparisons were made between responses by travelling parties with a disabled traveller and those without. Trip characteristics of special interest included: destination type, purpose of trip, nights away from home, method of travel, cost of trip, and self-evaluation of trip satisfactions.

Limitations in this particular study include the imprecise and simplistic grouping of disabilities. The authors did not examine the amount of advance planning, such as the identification of architectural barriers, necessary for travel with a handicapped person, nor the relative ease with which such planning could be accomplished. The sample size was 590 respondents with only sixty reporting a handicapped traveller. Such a small number necessarily limits the type of statistical analysis and the variety of experience that can be drawn upon. With larger, more representative samples, it would be possible to include more detailed examination of specific handicaps, and to extend the range of analysis so that travelling disabilities could be treated as another variable comparable to those considered elsewhere in this chapter.

Pull forces

People are attracted to a destination because it offers them something they cannot obtain where they currently are. Variations in the patterns of recreational travel reflect variations in the distribution of resources and in the distributions of tastes and preferences of potential travellers. To understand the attractions of different destinations, it is necessary to examine both the resource base and how travellers perceive these resources.

Resources

The traditional geographic method for analysing the effect of resources on motivating and directing travel is to identify and examine the destinations of travellers and the resources that seem to distinguish different groups of travellers and different destinations. Selke (1936) traces this type of systematic inquiry into vacation travel back to Mariotti's 1927/28 examination of the Italian tourist industry (*Lezioni di Economia Turistica*). Selke's own work, however, is more directly in the traditions familiar to modern geographers. As part of his analysis of the German travel industry in the 1920s and 1930s, he identified several resources spatially or temporally associated with recreational travel that have become *de rigueur* for geographic analysis of vacation patterns: seasonality, especially temperature, length of daylight, and the availability of snow; topography; ground water phenomena, especially mineral springs; running water features; glacial morphology; seashores; volcanic phenomena; diastrophic phenomena; flora and fauna; and 'human factors' such as museums, architecture, and industrial plant tours. Each of these was given separate attention – distribution, magnitude, and concentrations were described and mapped. For each one, the levels of visitation, types of associated accommodation and activities, and a bit of history or other background material was also provided. The combined effect was a wide-ranging narrative of the environment of German tourism, domestic and international, that provided the context for an analysis of the economic effects of tourism development around the country.

Another narrative approach is to focus on types of travellers rather than on types of resources. From this perspective, one 'follows' travellers from their various origins to specific destinations to identify those variables that influence the choice of routes and specific sites within the general destination region. Deasy's (1949) analysis of the tourism industry in a north woods county in Michigan (USA) is one of the earliest and best known examples. On the basis of previous experience, Deasy divided all visitors into five categories: (1) summer campers and fishermen; (2) autumn deer hunters; (3) sightseers; (4) transients; and (5) a gallimaufry of hay fever sufferers, partridge hunters, artists, and 'others'. Each group formed a separate section for discussion. Spatial distributions of origins, routes of travel into and within the region, types of preferred accommodation and activities, the type and distribution of the resources that support those activities, and some estimate of the total number of visitors provided the rubric Deasy worked in.

A narrative approach, of course, is not limited to the early studies of tourist travel. Matley (1976) has used narration to good effect in his examination of the forces shaping international tourism in the 1960s and 1970s. The time is current, the scope is broader, but the approach is the same as that of Selke and Deasy. A series of resources and destination areas provide the outline for a discussion of the patterns of travel, the development of international travel and accommodation, and the forces that influence these phenomena. Despite forty years between Selke and Matley, little has changed in the selection of important recreation resources: climate; water; topography; landscape; flora and fauna; mineral springs; and man-made attractions.

Matley distinguished several more precise classifications of manmade attractions. European cities are singled out as a special type of attraction, in contrast to Christaller's opinion that European cities are relatively unimportant destinations. Religious shrines, especially Christian and Muslim, are also seen as important international attractions. Battlefields, estates, chateaux, and farms are popular rural attractions, as are the sites of ancient ruins. Some modern 'ruins' are also significant tourist features, such as Second World War concentration camps.

Other man-made attractions of major tourist importance are the Olympics, the Commonwealth Games, international soccer matches, and to a lesser degree, international tennis and golf championships. National and regional sporting events can be generators of domestic recreational travel. Theme parks such as Disney World (USA), large urban parks such as Tivoli (Denmark), 'open air' museums such as Greenfield Village (USA) and Skansen (Sweden), and international exhibitions and world fairs are also attractions generating both domestic and international pleasure travel.

Another source of tourist travel that is frequently overlooked is the border town. Low prices for some goods such as cigarettes, gasoline, or liquor, or the availability of banned products, such as prostitutes, in neighbouring political units can generate locally significant travel volumes.

A different approach to understanding the influences on travel is to examine actual levels of tourist travel in comparison to some measure of expected travel. If there is a significant variation between the two, it may be possible to identify probable causes. These causes, in turn, lead to better understanding of the forces affecting the decision to travel. An example of this logic can be found in Williams and Zelinsky's (1970) study of international travel flows.

Williams and Zelinsky applied Goodman's hypothesis of indifference (Goodman 1963) to estimate the expected number of visits between any two countries. If one country receives 10 per cent of all international travel, for example, the hypothesis of indifference suggests that it should receive 10 per cent from each origin country. After obtaining a set of expected flows among fourteen countries, they found numerous examples where the observed and the predicted flows were significantly different. They then tested several hypotheses to explain these patterns.

1. The closer two countries are geographically, the more likely travel between them will exceed that predicted. Similarly, the greater the his-

83

torical, cultural, or trade connections between countries, the greater the actual flows *vis-à-vis* the expected. On the other hand, political and cultural difference can diminish the actual flows below that expected.

2. Attractive resources, especially a mild and sunny climate, will create a disproportionately large flow between certain pairs of countries. The heliotropic/boreaphobic drive (in the words of Williams and Zelinsky) or sunlust (in the words of Gray) is especially important in explaining travel to the south by Canadians, Scandinavians, and others living in cold climates.

3. Differences in prices and the availability of charter fares to certain destinations can create unexpectedly large flows.

4. Finally, special events such as world fairs can be used to boost tourist travel for a temporary period.

The authors found isolated examples where every hypothesis seemed to explain the differences observed, and concluded that, within the limits of available data, the hypotheses were supported.

Deasy and Griess (1966) also used this logic of discrepancy. In their project, they made predictions about the size, shape, and extent of the hinterland around a tourist attraction. Under ideal conditions, Deasy and Griess reasoned, travellers to an isolated attraction would come from a circular hinterland. If two similar, competing attractions had overlapping hinterlands, a boundary would form between them along the line of equal travel cost, and this would form a 'tourist-shed', analogous to a watershed. Travellers living on one side of the line would go only to the attraction on the same side. This is essentially the same logic used in Reilly's law of retail gravitation, and just as in retail geography, the ideal pattern is seldom observed. After mapping the origins of visitors to two competing tourist attractions in Pennsylvania (USA) – the Pioneer Tunnel Coal Mine and the Seldom Seen Valley Mine – Deasy and Griess observed that significant numbers of people choose to pass by the nearer attraction in favour of the more distant one. Moreover, the general shape of the hinterlands was highly irregular. Several hypotheses were formulated that might explain these patterns.

The first hypothesis concerned a 'regional identity'. The authors thought that western Pennsylvania, which included the Seldom Seen Valley Mine, might belong to a Lower Lakes Region, characterized by much travel throughout the region, with relatively little travel to other regions. The same thought would apply, of course, to the Pioneer Tunnel Mine in eastern Pennsylvania and the Middle Atlantic Region of which they were a part. Testing for the existence and influence of a regional identity is difficult. An approximation was made, however, by the following method.

Residents who lived in counties surrounding the two mines in 1955 but who had moved out by 1960 were identified from census records and their new county of residence mapped. The pattern of residential change was used to infer the extent of any regional sense of identity – assuming that residential migration would more or less resemble recreational migration in extent and direction. Patterns of residential relocation did emerge, and there was a rough correlation with the patterns of tourist travel to the two mines.

·   A related concept was also developed and tested: the familiarity of potential visitors with the products of the two mines. The Seldom Seen Valley Mine is promoted with an emphasis on coal, a widely-familiar concept. The Pioneer Tunnel, though, is promoted as an anthracite mine, a less common concept. The authors obtained estimates of regional anthracite sales in the North-east and Middle Atlantic Regions and observed a moderately strong correlation between the regional patterns of anthracite coal sales and *per capita* visitation to the mine. No special pattern was observed for bituminous coal sales and visits to the Seldom Seen Valley Mine.

Extending the concept of 'familiarity' still further, the authors next examined the effects of advertising on the generation of trips to the two mines. Both the location of newpapers carrying paid advertisements and the cost of the advertisements were mapped. The patterns of advertising distribution and of visitor origins revealed a very good match (see Fig. 4.2), and the authors concluded that advertising was probably a key determinant in the development of the facilities' hinterlands. They did not examine, though, the influences on the decisions to locate advertisements in certain areas – it is possible that the pattern of visitation existed first, and that advertising was tailored to fit the established pattern.

Another method employed in the search for explanations of travel is the use of a generalized conceptual model of the utility of attractions. One basic model was first developed by Luce (1959) to explain individual choice behaviour and was later extended by Huff (1963) to consumer decision-making, and finally applied by Wennergren and Nielsen (1968) to recreational travel. This model explains the choice of any destination from a set of alternatives as a function of the perceived utility of that destination in comparison to all other destinations. More precisely, the probability of any destination being chosen is proportional to its utility divided by the total utility of all possible destinations. In the work of Wennergren and Nielsen the destinations were reservoirs used for boating. A fundamental question was how to objectively measure the utility of a reservoir for boating. Their solution was to combine two easily measured variables: the surface area of the reservoirs, and the distance between eight origin regions and each reservoir. The first variable is positively related to utility; the second, inversely. In other words, the bigger or closer the reservoir, the better.

The utility of each reservoir was determined by dividing the surface area of that reservoir by the distance between that reservoir and a given origin. This was done for all reservoirs with respect to each origin; the total of these individual utilities is a measure of the aggregate boating utility for a traveller at a given origin. The probability he will make a trip to any particular reservoir is given by the ratio of the utility of that reservoir to all reservoirs:

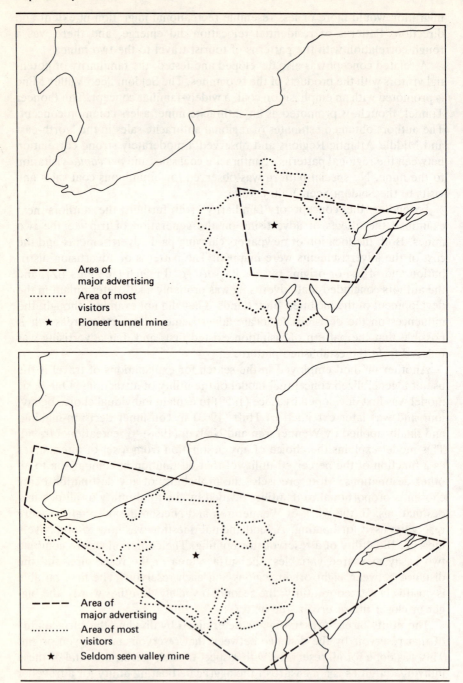

Figure 4.2 Spatial relationship between advertising and patterns of tourists' origins: two Pennsylvania tourist attractions (after Deasy and Griess 1966)

$$P_{ij} = \frac{S_j^a/D_{ij}^b}{\sum\limits_{k=1}^{n}(S_k^a/D_{ik}^b)} \qquad\qquad [4.1]$$

where: P_{ij} = probability of a person at origin i selecting reservoir j
S_j = surface area of reservoir j
S_k = surface area of all reservoirs k
D_{ij} = distance between i and j
D_{ik} = distance between i and k
n = number of reservoirs
a, b = empirically estimated parameters

By multiplying P_{ij} by the number of boaters at any origin, the authors were able to estimate the likely number of boaters travelling between individual pairs of origin and destination. A comparison of their estimates with actual figures was significantly close.

The last approach considered here is the analysis of correlations between travel patterns and socio-economic variables collected through on-site interviews. On-site observations of individual travellers are correlated with other observations such as the *per capita* rates of trips by origin, distance travelled, and site quality. Mercer (1972) used this approach in his study of travel to Melbourne (Australia) area beaches.

After collecting and organizing data from a series of beach interviews, Mercer regressed the variable 'distance to nearest beach' with 'visits per thousand population', using the municipal divisions of Melbourne region as units of analysis. This regression confirmed Mercer's belief in the importance of distance as an explanatory variable. The correlation between distance and visitation rates was not perfect, however. An analysis of the differences between the rate observed and that predicted by the regression analysis disclosed additional information. Many littoral suburbs had visitation rates far exceeding the predicted, even when their proximity to beaches was taken into account. Other seaside neighbourhoods had travel rates significantly lower than expected. The same discrepancies appeared for some inland communities. Upon closer examination of these anomalies, Mercer noted that positive residuals (unexpectedly high rates) were often associated with communities with above average incomes and large numbers of children and teenagers. Low rates of travel were spatially correlated with low incomes and high concentrations of the elderly and recent immigrants.

Further detail was added to the analysis by the tedious task of plotting the origins of each respondent at each beach. Individual distance decay curves were graphed for each beach, and the hinterlands delineated. Examination of the curves and the hinterlands pointed to the influence of highway accessibility, variations in perceptions of distance, and the central business district as a barrier as possible additional influences on travel.

Perceptions

Analysis of the perceptions of potential travellers of alternative destinations is as important as the analysis of 'reality'. In a sense, it might be said that resources exist only in the minds of those who use them. Knowledge and favourable evaluation of a resource are the *sine qua non* for its use. One technique used to explain the relationship between perceptions and travel behaviour is the Fishbein choice model (1963, 1967). Fishbein suggested that the choice of a particular good, such as a vacation destination, is the result of a comparison of the attributes of that destination with the person's set of preferred attributes. The alternative that most closely matches the ideal will be selected. The model involves two steps: (1) identification of desired characteristics; (2) measurement of the degree to which each destination possesses these. Because the characteristics define the utility of the destination, the Fishbein model is similar to the Wennergren–Nielsen model. The primary difference is that the Fishbein model uses a subjective reality, while the Wennergren–Nielsen model uses an objective reality.

The specific tasks necessary to use the Fishbein model for the choice of a destination are:

1. Compile a list of destination characteristics potentially desired and a separate list of destinations potentially chosen.
2. Have a random sample of respondents, representative of the population under study, indicate the relative importance of each characteristic on an appropriate scale.
3. Average all respondents' ratings from Step 2 for each characteristic.
4. Have the same respondents indicate the degree to which each destination possesses each characteristic on an appropriate scale.
5. Average the ratings from Step 4 for each characteristic at each destination.
6. Multiply the averages obtained from Step 3 and 5 for each destination to obtain the average perceived utility of each destination.

Comparisons of the utilities among all destinations provides relative rankings of different destinations. Goodrich (1978) has applied this procedure to a comparison of nine Western Hemisphere resort areas: Florida, Mexico, California, Jamaica, the Virgin Islands, Puerto Rico, the Bahamas, Barbados, and Hawaii. After obtaining the relative rankings of these areas, he compared the rankings with the expressed travel preferences of the same respondents. The result was a very close match between the perceived utility estimated from a Fishbein model and the expressed preferences of travellers.

A different method that is also useful for explaining variations in the perceptions of travel dimensions is multi-dimensional scaling. Like the Fishbein model, multi-dimensional scaling requires a list of potentially important destination features, as well as respondent assessments of the degree to which a series of destinations possesses these features. The actual analysis of the data is rather complicated and is usually accomplished via electronic data processing. A useful overview of the method can be found in Green and Carmone (1970).

An important feature of multi-dimensional scaling is that it places different destinations at positions along a small number of scales or dimensions that summarize the total variation among the destinations. The relative location of each destination reflects the particular characteristics of that destination. The closer two destinations are on the dimensions, the more similar they are. This also allows the identification of potentially substitutable or competitive destinations.

Mayo (1975) used multi-dimensional scaling for an analysis of eight tourist regions in the United States plus the national parks (considered as one 'region'), Indian reservations (also considered one region), and a hypothetical, ideal destination. Three dimensions resulted from his respondents' assessments of the qualities of these different regions: the relative level of congestion, scenic quality, and climate. The relative attractiveness of each destination in terms of these three general qualities was measured and five clusters of similar types of destinations defined. The distance (similarity) between each actual region and the ideal region was also observed and measured.

Mayo then asked his respondents to rank each ideal region on the basis of its relative attractiveness using a seven-point scale. Ratings for each were obtained and these were correlated with the levels of agreement to eighty-five psychographic statements. Eighteen of the eighty-five statements were significantly related to the perceived attractiveness. These eighteen statements were then factor analysed and seven personality traits identified that summarized different types of personalities that preferred each type of destination.

Multi-dimensional scaling and the Fishbein model are based on several shared assumptions. First, the researcher assumes he has identified all relevant locational characteristics. Obviously, if any characteristics have been left out, these cannot be included in the final conclusions. More fundamentally, both techniques are based on the assumption that respondents are able to form reliable, consistent images of various destinations, or conversely, that regions produce simple, identifiable images in the minds of potential visitors. This is obviously a moot point in the case of 'regions' such as the entire set of USA national parks. The validity of this assumption is supported, in part, by research that correlates the quality of an image with the perceptions of the characteristics of that region. In other words, researchers (e.g., Goodrich) sometimes test the validity of their models by asking potential travellers to what degree Region X has all the things a desirable vacation area should have. The answer is then compared to the expressed attractiveness of Region X. The usual result of this 'test' is a close match. Apparently few people are likely to indicate a region has everything they want in a vacation destination and yet say they would not like to go there. The 'test' thus says more about respondents' psyches than about the model itself.

The final method we will consider in the context of measuring the perception of destination and their qualities is based on the concept of cognitive dissonance (Brehm and Cohen, 1962; Festinger, 1964). Cognitive dissonance is the undesirable mental condition of believing contradictory 'facts' and being aware of that contradiction. An illustration will help to clarify this.

Adams (1973) undertook a study of the effects of uncertainty in weather forecasts on the decision to make a trip to the beach. His problem was this: if someone decides to go to the beach, and then learns that the weather prospects are unfavourable, he is put in a state of cognitive dissonance. To resolve the dissonance, two strategies are available. The traveller can cancel the trip. This makes his actions consonant with the information he has received, but it can lead to disappointment. Alternatively, he can alter his perceptions or interpretation of the information and still make the trip as planned. If his new interpretation turns out to be incorrect, he may still be disappointed, but at least he has removed any dissonance. Adams tried to determine whether or not some beach travellers actually distorted the information contained in an uncertain weather forecast to justify a preferred course of action. The research design to answer this question was composed of eight steps.

1. A sample of beach users was randomly selected at a series of beaches in the USA New England Region, and the sample was randomly divided in half.
2. The first half was asked if they would have made the decision to come to the beach if the weather forecast the night before gave a 60 per cent chance of rain. The answer, 'yes' or 'no', was termed the behavioural commitment.
3. The same respondents were asked to express, on a qualitative scale, ranging from 'not likely' to 'almost certain', the chances of rain represented by 60 per cent.
4. Both halves of the respondent group were asked whether they would go to the beach if the weather forecast showed a 50 per cent chance for good weather and 50 per cent chance for bad weather. The answer was termed the tentative commitment. Those who said they would go were defined to have strong tentative commitment, while those who said they would not go were said to have weak tentative commitment (see Table 4.3).

Table 4.3 Behavioural commitment versus strength of tentative commitment

Forecast	Strength of tentative commitment	Behavioural commitment:	
		Go to beach (%)	Cancel trip (%)
60% chance of rain	Strong	60	40
	Weak	19	81

Chi squared = 10.65, significant at 0.01

Source: Adams

5. The strength of the tentative commitment for each respondent was cross-tabulated with their behavioural commitment. The resulting pattern gave evidence of a strong desire for cognitive assonance (the opposite of cognitive dissonance). In other words, those who has a strong commitment to go were optimistic about the chances of good weather under the conditions of a 60 per cent chance of rain. Those with weak commitment hypothetically cancelled their trip (see Table 4.4). There is still a question, though, about which is the cause and which the effect. Does optimism about good weather lead to a strong commitment, or does a strong commitment lead to an optimistic interpretation of the forecast? Three more steps were taken to answer this.

Table 4.4 Perceived likelihood of rain versus behavioural commitment

Forecast	Behavioural commitment	Perceived likelihood:			
		Almost certain (%)	Likely (%)	A chance (%)	Not likely (%)
60% chance of rain	Go to beach	16	30	40	14
	Cancel trip	46	40	12	2

Chi squared = 21.84, significant at 0.001

Source: Adams

6. The second half of the respondent group formed a control group. They were asked what a 60 per cent chance of rain meant, without reference to a beach trip. They expressed their answers on the same qualitative scale used in Step 3.
7. The perception of the control group was compared to the perceptions of those with weak and those with strong tentative commitments from the other group. The control group was more pessimistic than those with strong commitments and more optimistic than those with weak commitment, thus reinforcing the hypothesis that some distortion of weather information had occurred among beach travellers to reinforce a previous desire (see Table 4.5).
8. Finally, the strength of the tentative commitment for the control group was tabulated with the perceived likelihood of rain when the forecast was for a 60 per cent chance of rain. There was no difference between the responses of those with strong commitment and those with weak commitment (see Table 4.6).

From these results Adams concluded that the desire for travel can cause a potential traveller to distort his perception of weather forecasts. More generally, this study gives evidence that a person's predispositions can sometimes lead to distortions of environmental information. This may provide a partial explanation of why people sometimes behave apparently irrationally when

Table 4.5 Perceived likelihood of rain: control versus test groups

		Perceived likelihood:			
Forecast	*Behavioural commitment*	*Almost certain* (%)	*Likely*(%)	*A chance* (%)	*Not likely* (%)
60% chance of rain	Go to beach	16	30	40	14
	Control	31	32	27	10
	Cancel trip	46	40	12	2

Chi squared = 16.88, significant at 0.01

Source: Adams

Table 4.6 Perceived likelihood of rain: control group stratified by strength of commitment

Forecast	*Strength of tentative commitment*	*Almost certain* (%)	*Likely* (%)	*A chance* (%)	*Not likely* (%)
60% chance of rain	Strong	31	31	28	10
	Weak	32	36	25	7

Chi squared = 0.25, not significant at 0.05

Square: Adams

confronted with the potential for environmental disaster in the form of floods, hurricanes, blizzards, or volcanic eruptions. To some degree, people make up their minds early and distort new information to allow them to feel justified to continue doing what they wish.

Travel behaviour

A frequent result of the combination of push and pull forces is that someone makes a trip. Two aspects of this action are of special geographic interest: (1) the choice of transportation mode (type of vehicle); and (2) the choice of route and destination.

Modal choice

Although some complex models have been developed to explain how travellers select one mode of transportation from a set of alternatives (Watson 1974), basic tabulations of actual versus preferred modes, expressed reasons for the choices, and travellers' characteristics also provide useful information.

Three variables influence the choice of mode: (1) the range of alternatives, including the location of terminals and the scheduling of trips; (2) the finances of the traveller, including fare schedules and income; and (3) personal preferences, including the quality of different modes and the desire for novelty. The influences of each of these variables may be examined from the perspective of the traveller or of the supplier of the transportation.

In the latter case, important questions include why an entrepreneur entering the common carrier business might choose to specialize in a particular form of mass transportation. One might also examine the ways in which several modes can be combined by a common carrier or a travel agent to make a tour package especially attractive to different market segments. The development of competitive and profitable fare schedules, trip schedules, location of terminals, the level of services and luxury on offer, and the choice of regular routes are also important research questions. Very little work has been done to date on these problems by recreation geographers. Lansing and Blood (1964) provide a good (albeit dated) overview of some research design issues related to modal choice.

An example of a study focusing on the travellers' side of the question is that of Earp, Hall, and McDonald (1976). A survey of travellers crossing the Solent (England) to the Isle of Wight during the peak holiday season was made to identify the reasons for their choice of mode of crossing, knowledge of alternatives, action if services were unavailable, and income.

Choices available to travellers included high-speed, high-cost modes (a hovercraft and a hydrofoil) and low-speed, low-cost modes (two conventional ferries), operating in two different corridors. The authors compared the responses to the variables described above by modal choice to identify possible influences on the selection of each mode. Estimates of the value of time saved by comparing cost versus time between modes were also made. However, this process of reasoning was subject to severe limitations. Most travellers did not have good knowledge about differences in fares or times, or even the availability of different modes. Moreover, some of the slower modes had travel schedules more convenient for many travellers, and this further complicated interpretations about trade-offs between time and money.

Route selection: mental maps

The choice of route and of destination are often difficult decisions to explain. When an individual travels into a new area, he uses maps and public information (Nolan 1976, discusses the use and evaluation of various travel information sources) as well as trial-and-error searching. Although some unfortunate decisions about route or destination inevitably occur, the traveller also makes some fortunate guesses and perhaps a few serendipitous discoveries. These results produce satisfactions, and with increased experience and knowledge, they become more frequent. One other result is that the resulting travel behaviour becomes more regular.

This description of the process of travel 'education' applies fairly well to non-discretionary and frequent trips, but several factors can vitiate its application to recreational trips. Travellers who make one major vacation trip per year to a different destination do not develop a habitual pattern of vacation travel. Many travellers seek novelty and variation and thus avoid using the same routes. Further, a substantial portion of all recreation trips are made without preplanned destinations or route selection. Colenutt (1969) in the British Forest of Dean region and Mercer (1971b) in Australia's Ferntree Gully National Park found that about 40 per cent of the visitors had not originally planned to stop at that site.

To better understand how people choose routes, whether or not they have a destination in mind, and to learn more about how people learn about the space around them, geographers have developed several closely related concepts known as mental maps, action spaces, activity spaces, and spatial search behaviour. Generally, these refer to one systematic way of describing and explaining how people interpret environmental and spatial information to make decisions about routes and destinations.

A mental map is a psychological construct that describes how a person views the world around him. It includes distance, spatial relationships, travel time and ease, the presence or absence of different facilities and barriers, and measures of the relative usefulness of different destinations. These are all measured in perceptual terms and thus do not necessarily conform to objective reality, or to the perceptions of other people. Some geographers such as Lewin (1963) and Goodey (1970) prefer to use the term 'action space' to describe this mental view of the world around a person. The preference for 'action space' over 'mental map' is based on the emphasis implicit in 'action space' on potential areas where behaviour might occur. Mental maps, to these geographers, include perceptions of spaces where the person may never travel.

Action space is shaped by trips made to work, school, stores, friends, and relatives, as well as through exploring. It is also influenced by advertising, maps, reading, and conversations with other people. One result of this genesis is that the level of knowledge of recreational supply and the travel landscape will be irregular. Some places and routes will be used often and will become well known; others will be used less often and will remain less familiar. Still other features may be known only by rumour. Aldskogius (1967) in his work on travel to vacation homes in the Siljan region of Sweden, and Maw (1969) in his work on travel to London swimming pools, were among the first geographers to draw special attention to the importance of variation in the knowledge of spatial relationships for recreation planning.

In addition to variations in the quality of knowledge are variations in the 'knowledge of quality'. An individual's action space is actually composed of two parts: the spatial extent of locations (this may be either continuous or discontinuous space); and the subjective utility of each place and route. Within the action space are a set of locations and routes actually used. This is the activity space and it represents revealed preferences. Relative level of utility can be inferred from the frequency of use of different routes or locations. Moreover, the activity space is sometimes used as a surrogate for the orientation and extent of the action space when it is not possible to actually identify the extent of a person's spatial knowledge.

The use of objectively defined activity space as a base from which to infer a subjective action space has been the strategy of a number of geographers. Some of the more important early contributions to the development of this concept have been by Marble (1967), Adams (1969), Brown and Moore (1970), Golledge (1970), Johnston (1971), and Horton and Reynolds (1971). Mercer (1971a) supplies an illustration of this work in recreational travel.

Many of the early studies of activity spaces of urban residents suggests that this space is typically a wedge pointed at the central business district, and centred on a person's residence. Other parts of the city are known vaguely, if at all. This shape develops from the usual pattern of travel to work along the most direct route as well as travel for shopping, socializing, and for school. Mercer believed this same wedge-shaped map might be identifiable in the context of urban recreational travel.

Data to test his belief came from a series of home interviews and on-site surveys in Melbourne. By examining origin – destination pairs, Mercer confirmed the existence of a wedge-shaped activity space. A similar pattern has been observed by Wolfe (1966) in Toronto, and by Duffell and Goodall (1969) in Birmingham (England).

In addition to identifying the existence and shape of the urban recreation action space, he identified groups of travellers who did not conform to that pattern. The first of these were residents who had recently moved into Melbourne and were spending much time travelling about to explore their new community. Another group were long-time Melbourne residents who had recently moved across town and still visited recreation facilities in their old action space. Finally, there was a small group of people who exhibited diffuse recreation travel intermittently – members of auto-touring clubs and those on car rallies.

The process of activity space formation and the patterns of spatial search were examined more closely by Murphy and Rosenblood (1974) among first-time visitors to Vancouver Island (Canada). Murphy and Rosenblood were especially interested in the relative importance of trial-and-error learning (also known as stimulus–response learning) versus conscious trip planning. A sample of visitors was interviewed on board a ferry from the mainland to the island. Information about twenty-four personal variables was obtained and grouped into five categories: personal characteristics, activity preferences, advanced planning efforts, spatial relationship to the island, and intervening variables such as weather conditions at time of arrival. Each respondent was also given a travel diary to maintain over the visit to the island describing routes of travel and activities during the stay.

Responses from all individuals were analysed with a method called 'smallest space analysis' (Guttman 1968; Bloombaum 1970). Smallest space analysis is similar to multi-dimensional scaling in that it describes the structure of a

95

data set in a small number of dimensions and locates each variable within the space defined by these dimensions. This permits the clustering of different travellers' characteristics to identify important influences on travel behaviour. Each variable was represented by a point in a multi-dimensional space. The distances between the points is proportional to the degree of correlation between variables. Murphy and Rosenblood found that a two dimensional space adequately explained a large percentage of the total variation and, further, appeared to be conceptually meaningful. Within this two dimensional space, four clusters of activity and participant variables were found: (1) planning characteristics; (2) shopping activities; (3) sight-seeing activities; and (4) travellers' profiles. Detailed examination of these clusters, other variables not used in the clustering, and the relative positions of all variables led to the conclusion that planning, information-seeking, and evaluation were much more important in explaining travel behaviour and the development of an activity space than so-called stimulus – response 'learning'.

The methodology chosen by Murphy and Rosenblood was influenced, in part, by the fact that their subjects had a limited time to develop an activity space. A different methodology would be possible if the population being studied were not short-term visitors to a resort region, but long-term residents. In such a case one can examine changes in destinations over an extended period of time to identify how an activity space evolves. Elson (1976) used this strategy in his study of the residents of Lewes in East Sussex (England).

Data were collected by a household survey of a random sample of car-owning heads of households who had moved to Lewes from another part of England. Sixteen informal recreation areas throughout East Sussex were identified at the start of the survey and these were used to gauge the extent and orientation of the activity space. Each respondent was asked if he had ever visited one of these areas, and if so, in which year after taking up residence in Lewes he had first visited it.

The form of the Lewes residents' activity space was first calculated by assigning to each destination a number equal to the percentage of respondents who had ever visited it. Contour lines were then plotted with these values as reference points. The resulting surface (Fig. 4.3) showed a steady decline away from the seashore.

To obtain a better picture of how this space evolves over time for an individual, Elson separated out those sites in each of the first four years of residence in Lewes. The fourth year was the last year chosen for study because most residents settled on a stable pattern of recreational travel after the fourth year.

Sites were classified as 'coastal', 'downs', or 'other inland'. The percentage of total new visits to each type of site in each of the first four years of residence was tabulated and a chi-squared statistic calculated to compare the types of sites visited in each year. A statistically significant difference was observed that suggested the typical search pattern begins with visits to coastal

some facts and relationships, and misses others. Ideally, several methods should be combined in any single project.

Two basic approaches are used to identify those forces that push travellers away from an origin and toward a destination: identification of psychological motivations and identification of socio-economic characteristics that influence travel. Psychological motivations are identified with three approaches. Reflective thinking is the least sophisticated, but quite common. With this method a researcher talks to travellers, examines the opinions of other researchers, and considers what might be sufficient motivation for a particular type of trip. Needless to say, there are substantial weaknesses in such an approach, but it does have the advantage of stimulating thinking and leading to new research questions.

An improvement on reflective thinking is to ask travellers themselves to suggest reasons why they travel. The reasons are then tabulated, ranked, and analysed. The advantages of this method are: (1) the results are 'objective' in the sense that any researcher would obtain the same answers to the same questions of the same subjects; and (2) one obtains information about what the subject of the research believes. On the other hand, travellers may be unaware of, or unwilling to vocalize deeper emotions and personal needs. To obtain that information, still more advanced methods are necessary. The most common of these in travel research is psychographics.

Psychographics were developed to assist advertising managers to develop more effective promotional campaigns, but the information they produce may also be of use in explaining some influences on human decision-making. The method uses a series of apparently innocuous statements to which a respondent is asked to indicate his level of agreement. These responses can, presumably, be combined to form a profile of an individual or group of individuals. The statements chosen relate to activities, interests, and opinions of potential travellers. The precise statements are designed on the basis of specific research questions. Some of these may concern themes to avoid in advertising, the importance of different types of constraints, the activities a person likes to engage in, and how a person views himself and those around him.

The use of socio-economic variables is the second of two basic approaches to describe push forces. Measurements of objective, personal characteristics such as age, sex, and occupation are correlated with objective measures of travel behaviour. The most recent work in socio-economic analysis of push variables is the identification and measurement of new variables such as fuel price and personal disabilities.

Another subject in which recent progress has been made is the analysis of complex travel behaviour. Many trips include multiple purposes and multiple stops. Early simplistic models focused on single-purpose, single-stop trips. Some work has been done to allow for the modelling of more varied trips, and more work needs to be done.

Pull forces refer to the attractions of a potential destination. These may

99

be studied either as objective phenomena or as subjective phenomena. Traditionally the description of resources was based on a narrative approach. A researcher identified a set of resources and a group of travellers, and then described, predominantly in qualitative terms, the distributions and relationships among resources, routes, and travellers.

A more quantitative method for the study of pull forces is to first develop a model to predict the level of travel. After comparing the predicted level with the observed level, discrepancies will usually be found. Systematic examination of these residuals will often lead to identification of potentially important discoveries.

Alternatively, one examines socio-economic variations among visitors at specific sites and relates these to differences at those sites. The unspoken hypothesis here is that differences in socio-economic characteristics may cause differences in the perceived attractiveness of different destinations. Identification of site characteristics associated with specific groups of travellers provides useful, supplementary information to broaden insights given by a study of the psychographics of travellers.

At a more abstract level, one can develop a model of the utility of different destinations using objective measures such as total site area. This is an adaptation of the Huff model of consumer behaviour. Central to this approach is the measurement of the utility of a resource by objective methods.

Utility is not purely objective, however. Several models of utility and travel decision-making that attempt to identify subjective utility have been proposed. Two of the most common are the Fishbein model and multi-dimensional scaling. The Fishbein model describes the selection of a trip destination as a two-stage process involving first the identification of desired site characteristics, followed by a comparison of the ideal to each actual site. Multi-dimensional scaling also is based on a list of site characteristics and produces a small number of dimensions that summarize a large number of site characteristics. Each potential destination can be described in terms of these new dimensions, and this allows the identification of clusters of similar or competing destinations, as well as their relative attractiveness.

A limited amount of work had been done in recreation geography on the interpretation of environmental information by travellers. This topic is important because the significance of a factual message that contains some degree of uncertainty can be distorted by a person to justify a desired course of action. This results from a condition called cognitive dissonance – a term describing the desire to do something in the face of evidence suggesting one should not do it. Mechanisms used by travellers to minimize cognitive dissonance are not fully understood and need to be explored more.

The usual result of the combination of a push and pull force is some type of travel behaviour. In practice, travel behaviour means the selection of a mode of travel and of route. Modal choice is the subject of extensive research in transportation engineering, and some of the basic methods are of relevance to recreation geography. The fundamental approach is to identify modes chosen by a large number of travellers and to cross-tabulate their choices with a variety of personal characteristics and other travel-related variables.

Selection of routes is usually studied by reference to mental maps, action spaces, and spatial search. The central idea is that people do not select a route on the basis of objective distance and pattern but rather on the basis of level of knowledge of distances, routes, travel time, the perceived quality of alternatives, and other factors. That much may sound like common sense, but the identification, measurement, and analysis of an action space is difficult. Inferences from observed travel behaviour to attitudes and perceptions about routes used and not used, from aggregate surveys to an understanding of one person's travel, and from hypothetical patterns predicted for uniform, ideal landscapes to the real world, present many challenges for future research.

Additional reading

Corsi, T. M. and Harvey, M. E. (1977) 'Travel behavior under increases in prices', *Traffic Quarterly*, **31**, 605–24

Hawes, D. K. (1977) 'Psychographics are meaningful . . . not merely interesting', *Journal of Travel Research*, **15**, 1–7

Heinritz, G. (1979) 'Ranges and catchment areas of selected recreation facilities in Bavaria', *Studies in the Geography of Tourism and Recreation Vol.II*, 177–86, Verlag Ferdinand Hirt, Wien, Germany

Hensher, D. A. and Stopher, P. R. (eds.) (1979) *Behavioral Travel Modelling*, Croom Helm, London

Huff, D. L. (1960) 'A topographical model of consumer space preferences', *Papers and Proceedings of the Regional Science Association*, **6**, 159–73

O'Rourke, B. (1978) 'Recreational travel to New South Wales beaches', *Australian Geographical Studies*, **16**, 53–64

Perry, A. H. (1971) 'Climatic influences on the development of the Scottish skiing industry', *Scottish Geographical Magazine*, **87**, 197–201

Stopher, P. R. and Meyburg, A. H. (1974) 'The effects of social and economic variables on choice of travel made for the work trip', in D. J. Buckley, (ed.) *Transportation and Traffic Theory*, Elsevier Scientific Publishing, Amsterdam

Wall, G. and Sinnott, J. (1980) 'Urban recreational and cultural facilities as tourist attractions', *Canadian Geographer*, **24**, 50–9

CHAPTER 5

Predictive research on location

When someone asks, 'What is recreation geography good for?', the answer is often a reference to the ability of geographers to select the best site for a business or public service centre. The methods available to help answer site-selection questions are the subjects of two chapters in this book. Site-selection techniques for private recreation enterprises are discussed in this chapter; techniques for public facility location are examined in Chapter 7, 'Normative Research on Location'. To some degree there are predictive and normative aspects in both private and public site selection, but the relative concentrations of these qualities are such that predictive models tend to be more relevant, in practice, to private enterprise site selection and normative models to public service site selection.

Methods for the prediction of private enterprise location come from two schools of thought: (1) locational theory; and (2) site selection methods. The former is frequently abstract and based on assumptions that simplify a complex reality. Elegant models have been produced and they are useful for identifying some of the forces that affect business success and central place vitality. These abstractions, though, are rarely helpful for actually selecting the best location for a new business. Site selection methods on the other hand, consist of techniques based on 'common sense' and experience. They are designed to solve problems, but their success often depends more on the intuition of the researcher than on their theoretical soundness.

A challenging problem for recreation geographers is to integrate locational theories with the practical methods of recreation site selection. The accomplishment of this task is beyond the scope of this book. For now we must limit ourselves to the state-of-the-art in the two schools.

Locational theory

Locational theory has come in three waves. Like real waves, the crests are easy to identify, but there is much mixing of beginnings and endings. The first wave came with the *transportation cost group*. This began with von Thünen's (1875) study of agricultural land uses around an isolated market centre. His assumptions and questions characterized much of the research that was to follow for the next century. Von Thünen's model was built on the dual concepts of transportation cost and land value. Land value was assumed to be an inverse function of transportation costs. In other words, the value of a parcel of land was inversely related to the distance between that parcel and the market centre. From this beginning, von Thünen sought an answer to the question: given a particular parcel of land, which crop would be grown on it? By simplifying the complex interplay of landscape features, resources and economic factors to a homogeneous plain with perfect mobility of capital and labour, uniform transportation costs, uniform fertility, and one central market, he reasoned that a series of concentric zones of crop production would develop. The crop grown in each zone has a characteristic value based on the intensity of cultivation, the market price of that crop, and the cost of transporting it to market. For example, garden vegetables, which command a high price per unit weight and which are grown intensively, would be planted close to the market. Firewood, which is bulky and has a relatively low value per unit weight, would be grown much further away because the producers of firewood could not successfully compete for the more expensive, central parcels of land.

Von Thünen's simple agricultural model has been the inspiration for a number of locational models for other industries. In recreation, Yokeno (1974) and Miossec (1977) adopted a von Thünen-type model for tourism development around cities. Vickerman (1975) used it to predict urban recreation business locations.

Weber (1909) extended the range of problems answerable with the transportation-cost approach by reversing von Thünen's original question. Rather than predict what would be produced at a given location, Weber wished to predict the best location for a given industry. He relaxed assumptions of a completely uniform plain by introducing variations in labour costs and resource distribution. He also recognized the tendency of some industries to cluster, and of some to disperse.

A more recent statement of the transportation-cost approach is found in the work of Hoover (1948). Hoover's contribution is not so much in his reformulation of the locational problem as in his penetrating analysis of agglomerative and deglomerative forces in industries. His analysis of transportation and production costs as agglomerative and deglomerative forces goes far beyond that of his predecessors. Hoover also emphasized the importance of public utilities, insurance, labour supplies, and the availability of capital for locational decisions.

The second wave of locational studies came from the *locational interdependence group*. In 1911, Weber criticized fellow economists for ignoring the spatial effects of inter-industry business dealings; Hotelling repeated the

103

charge in 1929. By 1935, Ohlin developed a crude theory to extend the concepts of inter-industry and inter-regional trade to the questions of location. He adopted a modified version of von Thünen's isolated state model, and replaced the central market with a central resource. He then predicted how location and clustering or dispersal of different industries would occur around the resource.

The most important and complete statements of location interdependence were not made by Ohlin, however, but by Christaller (1933) and Lösch (1944). Christaller laid down the principles of hierarchical locations and connections among towns and cities, and his work was to provide the basis for Lösch analysis of industries as well as that of subsequent geographers and regional scientists. These principles include the following:

1. There is a minimum population threshold below which a good or service will not be produced or offered for sale.
2. This threshold depends on the type of good to be produced. The willingness of people to travel to acquire that good also varies with the type of good. These two effects combine to produce differently sized market areas that are a function of each good. In general, those goods with higher thresholds will draw people from a greater distance than those with lower thresholds.
3. Central places (agglomerations of industries and people) form hierarchies based on the sizes of market areas. Small towns tend to offer only locally demanded goods; large cities offer both locally demanded goods and goods whose thresholds are much larger. Each higher ranked central place offers the goods of the lower ranked central places.
4. Free entry of business allows for a proliferation of competitors and a reduction in the size of market areas.
5. Uniform transportation and resource distributions cause competitors to locate as far away from each other as possible, and to expand their market areas as far as the competition will allow.
6. Inter-industry dependencies and the desire of firms to locate at places offering minimal transportation costs for customers cause complementary or non-competing enterprises to locate together.
7. The interplay of forces described in principles 4, 5, and 6 cause central places to develop hexagonal hinterlands. The hierarchies of central places produce hierarchies of hinterlands.

Lösch generalized central place theory by populating his theoretical world with a non-uniform scattering of buyers. His sellers have identical production costs, but different transportation costs, and they are able to exercise economic control over specific buyers by virtue of their location. Lösch also developed the concept of economic regions. These form around producers and are of a size that balances the need for an adequate market (which causes the region's boundaries to expand) with the effects of transportation costs (which cause the region's boundaries to shrink). On a homogeneous plain, with uniform transportation costs and resource distributions, these regions will take the shape of hexagons completely filling the space. On the real landscape, regions will merely tend toward hexagons, with distortions reflecting variations in the road network and the supply of resources, labour, and markets.

(Reilly's (1931) law of retail gravitation can be placed with the locational interdependence theories, although the 'law' is an analogy rather than a true economic law. Reilly wrote, 'Two centers attract trade from intermediate places approximately in proportion to the size of the centers and in inverse proportion to the square of the distances from these two centers to the intermediate place.' Mathematically:

$$\frac{T_a}{T_b} = \left[\frac{P_a}{P_b} \quad \frac{D_b}{D_a}\right]^2 \qquad [5.1]$$

where: $T_{a,b}$ = trade areas of the two centres a and b
$\qquad D_{a,b}$ = distances of a and b from an intermediate point
$\qquad P_{a,b}$ = population of a and b

In this form, the law of retail gravitation has limited use in predicting successful locations. Of more interest is the identification of the market boundary between two centres, i.e., the point where $T_a/T_b = 1.0$. This is determined by:

$$D_b' = \frac{D_{ab}}{1 + \sqrt{(P_a/P_b)}} \qquad [5.2]$$

where: D_b' = distance from centre b to market boundary
$\qquad D_{ab}$ = distance between a and b

Equation 5.2 can be used to delimit hinterlands among cities, and thus to estimate the potential market size for those cities. The equation can also be applied to the hinterlands of individual firms if their spacing is close enough to allow for some overlap. In this case, the attractiveness of the firms needs to be measured and used as a substitute for the population of the two cities. Retail floor space is often chosen for this purpose. Goodchild and Ross (1971) discuss other measures of retail attractiveness.

The third wave of location theories was generated by the *generalized market group*. Two names are pre-eminent in this group: Isard (1956) and Greenhut (1956). Although both worked at the same time and on the same task, their work took them along divergent paths. Isard sought a general model through a synthesis of the work of von Thünen, Weber, Lösch, Christaller, and others. His model was constructed as a more general model, embodying earlier models as special limited cases of his. Isard's work did not significantly depart from that of earlier researches; rather, he combined and broadened their work to all forms of land use and economic activity.

Greenhut, on the other hand, recognized certain weaknesses in the earlier research that could not be overcome by merely combining the strong points.

Among these weaknesses was the assumption that the individual firm, once established, would begin to act like a monopolist within its limited market area. Greenhut proposed a model that would allow a small number of firms to compete in a limited market area, thus forming a spatial oligopoly. Earlier models also assumed that individual producers had perfect knowledge of each other and of alternative locations. Greenhut introduced risk and uncertainty as site-selection factors. Previous locational theory was concerned with only financial costs and benefits. Greenhut recognized that site-selection depends not only on financial factors, but on personal preferences. In his terms, 'psychic income' must be added to pecuniary income if we are to more fully understand how locational decisions are made.

All these theories do provide some insight into the forces affecting regional development and locational choices. But because they achieve these insights by simplifying and abstracting the world, they are not easily applied to specific locational problems of actual recreation firms. Their chief application is the identification of certain general principles that should be considered in any site selection. These are:

1. A firm with relatively low transportation costs and a relatively large market area will have a greater chance of success than a firm with high transportation costs and a small market area.
2. Some trade-offs are possible between transportation costs, production costs, land rents, and market size.
3. Transportation costs include both the cost of bringing resources to the site of the firm, and the costs of distributing the product to the customer. The relative costs of transporting both resources and products determine, in part, where the firm will locate: high resource transportation costs pull a business close to the resource; high product transportation costs pull a business close to the market.
4. Some types of businesses seek to locate close to each other; some are indifferent to each other; some are repelled by each other.
5. Different locations will be attractive to different types of businesses. Attractiveness is based on resources; market location; transportation services; availability of capital, labour, and business services; and personal preferences of the decision-maker.
6. Firms in any given industry will tend to divide up the available market by selecting different locations to control different spatial segments of the market.
7. The size of the market and the number and location of competitors tend to limit the size of the potential development.

All of these forces need to be evaluated in the context of the individual firm. By themselves, and without a specific context, some of these lead to contradictory conclusions. Their relative importance and actual effect must be assessed in the context of specific industries. This is accomplished at present through a diverse collection of techniques called site-selection methods.

Site-selection methods

Site selection is site prediction. The choice of a site for any sort of recreation business, whether a tea room or a major league baseball franchise, is a prediction that the site will be a successful one. To make such a prediction, researchers rely not only on the abstractions of location theory, but also on the experiences of other researchers, planners, and developers. These are formalized through a feasibility study. Many of the basic ideas used in feasibility studies have been codified and published. Among the general guides relevant to recreation are Neal and Trocke (1971), Kotas (1975), and Mills (1977).

A feasibility study is superficially similar to the calculation of a benefit – cost ratio. If the benefits (profits) of a site are greater than the anticipated costs, that site is a plausible choice for a business. A developer may be interested only in whether a specific site can show a profit, or he may be interested in choosing the most profitable among a number of alternatives.

There are two major distinctions between formal benefit–cost analysis and a feasibility study. A site developer is interested in the net profit he can expect from a site, rather than in the ratio between money spent and money earned. The developer is also interested only in costs and benefits that show on a ledger sheet. In benefit–cost analysis, the decision-maker attempts to identify as many costs and benefits as possible, including secondary and intangible ones. This broad social concern is often not relevant to the decision facing a developer. Because of this, many governments have begun to require impact studies of major new resource developments. The purpose of these studies is to identify the probable effects of a decision on society, the natural environment, and the economy. Our focus in this chapter is on the economic aspects of recreation development. A fuller discussion of impact research is given in Chapter 9.

The contents of a complete feasibility study are extensive. Alternative sources of capital, management strategies, promotional campaigns, timing of development, and architectural design must all be considered. These are beyond the scope of this book, and they are topics in which geographers are not usually expected to be expert. On the other hand, geographers can contribute to at least five sections of a feasibility study: (1) the marketing strategy of the developer; (2) social characteristics of the market area; (3) economic characteristics of the market area; (4) transportation facilities of the market area; and (5) the physical suitability of the site.

Marketing strategy

Three strategies are available to a site developer that will influence which site should be chosen. One might attempt to identify the best market opportunity. This means trying to find both the product and location that will produce the greatest net return. Although this strategy offers maximum flexibility and potential success, the calculations necessary to compare all possible combinations of locations and products will defeat most attempts at a totally objective, rational analysis.

Alternatively, one might already have made a decision about the product and thus need only to select the location. This simplifies the decision by reducing the alternatives available. Or, one may already have a piece of property and only need to identify a good product. Again, this simplifies the decision by reducing the options and combinations to consider. Regardless which strategy is selected, one needs to consider certain variables described below. Their relative importance and interpretation will be influenced by the particular strategy adopted.

Social characteristics

Success in a recreation business depends on people. They must have money and must be willing to part with some of it. However, a measure of population wealth such as median income is not adequate by itself. Population demographics and the range of activities, interests, and opinions (AIOs) are also important.

Demographics The basic demographic variable for a feasibility study is the population of a region. Total population should be disaggregated by sex and age cohorts and by marital status. Average family size is frequently useful, too. This information is usually available from census sources, and it should be supplemented by forecasts of probable changes.

AIOs Current recreational activities and tastes are important parts of a community profile in a feasibility study. Educational levels, occupations, religions, and other social traits may be helpful in identifying preferences or resistances to certain types of products or promotional campaigns. Car, boat, and vehicle registrations; ownership rates of televisions, stereos, cameras, sporting equipment, and other recreational goods; plus membership in different recreational and social clubs, are indicators of the potential market for some products.

Community attitudes can affect the potential success of a business. If the community has conservative tastes and tends to be loyal to long-established, locally owned businesses, a franchise of a national chain that caters to those interested in the latest fads could be expected to do poorly. On the other hand, a community with a high turn-over in residents and little loyalty to local businesses, with a large university or with several large businesses that employ young, upwardly-mobile professionals will probably support boutiques offering the latest items in recreation, sport, and fashion.

Economic characteristics

The importance of median income has already been mentioned. Additional information on incomes, buying habits, regional economics, and inter-business relationships is needed to round out the picture of the economic environment of the market area around a possible site.

Incomes An increasing number of families have two working adults. Many teenagers are also supplementing family incomes. The frequency of and future trends toward multiple incomes in families in a potential market can be a valuable indication of potential sales. Two employed adults not only change the income of the household, but may indicate above-average demands for restaurants, recreational facilities offering day care services, and other businesses that cater to the tastes and needs of two-income families.

Median income is useful but it can be deceiving if some people have very high incomes in the community and others have very low incomes. A given median may represent a mix of high and low incomes or it may represent a nearly uniform distribution. Some measure of the distribution of wealth in the community is needed such as the standard deviation about the mean or frequencies by income category. Further, incomes of any size may be offset by high debts. Estimates of personal debt and disposable income can be much more valuable than raw income data.

Buying habits How many people in the market area buy on credit? Generally, the more potential credit customers around a site, the more successful a new business will be. Credit customers tend to buy more frequently and to spend more. The number of impulse buyers could be valuable to know, especially in comparison to the number who buy cautiously. Different businesses do better with different styles of shoppers.

An understanding of the timing of purchases by shoppers can be useful. Is there a local tradition of eating out only on weekends, or do people patronize restaurants throughout the week? When local residents, seek recreation, do they look for it locally on a daily basis or do they wait for a holiday and then leave town? Is the community a 'one industry' town whose major employer provides a company store that competes strongly with local retail firms? Examples of this situation are found on military bases and in remote mining communities.

Regional economics Economic data that describe the business environment are as important as those that pertain to local residents. The availability and cost of land, labour, and capital need to be determined. There can be substantial regional variations in the availability of open space and venture capital for new businesses. Most recreational firms tend to be labour-intensive, and the size and skills of the local labour pool may be critical. If a sufficient number of employees are not available locally, can more be imported? The adequacy of local sources of banking, insurance, and accountancy services should also be examined.

Inter-firm relationships Some recreation businesses benefit from being located close to each other; others suffer. Two racquet clubs probably do

109

best by avoiding each other to minimize spatial competition. On the other hand, two hotels probably increase the drawing power of each other. Together they become a more obvious destination for passing traffic. They can give referrals to each other when one fills up, and they can combine services to attract conventions that neither could host alone.

There is no well-developed theory to predict which types of recreational firms complement and which compete. Limited predictions have been made on the basis of observation and experience. Figure 5.1 is a summary of some

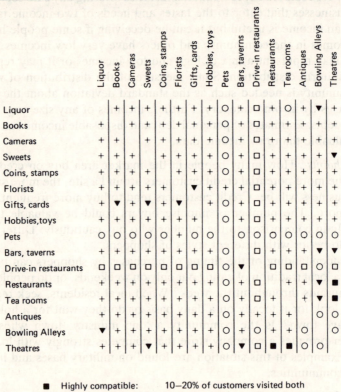

	Liquor	Books	Cameras	Sweets	Coins, stamps	Florists	Gifts, cards	Hobbies, toys	Pets	Bars, taverns	Drive-in restaurants	Restaurants	Tea rooms	Antiques	Bowling Alleys	Theatres
Liquor		+	+	+	+	+	+	+	○	+	□	+	○	+	▼	+
Books	+		+	+	+	+	+	+	○	+	□	+	+	+	+	+
Cameras	+	+		+	+	+	+	+	○	+	□	+	+	+	+	+
Sweets	+	+	+		+	+	+	+	○	+	□	+	+	+	+	▼
Coins, stamps	+	+	+	+		+	+	+	○	+	□	+	+	+	+	+
Florists	+	+	+	+	+		▼	+	+	+	□	+	+	+	+	+
Gifts, cards	+	▼	+	▼	+	▼		+	○	+	□	+	+	+	+	+
Hobbies, toys	+	+	+	+	+	+	+		○	+	□	+	+	+	+	+
Pets	○	○	○	○	○	+	○	○		○	○	○	○	○	○	○
Bars, taverns	+	+	+	+	+	+	+	+	○		□	+	+	+	▼	▼
Drive-in restaurants	□	□	□	□	□	□	□	□	○	▼		□	□	□	○	□
Restaurants	+	+	+	+	+	+	+	+	○	+	□		+	+	▼	■
Tea rooms	+	+	+	+	+	+	+	+	○	+	□	+		+	▼	■
Antiques	+	+	+	+	+	+	+	+	○	+	+	+	+		○	○
Bowling Alleys	▼	+	+	+	+	+	+	+	○	+	○	+	+	○		○
Theatres	+	+	+	▼	+	+	+	+	○	▼	□	■	■	○	○	

■	Highly compatible:	10−20% of customers visited both
▼	Moderately compatible:	5−10% of customers visited both
+	Slightly compatible:	1−5% of customers visited both
○	Incompatible:	negligible joint use
□	Deleterious:	one business harms the other

NB: Table is not symmetrical because compatibility is not necessarily symmetrical. The table is designed to refer to effect on business listed in left-hand vertical column. Thus, tea rooms have a slightly compatible effect on liquor stores, but liquor stores are incompatible with tea rooms.

Figure 5.1 Inter-recreation business relationships and complementarities (after Nelson 1958)

observations Nelson (1958) made of different types of shopping behaviour at retail locations in downtown shopping districts in his attempt to identify inter-business relationships. Five levels of compatibility were identified on the basis of the percentage of shoppers that reported visiting both types of business on the same trip.

Transportation characteristics

Volume The number of people passing a proposed site reflects both its accessibility and the surrounding population. Traffic counts, though, need to be interpreted with caution. A multi-lane, limited-access highway with a 100-kilometre-per-hour speed limit may carry a very large number of vehicles per day, but if there is no exit, the large volume might as well be miniscule. Daily, weekly, and monthly variations should also be measured. A commuter route may have a relatively large daily traffic volume, but if most of the volume is generated during the morning and evening rush hours, the total can be mis-leading. A street with a smaller daily total, but with a more uniform distrib-ution over the day actually may be a better site. Some rural highways are heavily travelled only on weekends and holidays. This pattern may be accept-able for seasonal recreation businesses such as general stores in resort areas, but it could signal financial collapse for others.

Highway design Current and planned highway design features strongly affect the probability that travellers will stop at a business site along the high-way. Multiple lanes, high speed limits, turn restrictions, impassable lane dividers, and one-way traffic are serious barriers to diverting some of the vehicles into the parking lot of a recreation business. Parking, both on-street and off-street, as well as congestion around the entrance to a parking lot also affect the chances that a traveller will become a customer.

Transportation modes The mix of different forms of travel should be con-sidered. A heavily travelled route that is predominantly truck and commercial traffic will contain only a small number of potential recreation customers. Conversely, a street with a light traffic volume still may have a large number of potential customers if most of the available traffic is private cars, pedes-trians, and buses carrying shoppers.

Site typologies Several authors have suggested that potential sites be class-ified according to their relationship with the transportation network. These classifications can help guide the identification of potential sites, and can stim-ulate more precise thinking about the nature of the business and of the types of customers the business should attract. Canoyer (1946) was the first to propose a five-category typology that has been adapted for use in other stud-ies:

1. central shopping districts: the downtown core of a city;
2. sub-centre districts: peripheral or suburban; shopping centres;

3. string streets: locations along major traffic arterials;
4. neighbourhoods: local shopping centres and plazas;
5. isolated sites: single stores in residential, industrial, or commercial areas.

Canoyer's typology is founded on the observable transportation network. An alternative is to consider the subjective relationships between travellers and their use of sites. For example, Nelson (1958) divided sites into generative sites and suscipient sites. Generative sites are those that attract customers directly from their homes for the purpose of doing business. The best generative sites are those that have the maximum number of potential customers around the site. Suscipient sites, on the other hand, are chosen so as to take advantage of impulsive shopping behaviour. As a result, they are usually located on major streets or in other areas of heavy vehicular or pedestrian traffic. Examples of suscipient businesses include some fast-food outlets, florists and gift shops located in airports, and carnivals that locate at shopping malls.

Berry (1967) developed a hierarchical grouping of intra-urban retail site from the postulates of central place theory. These were modified to allow for non-central places such as highway-oriented firms (petrol stations) and specialized areas (theatre districts).

Physical characteristics

Social, economic, and transportation characteristics of potential sites are external to the sites themselves. As important as these are, they are not sufficient to make a site successful. Physical qualities must also be examined, the variety of these characteristics and the exact nature of each that is desirable depends on the particular business, its product, and the intended market. Six general site characteristics are important to most recreation businesses: (1) area; (2) topography; (3) soils; (4) water; (5) climate; and (6) flora and fauna.

Area A site must be large enough to accommodate immediate and future levels of business, and yet be small enough to be affordable. The size needs to allow for efficient spacing of the actual business floorspace, as well as for storage, administrative offices, and equipment. Parking, queuing, sitting rooms, and customer circulation must also be planned for. Site area should be estimated in terms of user-density as well as physical area because desirable levels of density will vary greatly. Golf courses and equestrian facilities cannot function if large numbers of customers are crowded in small spaces. In contrast, part of the experience of attending live theatre, nightclubs, and film premières is the crush of the crowd.

A site planner must also have some knowledge of the probable temporal distribution of use in order to recommend an optimum level of development. For example, some fast-food outlets often experience long lines during the luncheon hour, with delays of fifteen minutes or more, common. While it is usually possible to expand the number of sales people and the counter space to reduce the wait to less than one minute, the cost would be prohibitive and the counter space would be unproductive during most of the day. Churches are not designed for Easter Sunday, highways are not designed for Friday rush hour, and most recreation businesses cannot be profitably designed for their peak business load.

Topography Many recreation businesses have no special topographic requirements other than that the site be level enough to build on. Even this means, in practice, wide variation in acceptable slopes. Heavy earth-moving equipment can be used to alter the terrain of hundreds of hectares if necessary. Some enterprises, though, do have special requirements. Airports require expanses of virtually flat land, while ski resorts need several hundred metres of local relief at a minimum to be feasible.

Soils Any recreation enterprise requiring major construction needs well-drained, stable soils. Beyond this, soil type and composition are often of minimal concern. There are some exceptions, though. 'Pick-your-own' farm operations require soils suitable for the crop being cultivated. Camp grounds and other outdoor recreation enterprises using septic tanks or pit toilets need soils of proper porosity and with acceptable water table levels.

Water Almost every recreation business benefits from the presence of water. The desirable form of water depends on the specific business. Camp grounds and vacation homes do well near large bodies of water suitable for swimming and boating. Resort hotels are often located at the seashore. Spas locate at hot springs. Hunting lodges require good wildlife habitats, which may include wetland. Restaurants can draw customers from relatively large distances if there is a picturesque millrace or waterfall outside a dining room window. Ski resorts may need ground water to supply snow-making equipment. A developer must identify the precise form of water required as well as its quantity, quality, and cost.

Climate Climatic and seasonal variations are especially important to tourism and outdoor recreational enterprises. Sun and mild year-round temperatures are two of the most valuable resources a tourism region can have. Cool or cold weather, though, is not always a liability. Winter sports require reliably cold temperatures and adequate snow for success. Some communities such as Quebec City, Canada, use the cold, darkness, and snow as an occasion for a large mid-winter festival. The shoulder seasons of spring and autumn offer other attractions and opportunities for tourism entrepreneurs. Spring flowers and blossoms, migrating birds, autumn colour, harvests, and the production of new wine and beer are occasions for fairs and tours in many countries.

Weather conditions are significant factors for a site developer, despite their transitory quality. In addition to estimating probable rain and temperature, one needs to identify the potential for floods, gusts created by high buildings or local topography, frequent thick fogs, heavy winter snowdrifts, blowing

113

sand, vulnerability to tornadoes and hurricanes, and the occurrence of Föehn and mistral winds.

Flora and fauna   Of all site characteristics, flora and fauna are probably the easiest to modify. Ornamentals and shade trees can be planted; noxious weeds can be removed. If necessary, many animals can be trapped humanely and moved to other locations. Dangerous insects can be exterminated. Birds, especially starlings and pigeons, are difficult to control, but these are usually maintenance nuisances rather than serious development problems.

Animals can also be imported to a site. Zoos and aquaria will, of course, have major animal acquisition programmes. Country clubs, vacation-home developments, camp grounds, hunting and fishing clubs, and other rural rec-reation businesses whose sales might be enhanced by the presence of certain species, may find it desirable to release carefully selected animals if the native populations are depleted.

Analytic techniques

Several different techniques are available for the analysis of information gath-ered for the above characteristics. Among the better known are (1) scaling methods, (2) multiple regression estimation, (3) Huff's net profit estimation, and (4) Gruens' customer behaviour method.

Scaling methods   Scaling methods compare and rank sites on the basis of previously identified characteristics. Scaling cannot predict total business, nor can it indicate if a site has the potential to make a profit. If a developer is confident that at least one of several sites could be successful, scaling can systematically identify the most promising ones, and eliminate those that are unsuitable.

The first step is to identify critical site characteristics – those qualities whose presence or absence will immediately remove a site from further con-sideration. Locations on a flood plain, astride an active geological fault, on unstable soil, or in the path of a planned highway extension, are examples of unsuitable locations.

Once these have been eliminated, the second step is to identify other rel-evant site characteristics, and to rank these in order of importance. Each quality should have a weight assigned to it to reflect its relative importance. Once this has been done, each site is then evaluated on each characteristic and a score assigned to reflect its relative quality on that characteristic. The individual scores are multiplied by the weights previously defined and a total score calculated for each site. The site with the highest total is the preferred site. Brick (1978) and Applebaum (1968) provide examples of this method in retail sales.

Multiple regression estimation   Multiple regression statistically combines several independent variables (site characteristics) to predict a single dependent variable (sales volume). This analysis does not necessarily assume a cause-and-effect relationship, but one must be able to assume that the observed statistical relationship will continue for a reasonable time in the future.

To date, most examples of multiple regression estimation of business levels in recreation have been for the demand for travel. These are discussed at length in Chapter 6. Green and Tull (1975) have used multiple regression to analyse consumer preferences for many types of retail goods. Smith (1978) used this method to estimate trends in wagers and gate receipts at *pari mutuel* race tracks.

Huff's net profit estimation   Huff (1966) suggested a 'programmed' solution to identify the optimal location for retail businesses. Two conceptions are fundamental to Huff's technique. The location of each potential site in a list of alternatives affects the potential sales; and each potential site has an inherent size limitation that affects both operating costs and sales. The best site is the site with the greatest net profit. Six steps are necessary to identify the optimal location from a set of choices.

1. Estimate the sales for specified scales of operation up to the maximum scale possible for a given location.
2. Estimate costs for specified scales of each operation up to the maximum scale possible for that location.
3. Estimate the net profit by subtracting costs from sales for each scale of operation for that location.
4. Identify the largest net profit among the various scales of operation at the location being studied.
5. Repeat steps 1 through 4 for each location.
6. Identify the greatest net profit among the possible locations.

Huff also suggested using a variant of the gravity model to estimate sales from population and retail floorspace figures.

Gruens' customer behaviour method   The Gruens (1966) developed a 'behavioural' approach for the identification of market potentials. If one has a profile of the typical customer of a business, it is possible to extrapolate from that profile and from census data to estimate probable sales. To do this, four general tasks must be completed; each requires several specific steps.

1. What is the customer base?
   (a) Survey the population in the intended market area to identify customers (those who made a purchase in the previous year) and non-customers.
   (b) Identify the profile of the average customer on the basis of age, sex, income, and other relevant variables.

    (c) Calculate the following ratios:

        (i) Number of respondents who fit profile and are customers

           Number of respondents who fit profile regardless of customer status

        (ii) Number of respondents who do not fit profile but are customers

           Number of respondents who do not fit profile regardless of customer status

2. What are the customers' motivations and preferences?

    (a) What does the average customer prefer in a location for the type of shopping being proposed: parking, pedestrian precinct or not, availability of services and other stores, etc.

    (b) How would each location under consideration affect the identity of the retailer in the eyes of the average customer? Would they be impressed or turned away by a particular location?

3. How many customers can be expected?

    (a) Delineate the probable market area on the basis of a survey of travel patterns of customers at similar stores and in the market area under study. Do not use a single distance measure to draw circular hinterlands.

    (b) Estimate the number of people in the market area who fit the profile and estimate the total population in the same area. Apply ratios from (i) and (ii) above to estimate the likely number of customers.

    (c) If there are competing retailers, artificially define mutually exclusive market areas around each retailer and around the proposed site. Bisect the area of overlap and assign populations in each portion to the nearer site.

    (d) Estimate the number of customers likely to travel from one market area to another in response to motivation and preferences described above.

    (e) Sum the total expected customers in each market area from within that area and from more distant areas for each site.

4. What sales volumes will be generated by the expected customers?

    (a) From sales records, estimate the percentage of charge customers and their average annual purchase. Estimate the total number of charge customers in the market area and multiply by their average annual purchase.

    (b) Repeat 4(a) for cash customers.

    (c) Sum 4(a) and 4(b) to obtain total sales.

5. Which is the best site?

    (a) Repeat steps 4(a) to 4(c) for each site.

    (b) If a new site would compete with one of your own stores, decrease the revenue at one to adjust for the diversion of old business.

    (c) Estimate the expected costs for each location and calculate the net profit for each. Select the site with the greatest net profit.

Certain limitations in the Gruens' approach should be mentioned. The method requires a market survey, sales records, and previous experience in each possible market area (or at least, in very similar markets). Obviously, if this information is not available, the method cannot be used. Another weakness is the delineation of autonomous market regions. This is arbitrary and often unwarranted. As noted before, some businesses actually benefit from proximity to each other.

The Gruens' method does not explicitly allow for variations in the size of operation although this could be incorporated by considering each size as a separate location. More serious is the lack of explanation of how a researcher is to estimate the effect of competition in the opening of a new business. Although there is a recognition that self-competition can have a deleterious effect, inter-firm competition is largely ignored. This subject needs more research.

Finally, the identification of both capital and operating costs is left to the researcher's own methods. Measurement of spatial variations in the costs of development, of utilities and business services, of labour, as well as variations in risk and uncertainty among different locations is not an easy process. Practical guidelines for estimating these would be very desirable.

Selected examples Most feasibility studies are done under contract for clients, and the methods and results usually are not published. The need for confidentiality of sales figures, management strategies, and other private information outweighs the benefits to be derived by academics and students from release of this information. Some suggestions for the conduct of site-selection analyses and feasibility studies nevertheless have been published in several sources. These are often a part of a larger study examining the health of an entire industry; other times they are abstracted from many sources and are presented as general guidelines. Some examples of use to recreation geographers include:

Airports: Bambiger and Vandersypen (1969); Sealy (1976)
Restaurants: Wyckoff and Sasser (1978)
Hotels, motels, resorts: Podd and Lesure (1964); Hodgson (1973); Scholz (1975)
Travel agencies: Brownell (1975)
Camp-grounds: Nulsen and Nulsen (1971); Colgan (1972); Canadian Government Office of Tourism (1978)
Sports franchises: Aldini (1977)
Sports centres: Ackroyd (1970); Gimmy (1978); Ontario Ministry of Culture and Recreation (1979)
Winter sports resorts: Lucas (1969)
Vacation homes: Ragatz (1969); Burby, Donnelly, and Weiss (1972)
Gasoline stations: Brick (1978); Claus and Hardwick (1972)
Urban river-fronts: Gunn, Hanna, Parenzin, and Blumberg (1974)

Golf-courses: Cook and Holland (1967); Jones and Rando (1974)
Marinas: Adie (1975)

Summary

More work needs to be done on all aspects of site selection for recreation enterprises. A few problems and challenges have already been identified, and several more can be noted.

1. The threshold of a business is a familiar concept in both locational theory and site selection, but actual methods for measuring the minimum population necessary to support a specific type of business are few and unreliable. Because recreation businesses rely strongly on personal tastes and preferences, simple population estimates may never be adequate. A threshold may have to be defined in terms of particular types of people such as the number of teenagers or the number of young professionals.

The potential demand for a particular recreation business is also a function of the presence of other businesses. A city of 250,000 with few art galleries and no professional theatre may find it difficult to support a symphony orchestra because there is no local precedent for widespread popular support of cultural activities. On the other hand, a city of the same size with a well-developed art gallery system, several small amateur and professional theatre groups, and perhaps a chamber music group will probably have enough people interested in high culture to also support a small symphony orchestra. In practice, this may mean that the 'threshold' for the first business of a new type will tend to be larger than the 'threshold' for subsequent units of the same type. The number of customers needed by the first and subsequent units may be the same, but the size of the population required to generate these customers will vary. The relative importance and the effects of different variables need to be examined to better understand the mechanisms behind thresholds.

2. The population available to a business as a source of consumers is partially determined by the willingness of people to travel to purchase the good being sold. More information is needed about the drawing power of different types of goods. These vary, not just in type, but also in quality. A gift shop specializing in locally produced, authentic handicrafts may have a better drawing power than one providing cheap, tasteless curios. A championship sporting event will draw people from a much further distance than a mid-season match between two mediocre teams. A Picasso exhibition will attract viewers from origins more distant than will the work of a local, unknown artist.

Reputations of establishments also affect their drawing power, and, in turn, are enhanced by their ability to attract people from great distances. Bronner's, a Michigan (USA) gift shop specializing in Christmas decorations, attracts shoppers from a 500-kilometre radius. Although many of the items found at

Bronner's could be purchased closer to home in the Christmas season, Bronner's year-round display, diversity of stock, heavy advertising, and unusual store decor has made it a regional phenomenon in the American Mid-west. Harrod's, a London department store, has an international clientele by virtue of its high quality, professional sales services, diversity of stock and its reputation for being an international attraction. And certainly some people like to buy at Harrod's for the perceived privilege of being able to truthfully say, 'I got it at Harrod's'. The forces that allow a business to build a reputation and to extend its competitive advantage far beyond its expected range need to be systematically identified.

3. The tendency of different firms to locate together and others to disperse has been well-established, but the actual forces are only crudely known. The effects of capacity, accessibility, market size, and product type on agglomeration and deglomeration are topics for additional research that could lead to practical rewards in the form of more efficient marketing and more successful business location.

4. Businesses, like people, change over time. Methods to incorporate the element of time into feasibility studies should be improved. The current-value (present-value) formula used in benefit–cost analysis is one such method, but it depends on the ability of the researcher to forecast changes in benefits and costs. This is where many benefit–cost analysis and feasibility studies fail. Reliable forecasting methods are hard to find. The notion of a product life cycle from marketing theory that described the introduction of a product, its subsequent acceptance and expansion, followed by a decline, may be a useful beginning for recreation business forecasting.

Recreation businesses are part of the landscape, and their morphology and relationships to other landscape features evolve over time. Once fashionable sections of large cities decay and become slums; former slums are rehabilitated and become fashionable shopping and dining districts. Are these changes predictable? When an international airport is constructed on the outskirts of a metropolitan region, is it possible to forecast land use changes? Other models might be developed for reservoirs, along sections of coastline recently made accessible by new roads, and around theme parks.

5. The methods for predicting total business volumes need to be strengthened. This work is needed for all types of businesses, but certain types may require more work than others. For example, some firms are especially vulnerable to fads and changes in tastes – specialized physical recreation facilities, health clubs, nightclubs, restaurants, theme parks, motion picture producers and distributors .

6. Related to the problem of predicting total business sales is the question of market definition and segmentation. Any single type of business may have numerous types of customers, each with their own special demands, pur-

chasing habits, and preferences. A useful contribution to the study of recreation businesses would be better identification of specific market segments for each type of good and service.

7. Finally, many of the principles presented in the chapter are based on work originally done for other types of retail firms. Understanding of the locational forces affecting recreational firms might progress more quickly if we could identify similarities among recreation and non-recreation businesses. For example, the factors affecting motel location may be similar to those affecting petrol station location. If so, a geographer interested in motel location should study the literature already available on petrol station location. Similarly, some hotels might mimic other CBD businesses and resorts might mirror, in part, certain resource-based industries. If other industries are faced with the same problems as certain recreation industries, there may be much we can learn from other specializations in geography.

Additional reading

Anonymous (numerous years) *Leisure Industries Review*, Gower Press Ltd, Epping, Essex

Applebaum, W. (1966) 'Methods for determining store trade areas, market penetration, and potential sales,' *Journal of Marketing Research*, **3**, 127–41

Applebaum, W. (1968) 'Store characteristics and operating performances', in Kornblau C. (ed.) *Guide to Store Location Research*, Addison-Wesley, Reading, Massachusetts

Berry, B. J. L. (1964) *The Geography of Market Centers and Retail Distributions*, Prentice-Hall, Englewood Cliffs, New Jersey

Cohen, S. B. and Applebaum, W. (1960) 'Evaluating store sites and determining store rents', *Economic Geography*, **36**, 1–35

Hand, H. H. (1979) 'Economic feasibility analysis for retail locations', *Journal of Small Business Management*, **17**, 28–35

Franckowiak, E. N. (1978) *Location Perception and the Hierarchical Structure of Retail Centers*, Department of Geography, University of Michigan, Ann Arbor, Michigan

Gosling, D. and Maitland, B. (1976) *Design and Planning of Retail Systems*, The Architectural Press, London

Martineau, P. (1958) 'The personality of the retail store', *Harvard Business Review*, **36**, 47–55

Redinbaugh, L. (1976) *Retailing Management*, McGraw-Hill, New York

CHAPTER 6

Predictive research on travel

When everything has been said and written about recreation planning, one fact remains: recreation means travel. Whether across the street or around the world, people must travel to enjoy most forms of recreation. Even the apparent exceptions often have some form of travel hidden in them. Reading at home presupposes a trip to a library or a bookstore; watching television implies a trip to purchase or rent a television set and travel of a signal from the studio to the receiver.

The centrality of travel was graphically portrayed in an influential article by Wolfe (1964). He tried to sort out the relationships among the key elements of recreation: population, affluence, urbanization, mobility, democratization of leisure, research, and planning. Only by placing mobility in the centre of his diagram (Fig. 6.1) was Wolfe able to bring order to the confusion of recreation facts, variables, relationships, ideas, and activities.

Centrality, however, should not be confused with importance. The most important element in recreation is people. Virtually every consideration and problem in this book is raised because it is, in some way, important to people – their pleasure, their well-being, or their jobs.

Mobility is central because the supply of resources does not match the location of those who would use them. There is a spatial imbalance between the demand for recreation resources and their supply. To rectify that imbalance, either the resources or the people must move.

The body of research that concerns predictions about the movement of people to recreation resources is the product of two schools of thought. The first is the development and use of predictive models; the second is the study and evaluation of model components. The distinction between the two is the familiar and imprecise distinction between 'applied' and 'pure' research. In practice, it is often impossible to say where estimating model components stops being a theoretical or academic exercise and becomes part of practical model development. Although the boundary is difficult to define, the conceptual difference is real. Work discussed in this chapter belongs to the first

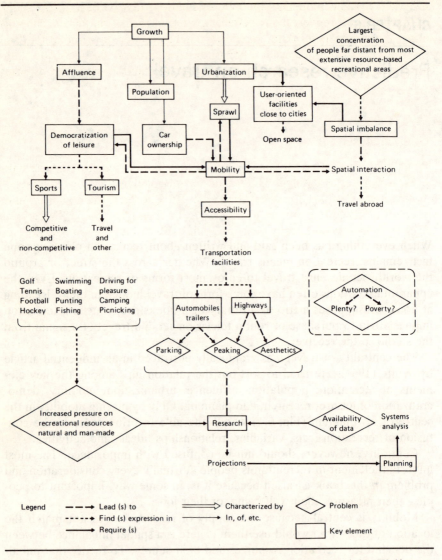

Figure 6.1 The key elements in the demand for outdoor recreation (after Wolfe 1964)

school – the use of practical tools for predicting travel. When we digress into the more technical subjects of statistical estimation and empirical definition, it is because the practical uses of recreation geography depend on theoretical and statistical knowledge.

Prediction techniques discussed in this chapter have evolved along three lines: (1) trend analysis; (2) gravity models; and (3) intervening opportunity models. A fourth line of research, the development of systems models, is not included. Systems modelling involves calculations that go beyond the scope of this book. Moreover, many systems models in recreation have such exorbitant requirements for data, manpower, and computer storage that they are rarely applied. After a consideration of the three groups of models, the chapter closes with guidelines for model development and a discussion of unresolved issues.

Trend analysis

Trend analysis is based on the assumption that there is regularity in the data a researcher has assembled. The reason for the regularity may be some controlling mechanism or it may be accidental. If the former, the regularity may be safely assumed to continue. If the latter, the researcher cannot be certain. Because a researcher usually cannot tell the causes of any regularity, he usually assumes there is some controlling mechanism, but avoids making long-term (ten years or more) forecasts.

In its simplest form, a trend analysis can be made with pencil and paper. By plotting the number of travellers in each of several years it is often possible to visually plot a line that approximates to the long-term trend in the data. The scatter of points around the plotted line is 'error'. This error may be measurement error, the result of other causal variables, or a combination of the two. If the error is not too great, this method can produce acceptable forecasts for certain situations. Consider the travel patterns (anonymous 1974b) of West Germans to Jamaica from 1961 to 1972 (Fig. 6.2). There was a slow rise from about 1,000 travellers in 1961 to about 3,000 in 1972. A straight line fitted to the data and extended to 1973, results in a forecast of also about 3,000 visitors. This is quite close to the actual level reported.

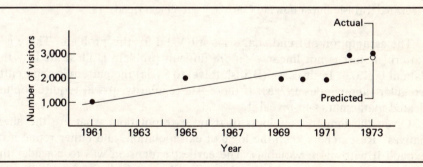

Figure 6.2 West German tourist flows to Jamaica: a linear trend

There are, of course, limits to this technique. The further a researcher tries to forecast into the future, the less reliable the forecast. Further, this particular method is usually based on the assumption that the trend is linear. If the relationship is curvilinear, straight-line forecasts can produce substantial errors. An example of this can be seen in the following forecast (anonymous 1974a) of the number of British travellers to Canada (Fig. 6.3). If a researcher were to look at the period from 1961 to 1965, he would probably assume a straight line relationship; a linear forecast to 1973 would yield an estimate of 95,000 travellers. If the estimate were made with more recent data, say for the period 1969 to 1971, the estimate would be 200,000. As widely different as these two forecasts are from each other, they are just as far from the actual figure of 340,000.

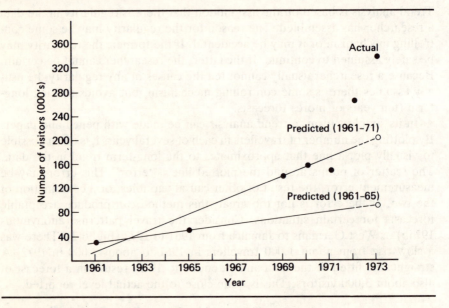

Figure 6.3 British tourist flows to Canada: a curvilinear trend

The assumption of trend analysis is still valid for this problem. There is a pattern; it just is not linear. A more difficult problem is illustrated by the data in Fig. 6.4. In this case (British travel to Syria) the pattern is apparently irregular (anonymous 1974a). If there is a regularity, it will require sophisticated mathematics to reveal it.

Given the limited usefulness of trend extrapolation, what are the alternatives? Researchers keep the logic of extrapolation, and either refine it or expand it with more variables. The earliest expansion was to consider the effects of distance on travel. As shown in Chapter 4, distance measures are among the most useful independent variables in explaining travel behaviour. To switch from explanation to prediction, a researcher develops an explanatory model relating distance to past travel and then applies it to predict future travel at a proposed facility.

An application of this method is the work of Ullman and Volk (1962) on

124

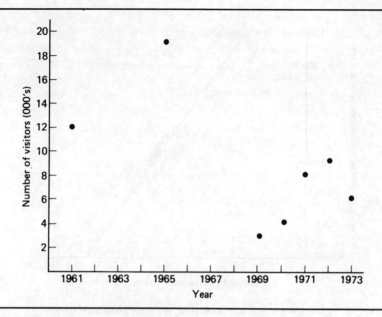

Figure 6.4 British tourist flows of Syria: no obvious trend

forecasting trips to selected reservoirs in the state of Missouri (USA). Plotting the log of the number of trips *per capita* from each county to a reservoir against the distance, revealed a strong linear relationship. This pattern was formalized by plotting what the authors called a 'regression line' through the data, with two parallel curves reflecting the effects of variations in income and intervening opportunities.

Future attendance at a proposed reservoir was predicted by calculating the distance from each county to the proposed site, and then noting the expected *per capita* attendance associated with that distance. Once *per capita* rates were obtained, they multiplied the rate by the county population to obtain a county total. The sum of these county totals gave the expected annual attendance at the reservoir.

This method can be simplified, as Ullman and Volk noted, by constructing a set of concentric zones around the proposed site. Because *per capita* rates decline with the logarithm of distance, a series of estimates of average travel rates for each zone of travel can be made by referring to the regression line in Fig. 6.5. If population estimates are available for each zone, one proceeds as before to make a forecast. Table 6.1 is a summary of some hypothetical calculations by Ullman and Volk for this type of problem.

Their method has several disadvantages or weaknesses. The most apparent is the use of really only one explanatory variable, distance. The parallel curves adjusting for income and reservoir competition are quite simplistic and fail to adequately account for these effects. But then, this was one of the earliest travel forecasting models.

125

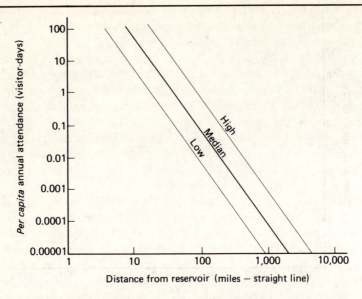

High — curve applying to urban, high income areas or areas with no
  reservoirs

Low — curve applying to rural, poor areas or areas with many
  reservoirs

Figure 6.5 Ullman and Volk's reservoir use 'regression' curve (after Ullman and
  Volk 1962)

Table 6.1 Estimated attendance at hypothetical major impoundment fifty miles from
  St Louis: an example of the Ullman and Volk method

Distance zones from hypothetical reservoir	Zonal population	Per capita category	Annual visits	Total annual user days
0–10	20,000	median	15+	300,000
10–20	40,000	median	10+	400,000
20–40	90,000	high	10+	900,000
40–60	2,000,000	high	4	8,000,000
60–100	300,000	low	0.4	120,000
100–200	2,000,000	median	0.03	60,000
200–300	10,000,000	median	0.005	50,000
300–500	30,000,000	median	0.001	30,000
Beyond 500	(rest of USA)	estimate		50,000
			Total	9,910,000

Source: Ullman and Volk

The definition of distance as straight line was also questionable. It may be an adequate estimation in the mid-western United States, but for many other locales this could introduce substantial error.

The prediction obtained by the Ullman and Volk method is 'static'. It is, implicitly, for the first season of use. Attendance at some reservoirs may rise dramatically as they become better known. Others may experience an initial surge of use as visitors come to see the new attraction, and then experience a decline in use as the novelty wears off.

Ullman and Volk reported a linear relationship. However, they did not statistically measure that relationship. Their 'regression line' was only a visually-fitted line. They did not have a measure of the goodness of fit, nor any idea if some other curve might be better.

Recognizing both the problems and the potential usefulness of this method, the US Army Corps of Engineers (1974) adapted it for use for their own reservoir planning. *Per capita* use rates were collected for counties surrounding a large number of reservoirs. Graphs were again plotted, but this time a separate distance decay curve was made for each reservoir. The line was plotted statistically, using a power function to allow for a curvilinear fit. Distance was measured in road miles. Inventories were made of the resources at each reservoir to provide planners with an idea about facility differences. Finally, all this information was made available to planners in the form of a manual. Figure 6.6 and Table 6.2 are examples of the type of information for each reservoir. From this, a planner can forecast initial use by following these steps:

1. Evaluate the proposed project characteristics.
2. Select a similar project by comparing the proposed project with existing reservoirs.
3. Estimate the day-use market area of the similar project.
4. Estimate the day-use market area of the proposed project.
5. Select a *per capita* use curve for the similar project.
6. Modify the curve to reflect dissimilarities between the similar project and the proposed project.
7. Determine the county populations within the day-use market area for the anticipated year that the project operation will begin and derive *per capita* use rates for each county by measuring road distance from the most populous city in the county.
8. Calculate the annual day-use from each county by multiplying the *per capita* rate by the county population.
9. Sum the contributions from each county to find initial annual day-use for the project.
10. Determine the percentage of total use which the foregoing presents. If 100 per cent, use as is; if less, adjust accordingly by adding camping use to get total use.

Table 6.2 Example of data used in US Army Corps of Engineers method for forecasting reservoir use

---

Tenkiller reservoir

---

1. *Reservoir description* The project is located on the Illinois River about 5 miles (8 km) north-east of Gore, Oklahoma, 22 miles (35.4 km) south-east of Muskogee, Oklahoma, and 40 miles (64.4 km) north-west of Fort Smith, Arkansas. The terrain in the reservoir area is hilly to semi-mountainous, characterized by wooded ravines and at many points by steep rock bluffs. With the exception of a few upland pasture tracts, forest covers most of the area. The forest trees, while not of commercial value, greatly enhance the scenic value of the reservoir. The government-owned area above the 12,500-acre (5,050 ha) lake is 18,278 acres (7,384 ha) making a total area of 30,778 acres (12,434 ha) available for recreation.

2. *Reservoir resources* Access to the area is provided principally by US Highway Nos. 62 and 64 and Oklahoma State Highway Nos. 82, 100, and 10A. County roads branch off at many points along the principal highways to provide excellent access into all reaches of the lake. The climate of the reservoir area is characterized by moderate winters and comparatively long summers. The reservoir supports one of the most popular and important fisheries from the standpoint of angler use in the state. In addition to the many cottage and home sites on land adjacent to the project, there are five quasi-public groups with organized camp facilities, five private clubs, and three cottage sites on project land. There are also six guest establishments with rental units on project land. The total estimated population within a 100 mile (161 km) radius is, 1,250,000, the largest percentage being urban.

3. *Competing water-oriented recreation areas*

Name	Distance zone (miles)	Size (acres)	Recreation facilities		Annual attendance
			public	private	
Eufaula reservoir	25–50	102,000	yes	yes	2,001,800 (1967)
Fort Gibson reservoir	0–25	19,000	yes	yes	2,111,700 (1967)
Greenland State Park	0–25	930	yes	yes	unavailable
Markham Ferry Reservoir	25–50	unavailable	yes	yes	unavailable
Wister Reservoir	25–50	4,000	yes	yes	565,700 (1967)

4. *Other pertinent data*
   Name: Tenkiller   District: Tulsa
   Location:
       State: Oklahoma
       Counties: Sequoyah and Cherokee
       River: Illinois
       Major highway access: US 62 and 64; State 100, 82, and 10A
   Project purposes: Flood control and power
   Year impoundment begun: 1952

Pool size;
  Maximum: Acre feet: 1,230,000
               Surface acres: 20,800
               Shoreline miles: not available
  Average recreation: Surface acres: 12,500
                      Shoreline miles: 130
Number of access points: 18
Recreation facilities:
  Tent and trailer spaces: 997
  Day use areas capacity in
    (recreation days)   13,680
  Boat launch lanes: 39
  Attendance (recreation days): 1968   1,465,500
                         1967   1,372,600
                         1966   1,842,100
                         1965   1,781,900
                         1964   1,636,200

Per cent annual attendance during peak months of use:

Apr	May	June	July	Aug	Sept		Total
7.3	10.4	14.3	16.6	15.7	9.9		74.2

Source: Adapted from US Army Engineer IWR Research Report 74–R1

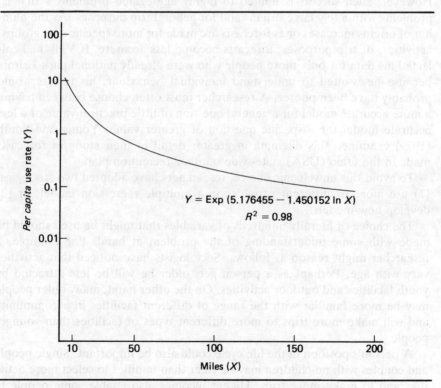

$$Y = \mathrm{Exp}\,(5.176455 - 1.450152 \ln X)$$

$$R^2 = 0.98$$

Figure 6.6 US Army Corps of Engineers' use curve for Tenkiller Reservoir (after the TWR Report, 74-Rl 1974)

The Corps of Engineers' procedure was a systematic improvement over Ullman and Volk's method, but there were still a couple of steps that were not as objective as they might be: the selection of a similar project; and adjustments made to existing curves to reflect dissimilarities between projects. Regional variations in demand and other variables were also left to the planner's informed judgement.

To account for some of these variables in his later work, Volk (1965) expanded his earlier analysis by including variables that were identified in the literature as probable influences on travel: median family income; the percentage of people living in urban areas; and *per capita* car ownership. Data were collected on a state by state basis, and compared with travel between individual states and national parks.

Every regression equation Volk computed (one for each park) explained at least 75 per cent of the total variance. Some explained as much as 95 per cent. In all cases, distance accounted for at least 60 per cent; the three new variables added only 3 to 20 per cent.

Given these results, one might conclude that if a planner knew nothing more than the distance between a proposed park and major population centres, he could make fairly good predictions. In fact, this is generally true. However, such success is limited to highly aggregated problems – that is, problems with a few large origins and for general trip purposes. As the number of origins increases or as forecasts are made for more specific user groups, activities, or trip purposes, forecasts become less accurate. If Volk had collected his data for only those people who were already national park visitors because he wanted to understand individual behaviour, his results would probably have been poorer. A researcher must often choose between having a more accurate model for a general question of little practical value or a less accurate model for a specific question of greater value. Young and Smith (1979) examined this dilemma in greater detail in their study of forecasts made in the Ohio (USA) state-wide outdoor recreation plan.

To avoid this unwelcome choice, researchers have adopted two strategies: (1) use more or different variables in a multiple regression model; or (2) develop new models.

The choice of literally hundreds of variables that might be used should be made with some understanding of the problem at hand. For example, a researcher might reason as follows. Sociologists have noticed that activities vary with age. Perhaps as a person gets older he will be less attracted by youth facilities and outdoor activities. On the other hand, many older people may be more familiar with the range of different facilities in a community and will make more trips to more different types of facilities than younger people.

A person's position in the life cycle could also be important. Single people and couples with no children may be freer than families to select more activities and to make more trips. Higher incomes also enable some people to make more trips. Foreign-born residents, especially recent immigrants, often earn less than native residents, and are thus less likely to make trips.

This, in fact, is the type of thinking Dent (1974) went through in his study of recreation day trips by Canberra (Australia) residents. Dent collected information about past trips and personal characteristics that may influence trip behaviour. These variables included the country of birth, number of children in the household, age of the eldest child, respondent's position in the household, type of dwelling, number of cars normally available, age, and occupation of head of household. Preferences for different facilities were also identified.

Dent wished to answer three questions for each individual: (1) What influences the decision to make at least one trip? (2) What influences the number of trips in one year? (3) What influences the number of locations visited in one year? Whereas most researchers had studied aggregated problems, Dent was interested in explaining what influenced an individual's behaviour.

After cross-tabulating each independent variable with three dependent variables: ((1) if a trip were made; (2) number of trips made; (3) number of locations visited), Dent selected the most important variables. These were then used to calibrate three multiple-regression models. These models were not successful as predictors. Only age and occupation had some influence, but the amount of variance explained (less than 10 per cent) was so small that the model had no practical value. These poor findings have been repeated by other researchers working with the same disaggregated questions.

There are at least two reasons why geographers have not been successful in explaining individual behaviour. The first is that the choice of variables may be theoretically correct, but the population studied (such as Canberra residents) are often homogeneous. There is not sufficient variation among the values of the independent variables to statistically explain variations in trip-making.

The second reason is more likely. Human mobility is subject to numerous constraints. Short-distance, short-term travel, such as recreation day trips, is constrained by supply, time, and distance, but is relatively free from other constraints. Long-distance, long-term moves are less sensitive to distance and time, but are constrained by other factors. A major change in residence, for example, is influenced by education, income, occupation, family ties, and familiarity with the destination. The problem for recreation geographers is to identify the constraining variables for the travel they wish to study.

Models produced by trend analysis are sometimes called *ad hoc* models. An *ad hoc* model is one developed for a specific problem, with no potential for further use, and usually no basis in theory. Multiple-regression equations are a common form of *ad hoc* models. On the other hand, gravity models represent a class of models that can be used in a variety of situations. The gravity model is based on a hypothetical statement of important variables and expected relationships, while trend analysis models are based on variables chosen because of convenience. As a result, gravity models are both more 'formal' in the sense that the basic structure is set, and also more 'flexible' because the basic structure can be redefined in myriad ways.

Gravity models

The gravity model, first discussed in Chapter 2, is based on an analogy to Newtonian physics: the strength of the attraction between two bodies is proportional to the product of their masses and inversely proportional to the square of the distance between them.

Although implicit formulations of the gravity model have been seen in studies as early as the mid-nineteenth century (Carrothers 1956, provides one of the best histories of the concept), formal presentation dates from Stewart (1948) and Zipf (1946) who independently and simultaneously developed the analogy. Zipf was interested in explaining the level of interaction (defined operationally as the number of rail shipments, telephone calls, and similar forms of social or economic exchange) between two cities. One formulation he found especially useful was $(P_1P_2)/D$: the product of the population of two cities divided by the separating distance. Zipf examined this ratio for all pairs of cities he was studying, plotted the level of interaction between the two cities against the distance on double logarithmic paper and found a linear relationship.

Stewart approached the concept as a conscious attempt to mimic physics. Noting that physicists' models have been developed for large numbers of particles (such as electrons) rather than for individual particles, he argued that the reason geographers had made such poor models of behaviour was that they were attempting to explain or predict individual behaviour. Laws of physics, Stewart argued, could never have been developed if physicists had tried to explain the behaviour of individual particles.

Newton's descriptive equation for gravitational force provided an analogy to 'demographic force,' the potential interaction between two areas. This analogy is applied in recreation modelling by replacing one mass with the population of an origin and the other mass with the attractiveness of a destination.

The population of origin component may be defined as the number of people in a city, county or other region. Alternatively, it might be the number of people who have made a particular type of trip in the past year. Or it might be the number of people likely to make a trip in the future. It might also be a combination of several variables. Cesario (1976) has defined the origin component in his version of the gravity model as 'emissiveness', a quality defined by several socio-economic variables related to the propensity to travel.

The destination component might be a measure of the aesthetic appeal of a park, the capacity of a concert hall, the space in a parking lot, a measure of a resort's fame or a combination of several variables.

Distance measures are almost as numerous as the other two components' definitions. Straight line distance, road distance travel time, the number of airplane changes, the cost of scarce fuel, and the number of busy street crossings have all been used.

Once the components have been defined, weights must be decided on. If a weight other than 1.0 is used, what should it be? Should several weights be used? The population component might be broken into income categories, for example, and a different weight assigned to each category to reflect the different demand for a particular type of recreation. Exponents rather than weights might be used; again one must decide what exponent is best, and how it should be estimated. Cheung (1972), for example, used three exponents to estimate the effect of distance on travel to Saskatchewan (Canada) parks.

There is no single, best answer to these questions. Some of the readings at the end of the chapter contain recommendations for actual values of weights or for how one might estimate the best value. The choice must eventually be made on the basis of what hypotheses are to be tested, the researcher's statistical ability, and the available literature and data.

An important characteristic of the gravity model is that the basic form is fixed. A gravity model can be applied to many problems through appropriate changes in coefficients and component definition. To estimate the coefficients, one begins with the basic model:

$$T_{ij} = G \frac{P_i A_j}{D_{ij}^b} \tag{6.1}$$

where: T_{ij} = the number of trips made in some time period between origin i and destination j

P_i = some measure of population of i

A_j = some measure of the attractiveness of j

D_{ij} = some measure of distance between i and j

G and b are empirically estimated parameters.

To calculate G and b, assume, for the moment, travel between i and j requires no time or effort: the effect of distance is zero. The number of travellers from i to j is thus proportional to the attractiveness of j. The combined attractiveness of all js is A. This might be, for example, the total number of seats in a sports arena, summed over all arenas. The relative number of trips from i to j is proportional to A_j/A. Thus, if there are 50,000 seats in all arenas in a region, and arena j has 5,000 of them, then 5,000/50,000 or 10 per cent of all arena trips from i will be to j.

If the total number of trips made is T and the total number of travellers is P, then T/P is the average number of trips per traveller. Let k signify this ratio. Total trips made by an individual from i to j is thus $k(A_j/A)$. For example, if the average number of trips per traveller is 15, then the hypothetical traveller from i would make 10 per cent of 15 trips per year to j, or 1.5 trips.

Given this estimate of expected trips between a particular origin and destination for one traveller, the number of trips for all travellers from i to j, V_{ij}, is the product of P_i and $k(A_i/A)$:

$$V_{ij} = k \frac{P_i A_j}{A} \qquad [6.2]$$

Now, relax the assumption about distance having no effect on travel. If the actual number of trips from i to j is T_{ij}, the ratio between the actual and the expected is T_{ij}/V_{ij}. If distance does not have an effect, this ratio is unity. If it does have an effect, the ratio will take a range of values.

The work done by Zipf, Ullman and Volk and others, suggests that the log of distance may be proportional to the log of the number of trips. If one assumes this, the following can be hypothesized:

$$\log \frac{T_{ij}}{V_{ij}} = a - b \log D_{ij} \qquad [6.3]$$

Removing the logs from equation 6.3:

$$\frac{T_{ij}}{V_{ij}} = \frac{a}{D_{ij}^b} \qquad [6.4]$$

Substituting 6.2 into 6.4, and setting $G = ak/A$:

$$T_{ij} = G \frac{P_i A_j}{D_{ij}^b} \qquad [6.5]$$

which is identical to the original formulation.

Data requirements for calibrating a gravity model should be spelled out. The gravity model is based on an implicit time period, defined by the period for which the data were collected, usually a year or a season. If the time period changes, the prediction changes. The model is calibrated from historical data; records of past trips are necessary. These records must include some measure of population, attractiveness, distance and number of trips made for each origin–destination pair. The number of calculations necessary for several origins and destinations rises as the product of the number of pairs. Thus for a province with 50 destinations and 80 origins, $50 \times 80 = 4,000$ separate predictions are needed. These would be summed appropriately to yield the total number of trips to each destination from all origins.

A study that has become a standard reference for gravity models is an analysis of camper flows to Michigan (USA) state parks. Van Doren (1967) used equation [6.1] to predict the number of campers travelling to each of fifty-five state parks from seventy-seven counties. Population was defined as the number of campers in each county. Travel time (with the addition of a one hour 'set-up' time to control for a tendency to over-predict short trips) served as the distance component. The coefficients were calculated as described in equations [6.1] to [6.4]. Attractiveness of the parks was a weighted sum of natural features such as vegetation, climate and topography;

134

manmade features such as boating facilities and beaches; and a location variable describing whether the park was on a Greak Lake or not. The model was able to predict camper flows with a standard error of about 32 per cent, comparable to apparent 'random' fluctuation in attendance at a single park from one year to the next.

A modification of this model was used to predict recreation traffic growth in Dorset County (England). Whitehead (1965) was interested in all trip purposes and wished to predict increases over a twenty-year period (which he believed to be the maximum length of reliable population growth projections) rather than for a single year. He compared this growth with projected road capacities to see if road building projects would equal future demand.

At the time Whitehead was working, an estimate of national traffic growth had been made and was widely accepted: 5 per cent per annum. However, this was aggregated for all trips, all drivers, all regions. Whitehead was faced with the dilemma described earlier – accept an accurate but general forecast or develop a possibly less accurate forecast that would more validly reflect local conditions. Because he believed local changes were sufficiently different from the national averages, he opted for the second alternative.

Whitehead began by accepting a recommendation for model development from another geographer, Tanner. Tanner (1957) suggested that more accurate forecasts could be realized if a power function were used in place of the simpler exponent in the distance component. This has the effect of allowing a varying influence of distance on the propensity to travel. The modification produces the model:

$$T = G \Sigma \left[\frac{P_i P_j \, e^{-\lambda D_{ij}}}{D_{ij}^b} \right] \tag{6.6}$$

where: P_i and P_j = populations of two towns, i and j
  e = the natural logarithm base
  λ is a parameter
and other symbols are as defined before.

Whitehead made three more modifications. Like Van Doren, he used driving time. The next modification reflects a potential weakness inherent in the model. Doubling the population of each town would increase the prediction of travel fourfold. To correct for what would probably be an over-prediction, he suggested the form:

$$T = G \Sigma \left[\frac{(P_i P_j' + P_j P_i') \, e^{-\lambda D_{ij}}}{D_{ij}^b} \right] \tag{6.7}$$

where: P_i' and P_j' = population estimates for some point in the future.

Finally, to minimize the tendency of the model to over-predict very short trips, Whitehead added an exponent to the distance component that would decrease with increasing distance:

$$T = G \Sigma \left[\frac{(P_iP_j' + P_jP_i')\, e^{-\lambda D_{ij}}}{D_{ij}^{(1 + 1/D_{ij})}} \right] \tag{6.8}$$

To apply the model to forecasting traffic growth, Whitehead first separated 'native traffic' (generated by local residents) from 'holiday traffic' (generated by tourists). Holiday traffic is seasonal, is expected to grow faster than local traffic, and causes local congestion. Data collected for the forecast included the numbers of vehicles in use for the origin component from all towns within 80 kilometres of Dorset. This radius, according to other surveys, includes about 90 per cent of all pleasure traffic origins. Coefficients were estimated, current diversion rates reflecting the percentage of all traffic that passes through local towns were obtained, and a forecast made. The estimates of future traffic levels were found to far exceed projected road capacities indicating that congestion problems would grow.

Both Whitehead and Van Doren found that their models tended to over-predict short trips and had to make adjustments for this. Other researchers have noted the same pattern, and some have found that gravity models tend to under-predict very long trips. The actual travel behaviour of populations, compared to the theoretical, appears to include an element of 'inertia'. Some individuals have such a large 'start up' inertia, they never make any trips at all. Others, once going, enjoy travel so much they tend to keep going. So that researchers could avoid having to arbitrarily adjust their models as Van Doren and Whitehead did, Wolfe (1972) suggested a systemic modification of the gravity model. Wolfe proposed an inertia model in which the reaction to distance is a function of distance:

$$T_{ij} = G \frac{P_iA_j}{D_{ij}^b} D_{ij}^{\left[\frac{\log D_{ij}/m}{n} \right]} \tag{6.9}$$

where: m and n are empirically estimated parameters and other symbols are as defined before.

Although there is no theoretical foundation to the model, it does simulate observed travel patterns better than the original gravity model.

The examples in the previous pages share a common characteristic; each is determined. Given certain populations, past levels of use and distances, future travel levels are mathematically determined. Travel, however, is not really so mechanistic.

A more conceptually sound approach is to estimate the probability that a traveller will make a certain trip. A forecast of the expected number of trips can be made by multiplying the probability of a particular trip by the total number of trips actually made. An example of this approach is given by Wennergren and Nielsen's (1968) study of recreational boaters. They defined the probability of a trip being made from a given origin to a given destination as the ratio of the 'utility' of that destination to the utility of all destinations. 'Utility' was defined as the ratio of the size of a reservoir divided by the distance to that reservoir. This probabilistic model thus has the form:

$$P_{ij} = \frac{\dfrac{S_i^a}{D_{ij}^b}}{\sum\limits_{k=1}^{n} \dfrac{S_k^a}{D_{ik}^b}} \qquad\qquad\qquad [6.10]$$

where: P_{ij} = probability of a boater at i selecting reservoir j $(0 < P_k < 1)$
   S_j = surface area of reservoir j
   n = total number of reservoirs
   a and b are empirically estimated parameters.

Probabilities of travel to each of twenty-two different reservoirs for boaters living in eight different cities were obtained. Unlike other models that used historical data, these probabilities are based on a theoretical statement about the utility of a resource. To apply this forecast to predicting levels of travel, one must return to historical data. Two approaches are possible. If one assumes no growth in the total number of trips made, the model can be used to allocate the existing trips among existing reservoirs by multiplying probabilities by total trips. On the other hand, if a forecast of total trips is available, that forecast may be used instead of existing levels.

We have considered two types of gravity models. One predicts the number of trips expected between one or more origins and destinations. This is an unconstrained model because there is no limit on the number of trips that might be predicted. The other type of model allocates a given number of trips among alternative destinations. This is a constrained model because there is a limit to the number of trips predicted. What would be useful is a generalized model to allow a researchers to combine the features of a trip-generation model and a trip-distribution model. Such a combination has been proposed by Cesario and Knetsch (1976):

$$T_{ij} = \left[G\, P_i\, K_i^{(a+1)} \right] \left[\frac{A_j\, e^{b(D_{ij})}}{K_i} \right] \qquad\qquad [6.11]$$

where: A_j = attractiveness of a given destination
   K_i = competitive strength of all other destinations

$$(j \neq k);\ K_i = \left[A_k\, e^{b(D_{ik})} \right]^a$$

and other symbols are as defined before.

The first set of brackets encloses the trip generation component. Total trips are influenced by some characteristic of the origin such as total population, a measure of the attractiveness of alternative destinations and the distance between origin and destinations. The second set of brackets distributes the total number of trips among the various destinations. The proportion going from a given origin to a given destination is influenced by the relative attractiveness and accessibility of that destination.

This generalization allows researchers to handle a couple of problems that simpler models do not. If the accessibility of a facility is increased by lowering entrance fees, improving access or if the facility is made more attractive or given a larger capacity, the model predicts both an increase in the total number of trips and a redistribution of existing trips from existing destinations to the improved one. In the language of economics, the model predicts an increase in the demand for travel in general and a decrease in the demand for the substitutes for a particular destination, that is, for its competitors.

The effect of building a new facility on attendance at other facilities is also predictable. Building a new facility is the same as increasing the accessibility of a facility from 0 to $A_j e^{b(D_{ij})}$. K_i thus increases by the same amount. A new, larger number of trips is predicted by the generation component while the distribution component predicts a new pattern of travel to all facilities.

Cesario and Knetsch calibrated the model with data from eleven Pennsylvania (USA) state parks and found a close correspondence between the expected and actual numbers of visitors at each park. They did not, however, apply the same model to a different year to estimate its predictive ability with other data sets.

All approaches considered so far make a certain assumption that might be challenged: forces affecting travel associated with origin characteristics can be separated from those associated with destination characteristics, and both of these can be separated from the effects of distance. It is more likely that travel decisions are based on interactions among population characteristics, the quantity and quality of facilities and the distance to them. Lintsen, in a study of travel to recreation facilities around Eindhoven (The Netherlands) calibrated a gravity model with an attraction index for each of twelve destinations specific to each of twelve different household types (Table 6.3, cited in van Lier, 1978). Although there are some general consistencies, such as the fact that areas 7 and 8 are usually the two preferred sites for each household type, the overall consistency is not as strong as one might expect if the assumption that facility attractiveness is independent of population characteristics were true.

This discussion is another form of an issue we considered in Chapter 4: the use of aggregated versus disaggregated modelling. The assumption that origin, destination, and distance effects can be separated from each other is defended by researchers such as Cesario on the grounds that empirical results indicate such a distinction can be made statistically even if not conceptually. Moreover, the statistical analysis of these effects is made on the basis of aggregated models, and not in an attempt to explain differences among individuals. Cesario (1978: 153) responding to criticism by van Lier (1978) for making this assumption just described, defended his approach by writing, 'The model proposed is purely descriptive (as is the standard gravity model) in that it is a procedure designed to merely sort out the factors giving rise to variations in aggregate trip-making patterns...only aggregate data were con-

Table 6.3 Attractivity – Indices of twelve recreation areas for twelve household categories, depending on income and family-cycle

Area	Household category											
	1	2	3	4	5	6	7	8	9	10	11	12
1	0.070	0.110	0.053	0.069	0.074	0.036	0.049	0.112	0.067	0.064	0.098	0.047
2	0.026	0.060	0.028	0.033	0.042	0.069	0.049	0.067	0.041	0.027	0.049	0.055
3	0.005	0.010	0.010	0.007	0.003	0.005	0.005	0.008	0.006	0.014	0.009	0.008
4	0.043	0.040	0.048	0.028	0.034	0.042	0.060	0.055	0.047	0.031	0.052	0.046
5	0.092	0.053	0.117	0.104	0.152	0.111	0.083	0.107	0.160	0.124	0.195	0.202
6	0.038	0.013	0.028	0.032	0.026	0.017	0.040	0.041	0.019	0.008	0.038	0.012
7	0.253	0.237	0.115	0.234	0.172	0.211	0.251	0.127	0.181	0.204	0.181	0.187
8	0.192	0.131	0.184	0.160	0.188	0.178	0.179	0.279	0.2k3	0.136	0.262	0.132
9	0.090	0.095	0.152	0.083	0.130	0.123	0.070	0.050	0.096	0.106	0.036	0.117
10	0.138	0.097	0.097	0.179	0.073	0.096	0.092	0.102	0.057	0.102	0.017	0.035
11	0.045	0.087	0.082	0.030	0.085	0.071	0.067	0.029	0.062	0.105	0.034	0.135
12	0.008	0.068	0.087	0.040	0.021	0.040	0.057	0.023	0.051	0.079	0.029	0.025

Source: van Lier 1978

sidered, any attempt to infer behavioral parameters of individual recreation seekers is meaningless.'

The desire of researchers to understand individual behaviour is very strong, though. Care must be taken to limit the discussion of the results of any analysis to the proper level of aggregation. For example, elsewhere in the same communication where Cesario cautioned against using aggregate models to explain individual behaviour, he yields to the ambition to push his model further than it should go. 'It should not be mistakenly implied that the methodology cannot be applied to a sample of individuals. All one has to do is to consider each individual as an origin and observe his recreation trip-making behavior over time.' Cesario also argued that his concept of emissiveness, which is also a statistical aggregate, can be disaggregated. 'It is perfectly sensible to speak of emissiveness of one individual with respect to another.' Such slips should serve as warning to all researchers not to infer more from their data than theory and evidence allow.

To conclude the discussion of gravity models, we turn to an alternative form of the distance component. Edwards and Dennis (1976) suggested a generalized form:

$$C_{ij} = \frac{(X_1)\,(X_2)\,(X_3) + (X_4)}{X_5}\, X_6 \qquad\qquad [6.12]$$

where: C_{ij} = cost of travel between i and j
 X_1 = cost of gasoline per litre
 X_2 = litres consumed per kilometre
 X_3 = average kilometres travelled per hour
 X_4 = value of leisure time per hour (defined as 25 per cent of hourly salary)
 X_5 = average number of people per car
 X_6 = travel time

This generalized cost is used in the following model:

$$T_{ij} = P_i A_j \exp(-\lambda C_{ij}) \qquad\qquad [6.13]$$

where: λ = an empirically estimated parameter
and all other symbols are as defined before.

A 'recreation pull', S_{ij}, of destination j on origin i is defined as:

$$S_{ij} = A_j \exp(-\lambda C_{ij}), \ \ S_i = \Sigma S_{ij} \qquad\qquad [6.14]$$

The generation component is defined as the product of the pull of all destinations on a potential traveller located at origin i, times the total number of potential travellers:

$$T_{ij} = P_i S_i^b \qquad\qquad [6.15]$$

The distribution component takes the form of a constrained gravity model:

$$T_{ij} = T_i \frac{S_{ij}}{S_i} \qquad [6.16]$$

Combining equations 6.12, 6.14, and 6.15:

$$T_{ij} = P_i S_i^b A_j \exp(-\lambda C_{ij}) \qquad [6.17]$$

Solving this equation requires some relatively sophisticated estimation techniques. Not only must the coefficients be determined, A_j must be estimated either statistically or with another model, and the equation with numerical values calibrated with non-linear least squares estimation. The interested reader should refer to the original article. Two non-statistical issues are discussed further here. The generalized cost component combines fuel costs, time loss, and distance decay. By incorporating out-of-pocket costs with opportunity costs of travel time, certain additional analyses can be undertaken. If one assumes that benefits from recreational travel are at least equal to the costs (if they were not, people would stop travelling), then the estimated costs to the individual are a surrogate for the economic value of travel to that individual. This individual, of course, is a hypothetical average individual. Because the statistics are based on aggregate populations, statements about costs and benefits should really be interpreted as aggregate statements.

By multiplying average benefits by the total number of people travelling, one can obtain the total economic value of recreation travel. Edwards and Dennis did this and found that the average traveller received a benefit equivalent to 45 pence (1970 prices) for each trip. With an average of three persons per car and a total of 5,760,000 recreation trips in south-western England, the estimated value of recreation day trips was £2.5 million.

The generalized cost component allows a researcher to estimate the economic benefits of highway improvements that shorten driving time or distance. Effects of changes in speed limits introduced in some countries to save fuel can also be estimated. Slower speeds do reduce fuel consumption and thus lower the cost of travel, but they also raise the time spent travelling, which raises its cost. These effects are further complicated by the general rise in fuel prices, local uncertainty about fuel availability and changes in salaries and wages due to inflation.

Edwards and Dennis, as other researchers, assumed that a single destination existed for each trip and that travellers wished to minimize costs. Not all recreation trips conform to these assumptions. Colenutt (1969), for example, identified three distinct types of Scottish travellers in the Forest of Dean area. Some visitors did come to the main tourist attractions by the shortest route. These were day trippers that gravity models are useful to describe. However, over two-thirds of all travellers in the Forest of Dean and the adjoining Wye Valley did not behave this way. Some toured the region without a specific destination. Still others made a tour of several destinations. When there is no destination, or when a route is chosen for its charm or numerous attractions, the previous model performs poorly.

This problem is largely unexplored in trip forecasting. Recreation geographers may be able to make an important contribution to travel research by studying this phenomenon. Almost all existing models forecast trips with single destination and with routes chosen for minimal costs, such as the journey to work. Recreation touring, with no destination and where travel is a benefit, not a cost, still challenges travel forecasters.

We have now come to an alternative consideration of the effect of distance. This new consideration is based on the proposition that, for some trips, the real influence on trip length is not the cost of travel, but the distance to the nearest desired facility. Put more precisely, the probability of going to a particular destination is inversely proportional to the number of comparable destinations closer to the origin. While it is easy to think of examples where travellers pass by nearer facilities in favour of more distant ones, the importance of intervening opportunities is a useful concept for trips to bathrooms, schools, grocery stores, dry cleaners, petrol stations (especially when the gauge registers 'empty'), libraries, theatres, and neighbourhood parks.

Intervening opportunities models

The intervening opportunity model, developed by Stouffer (1940) is a response to a weakness in the conceptualization of distance as the primary determinant of travel patterns. Consider two neighbourhoods in an urban region whose residents have similar educations, occupations, mobility, and tastes. With no major differences, their travel patterns for the same purposes would be the same. However, if one of these neighbourhoods is centrally located and the other is in the suburbs, the central neighbourhood will have access to, for example, more jobs than the suburban one.

If distance, *per se*, were the most important variable influencing travel behaviour, then one expects to see similar distance decay curves. The fact is, though, the curves are different. The decline in the number of trips to work over a given distance is much more rapid for central residents than for suburban residents because of the greater density of jobs in the central part of the region. Because trips to work must be made, the variable that shapes the travel patterns is not distance, but the number of opportunities.

This conclusion can be empirically demonstrated using an argument similar to the previous one. If opportunities are more important than distance for some types of trips, then one expects to find similar curves for two neighbourhoods when a measure of the number of opportunities is substituted for distance. Adequate information about the number of alternative destinations, origin, and the number of trips is difficult to find. An English study (Clark and Peters 1965) of urban travel offers some evidence that, in certain circumstances, distance does not matter.

A survey of journeys to work in two London boroughs, Kensington (central) and Deptford (suburban) resulted in the curves in Fig. 6.7. The two curves show the decline in the number of trips as the accumulated number of employment opportunities increases – both are quite similar.

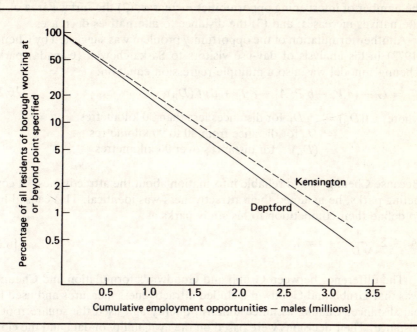

Figure 6.7 A graphic test for the effects of intervening opportunities (after Clark and Peters 1965)

Recreation researchers have usually incorporated the notion of intervening opportunities as a variable in combination with other variables. Grubb and Goodwin (1968), for example, included a measure of the effect of intervening opportunities among four other predictors in their study of Texas (USA) reservoirs:

$$T_{ij} = G P_i^a C_{ij}^b I_i^c S_j^d X_{ij}^e \qquad [6.18]$$

where: C_{ij} = cost of travel from i to j
   I_i = median income at origin i
   S_j = surface area of reservoir j
   X_{ij} = effects of competing reservoirs available to users at i on attendance at j
   a to *e* are empirically estimated parameters

The measure of intervening opportunities, X_{ij}, is defined as:

$$X_{ij} = \sum_{k=1}^{n} \left[\frac{\log S_k}{D_{ik}} \right] \quad j \neq k \qquad [6.19]$$

where: k is a competing reservoir
and other variables and symbols are as defined before.

The expected sign of X_{ij} is negative. Trips from i to j will decrease as: (1) the number of intervening opportunities increases; (2) the surface area of the alternatives increases; and (3) the distance to alternatives decreases.

Another formulation of the opportunity problem was suggested by Cheung (1972) in his analysis of day-use visitors to Saskatchewan (Canada) parks. Cheung's model was also a multiple-regression equation:

$$T_{ij} = G + (a\,P_i + b\,P_i\,A_j + e\,T_j + d)/f\,(D_{ij}) \qquad [6.20]$$

where: $f(D_{ij}) = \frac{1}{2}\,D_{ij}$ for distances less than 30 kilometres
$\qquad\qquad = D_{ij}$ for distance from 30 to 90 kilometres
$\qquad\qquad = (D_{ij})^{1.5}$ for distances over 90 kilometres

Because Cheung lacked reliable information about the attractiveness of competing parks, he assumed their attractiveness was identical. This caused him to define their competition to his study parks as:

$$A_i = \Sigma\,\frac{1}{\sqrt{D_{ik}}} \qquad j \neq k \qquad [6.21]$$

The difference between Grubb and Goodwin's formulation and Cheung's was that Grubb and Goodwin included attractiveness measures and used linear distance; Cheung assumed uniform quality and used the square root of distance. Their decisions were based on the availability of data and the closeness of the fit of alternatives to observed patterns. It is possible, though, to suggest some guidelines to provide a more theoretical basis for choosing different competing site measures.

First, any competing site measure should help a researcher avoid the usually unrealistic assumption that a given increase in supply will cause an exactly proportional increase in participation. Doubling the number of television sets would not double the number of people watching television. The only time an increase in supply would cause a proportional increase in participation is when existing resources are used to capacity and there is a large unmet demand. This condition is not very common. A competing site measure should describe the competitive strength of any given alternative site as a direct function of the site's relative attractiveness and accessibility. On the other hand, the competing site variable should predict that a site will experience greater competition as the number of alternative sites increases. Finally, the variable should be capable of reflecting the addition or subtraction of alternative sites.

Beaman and Smith (1976) suggested using a generalized version of Grubb and Goodwin's variable:

$$X_i = \left[\Sigma\,\frac{A_k}{D_{ik}^a}\right] \qquad [6.22]$$

where: X_i = competing site variable for some facility as seen from origin i
A_k = attractiveness of competing site k
D_{ik} = distance between i and k; a is a coefficient

The question now raised is: what value of a is most appropriate? The answer depends on what assumptions a researcher wishes to make about potential travellers. When a is less than 1.0, it is assumed that distance is not very important to travellers and that more distant sites will be relatively great competition to any given site. And because the number of alternative sites available to a traveller increases with increasing distance, the effect of cheap and easy travel (implied by $a < 1.0$) would be for travellers to be more likely to choose one of the more plentiful distant sites than one of the fewer local sites.

A different pattern emerges when the distance exponent is greater than 1.0. Distance and travel costs are assumed to be more important than before. As the value of the exponent goes beyond 2, the implicit importance of distance grows very rapidly. Large values of a (greater than 1.0) should be chosen when the researcher believes that accessibility concerns overwhelm the greater combined attractiveness of the large number of distant sites. Travel by small children, the elderly, or others with seriously constrained mobility might be best replicated with a large distance exponent. A smaller exponent would be more appropriate to people who enjoy travel, are relatively free in making travel decisions and who perhaps visit more than one attraction during a trip.

Guidelines for model development

Before beginning to develop a forecasting model, one needs to think through several issues. Some of these have been identified previously; others were hinted at. The following should help you focus on some of the key issues any researcher must deal with before making a forecast. Any model, regardless how complicated or sophisticated, will produce an inferior prediction if it is not appropriate to the task at hand. Informed judgement and a knowledge of the context in which a forecast is made is one of the most important resources a researcher can have.

1. The model should be sensitive to the researcher's objectives. One needs to be able to say why a forecast is needed, what decisions it will aid, the level of accuracy needed, the time period of the forecast, and what level of aggregation is appropriate.
2. The model should have a structure that produces realistic and firm projections. This does not mean the true explanation of the process is necessarily identified. Instead, it means that whatever form a model takes, that form is capable of reproducing the trends and relationships in the data.

145

3. Data requirements must be reasonable. The most powerful model in the world is useless if the data to calibrate it are not available. Data requirements include not just simple availability, but accuracy, reliability, format, plus the cost and time necessary to collect and maintain the data.

4. Calibration must be possible with available statistical techniques. Just as a lack of data will disable a model, ignorance of certain methods or not having access to a computer can severely limit the researcher's choices.

5. The coefficients derived should be stable. It is often possible to calibrate a model to accurately reproduce historical trends, but as soon as the model is used for a forecast, the coefficients change and accuracy is lost. Similarly, a model calibrated for one group or one type of travel is often not the best for other groups or other types of travel.

6. Note 5 notwithstanding, one should be alert to the possibility of modifying an existing model for a project. This can save time, effort and money. If an original model must be developed, it might be designed flexibly. A model to forecast trips to libraries may, with appropriate changes in the coefficients and variable definition, forecast attendance at art galleries. A model of inter-provincial tourist travel could also apply, with reworking, to convention travel.

7. Some models stand alone. Others require additional models or projections. Be aware which category a model falls in. The availability of other models and the accuracy of their data sources and projections can be an important consideration as one decides between alternative models.

8. Most models are deterministic, but a stochastic model is often more appropriate. Similar individuals under similar circumstances often make very different decisions. Deterministic models cannot allow for this. Stochastic models would predict similar probabilities for comparable people and situations, but allow for different outcomes.

9. Models based on multiple regression are vulnerable to three common problems; multicollinearity; autocorrelation; and heteroscedasticity. Multicollinearity (two or more independent variables are correlated) produces unreliable coefficients and may change their signs. Autocorrelation (observations are not independent) can artificially raise R^2 and lower the error estimate. Heteroscedasticity (size of the error varies with the size of the observation) distorts R^2. A researcher should at least be aware of these problems and the circumstances under which they can occur. A number of tests and some methods for treating the biases caused by the errors exist for each problem. These are often complicated and require the use of advanced statistics. Advanced statistics texts, especially those on regression methods, will provide more information. Some possible references include the following. For multicollinearity, see Walters (1968), and Farrar and Glauber (1967); for autocorrelation, see Malinvaud (1970); and for heteroscedasticity, see Goldfeld and Quandt (1965) and Beaman, Cheung, and Knetsch (1977).

146

Summary

Research in travel predictions will be likely to continue along the same lines as described in this chapter: continued refinement and variation of a few basic models. New measures for traditional variables, new variables and new methods for weighting them will be developed. One subject for inquiry that is a major departure from the past would be to study the interaction effects of variables.

This shortcoming in models is due to a limitation in statistics usually used to calibrate models. Once a variable has been used in an equation, it cannot be used again. This is not a serious problem if there is no interaction; but, as Parks Canada researchers learned in the Canadian Outdoor Recreation Demand Study (Parks Canada, 1976), interaction does occur in some circumstances.

An example will help clarify this point. A twenty-one year-old person today with a bachelor's degree may, with almost equal probability, be male or female; will probably come from a middle to upper income family; and will become a blue or white collar worker, go on to graduate school, become a homemaker or become unemployed. A seventy-one year-old person today with a bachelor's degree is much more likely to be male; to come from the dominant ethnic group; to have had an above average income; and to have been a white collar worker. The differences between the two individuals are due to the differences in society over the fifty years separating their graduations. Those differences would probably be missed if a model using age and education does not account for their interaction. Age and education imply more about a person than merely the sum of the variance explained by the two independently.

Work should expand on comparing different types of models. A few studies have already been completed. Ellis and Van Doren (1966) compared the use of gravity models and systems models for one type of travel. Okabe (1976), and Dison and Hale (1977) have compared the intervening opportunity model with the gravity model, but they did not do this for recreation travel. This initial work needs to continue.

Future models should be developed for more precise purposes, while still recognizing the potential problems of disaggregation. Some researchers have found, for example, improvements in predictions when separate models were made for males and females. Day-use models might be developed separately for weekday day-use and weekend day-use. Other travel models might distinguish between varieties of the same basic user group – canoeists, sail boaters and motor boaters might be more profitably separated than grouped together.

Another aspect of greater specificity in models would be to study travel behaviour for equivalent trips in different countries. Day tripping in the densely populated Netherlands might have significantly different coefficients than a model for day tripping in the sparsely populated Prairie Provinces of

147

Canada. Separate models would probably also have to be developed to accommodate differences between a Western country such as West Germany and a Marxist country such as East Germany. Not only are economic conditions different, there are important differences in recreation supply, social conditions, and freedom to travel.

All the variables considered so far, with the exception of 'attractiveness', are external to the recreation destination. The decision to travel to a particular destination is also influenced by 'internal' variables. These include the following. Entrance fees represent a travel cost often not included in the distance variables. The effect of a fee may not be the same on all visitors. Local users may be more sensitive to the establishment or increase of a fee than visitors who have come a further distance. For a tourist, the fee is only a small part of his travel budget, and he is thus not as sensitive as a local visitor who has virtually no other costs. Moreover, for certain public facilities, local visitors may feel they have already paid for the facility through their taxes and will thus object to the fee in principle.

Fees may also affect the length of stay. If someone has to pay to enter a facility, he is likely to spend a longer time in the facility than if it were free – to get his money's worth. Visitors who are willing to pay a fee are also more likely to be especially interested in the facility and thus represent a more receptive audience for information services and programmes. Free admission allows casual visitors to 'drop in' to wander around, relax, warm up or cool down in cold or hot weather, or to use the washrooms.

In a few cases the establishment of a fee may actually increase the attractiveness of a facility. Some consumers equate value with price, and the establishment of a modest price on an experience increases its value. The actual incidence of and circumstances surrounding this apparently irrational behaviour needs to be explored.

Much travel is done by private car. That means a parking lot. The capacity of a lot can often be an influential force affecting the total number of travellers who stop at a facility. This is especially true for people on a pleasure drive who might stop on impulse if there is adequate parking.

The location of parking is important. A lot separated from a facility by a railroad track or highway will turn potential visitors away. A lot too far away or very large (50 hectares or more), without some form of local mass transportation will also turn away potential visitors.

Predictions are often made for the initial year of a facility. If that facility is developed over several years, or if there are substantial changes in programmes over time, the effects on user levels can be substantial. Generally, new developments add visitors, but the nature of these developments might change the type of visitor attracted. The clearing of trees and brush from a small camp-ground to expand the number of sites will probably increase the number of campers, but they may change from a clientele interested in natural beauty to one interested in socializing with other campers. Adding a 'pops' programme to the schedule of a symphony orchestra may increase ticket sales, but will draw people less interested in the classics or virtuoso musicians. Attractive, semi-dressed cheerleaders at a sporting event will draw more spectators, but they may be less informed and less interested in the particular team or sport than the earlier audience.

Some types of recreation facilities depend heavily on changing programmes. Theatres, concert halls and art galleries change programmes or displays regularly to encourage repeat use. The attraction of cultural facilities to the general population is not large enough, and the costs too high, for them to be successful relying on one-time use. Public parks, on the other hand, need not change services every season. The latent demand for park use is so high, and the subsidized costs for public parks so low, that repeat use may not be a determining factor in their success.

Interpretive displays or historical exhibits, however, might need to attract repeat visitors to justify their being offered. The cost and effectiveness of changing programmes needs to be more precisely identified for different types of attractions. Such changes may attract a larger number of repeat visitors, but the number of first-time visitors will probably remain unchanged.

An unexpected effect of this might be a decrease in the average length of stay. Average length of stay is sometimes used as a measure of the quality of a programme. The higher the quality, the longer the stay. But if changing exhibits or programmes increases the number of repeat visitors, who tend to stay a shorter time than first-time visitors, the net effect could be a slight lowering of total average length of stay. A possible, but unwarranted, conclusion would be that changing exhibits lowers the quality of the experience. In fact, there would probably be no change, but the careless use of one or two aggregate statistics could miss that.

Travel models usually assume perfect knowledge of attractiveness, competing sites, distances and costs. This is usually false. Advertising, news stories, and word-of-mouth can affect all these things. Although people working in marketing assert that advertising is effective, there is little hard data in the travel research literature documenting advertising's effect on changing travel patterns.

A few researchers have attempted to measure the effects of images and knowledge on recreational travel. LaPage and Cormier (1977) have explored perceptions of different groups toward camping to identify barriers to the growth of the USA camping industry. Such work can be extended to recreational travel.

A country with a particularly vivid image problem, and one for which some statistics have been collected on the effects of image on travel, is Eire. International pleasure travel adds a substantial amount to Eire's economy each year. *Bord Failte Eireann*, the Irish tourist organization, estimates that 15 per cent of all Irish jobs are in tourism. When terrorist activities renewed in Northern Ireland in 1972, the violence of the northern neighbour dealt a severe blow to the Irish tourist industry. Aer Lingus lost £4 million. Hotel earnings fell by 20 per cent. The Irish Transport Company closed two of its travel offices in Britain. The British and Irish Line, a major shipping firm, lost a third of its passenger bookings to Ireland. Research into estimating the total effects of the image of violence on tourism could do nothing to offset the reverses in this situation, but it would help to more accurately measure the magnitude of the damage.

Turning specifically to the models we have considered, the gravity model is based on an analogy to a model that assumes mutual action between two bodies. In recreation travel the action tends to be 'one way.' Interaction between a residential neighbourhood and a theatre district is obviously 'one way', but what about interaction between two countries? A gravity model using population figures of two countries to forecast international tourism would predict an equal counterflow between two nations. But in the case of Austria and Italy, for example, the number of trips from Austria to Italy exceeded the reverse flow by 20 to 1. More precise model formulation is needed to account for these differences.

Another aspect of international travel is the effect of charter flights and package tours. These probably increase the number of trips, length of stay and, perhaps, distance travelled. The great number of British tourists travelling to the Balearic Islands and other Spanish resorts is due, in large part, to low-budget tours. During the winter months, Canadians represent the second largest national group in Florida because of inexpensive charter flights.

As more and more tourists come to a region, prices tend to rise. Eventually rising costs divert some tourists to other areas of similar attractiveness and accessibility, but with lower prices and smaller crowds. Brittany and Aix-en-Provence now divert tourists from the Riviera. There are few models that can reliably predict this effect, although it is well known in the travel industry.

Currency changes are another aspect of international travel ignored in travel predictions. Canada has long had a net travel deficit to the United States. The drop in the value of the Canadian dollar in the early 1980s kept more Canadians at home and attracted United States residents. The same effect has drawn Japanese visitors to North America as the value of the yen rises in comparison to the Mexican peso or the USA and Canadian dollars. Regardless of future relative levels of currencies, the need to understand and predict the effect of currency changes on travel patterns will continue to be important.

International travel can also be stimulated by special events such as a world fair or the Olympics. Williams and Zelinski (1970) note that the 1964 and 1968 Olympics in Italy and Japan increased the number of tourists visiting those two countries in those years and caused a long-term increase in international travel to the two countries. Expo '67, on the other hand, did not make a long-term improvement in international travel to Canada.

At the other end of the scale, literally thousands of local governments hold fairs, festivals and exhibitions to bring in tourists and money. Researchers will find little published information about methods for predicting the drawing power of either the Moscow Olympics or the Elmira, Ontario, Maple

Syrup Festival. Yet both are justified, in part, on the grounds that they will attract large numbers of travellers. Geographers could make a contribution to the feasibility studies behind these events.

Finally, one type of travel model has been ignored, not only in this chapter, but in almost all recreation literature: the notion that intervening opportunities are not barriers, but are stepping stones. The idea is the equivalent of the island hopping of plant and animal species down an archipelago. An analogy between the long-term, one-way migration of species and the fleeting phenomenon of recreational travel may seem tenuous. But the connection is stronger when one remembers travel brochures advertising '15 European cities in 14 days'. A certain type of travel personality seems to relish collecting as many destinations as possible in a limited time. Travel models that emphasize single destinations or overlook the pleasure of travel, even hectic travel, fail to account for a large number of trips.

Additional reading

Batty, M. and Mackie, S. (1972) 'The calibration of gravity, entropy, and related models of spatial interaction', *Environment and Planning*, **4**, 205–33

Carruthers, R. C. and Dale, H. M. (1971) 'The modelling of surface trips to the Third London Airport', *Regional Studies*, **5**, 185–98

Cesario, F. J. (1973) 'A generalized trip distribution model', *Journal of Regional Science*, **13**, 233–47

Cesario, F. J. (1974) 'More on the generalized trip distribution model', *Journal of Regional Science*, **14**, 389–97

Cicchetti, C. J. (1973) *Forecasting Recreation in the United States*, D. C. Heath and Company, Toronto

Howrey, E. P. (1969) 'On the choice of forecasting models for air travel', *Journal of Regional Science*, **9**, 215–24

Isard, W. (1960) *Methods of Regional Analysis: An Introduction to Regional Science*, The MIT Press, Cambridge, Massachusetts (see especially Ch. 11)

Neidercorn, J. H. and Bechdolt, B. V. (1969) 'An economic derivation of the "gravity" law of spatial interaction', *Journal of Regional Science*, **9**, 273–82

Thompson, B. (1967) 'Recreational travel: a review and pilot study', *Traffic Quarterly*, **21**, 527–42

Vickerman, R. W. (1975) *The Economics of Leisure and Recreation*, The Macmillan Press, London

Chapter 7

Normative research on location

In Chapter 5 we examined some of the methods used to select sites for recreation businesses. In this chapter we turn to the methods that have been developed for the selection of sites for public agency programmes and facilities, especially those concerned with users and activities, rather than with preservation or historical restoration. We will begin by looking at the nature of public services and facilities in general. This is followed by a discussion of different types of public facilities and the different objectives they might be designed to meet. Finally, we examine alternative methods for selecting sites.

Locational characteristics of public facilities

A public facility planner is concerned not only with the objective of the facility, but also with its externalities. Because the public at large will usually pay for a facility through taxes, many public groups will usually have something to say about how they are affected by that facility. A public park may not only provide the opportunity for recreation for residents of one neighbourhood, it may alter the property values adjacent to the park and may cause increased congestion on some streets. If one neighbourhood gets a new park, another neighbourhood may have to do without. Assessment of all the costs and benefits of a public recreation facility can greatly complicate the decision about where to build, or whether to build at all.

Unlike private enterprise, there is no economic Darwinism that governs the survival of a public facility. Failure to meet objectives does not cause it to go bankrupt and to cease operating. The relative security of general tax funds and of the jobs of civil service employees produces a certain 'inertia' or 'longevity' in most public programmes and facilities. Trends toward greater public accountability, programme evaluation, attempts to cut budgets, the implementation of 'sunset' laws, the use of zero-based budgeting, and the ability of the public to influence government agency operation through ref-

152

erenda and citizen participation, are having an effect on the operation of facilities, but these are slow and cumbersome compared to the effects of market-place forces on most small and medium-sized businesses.

In most communities, the producer of public recreation services is a single level of government. This can permit a monopolistic decision-making process to develop. Political pressures and a sense of public responsibility usually deter officials from behaving like private monopolists, but the lack of market-place competition causes other problems. Existing location theory is predicated on the belief that decentralized distribution of facilities produces a meaningful pattern. This pattern is described and explained through central place theory, but its efficiency and the ideal mix of different sizes and types of facilities is not addressed by central place theory or any other traditional locational theory. In the geography of the market place, one can assume that questions of efficiency are answered automatically by the operation of the market. Inefficient firms are eliminated without recourse to some formal evaluation procedure. For public services, however, one cannot assume that external forces obviate the need for evalution. Systems theories of public facilities and evaluation methods of their location are critical to effective planning and operation. As we shall see, these are only beginning to be developed.

Types of public facilities

It is useful to define, at this point, what is meant by a public facility. At the most general level, a public facility is one that provides a public good or service. A public good may be defined as one that is offered by the government. A public facility is therefore any facility that is owned and operated by some level of government. However, almost every type of facility and good has been provided by a government at some time, somewhere in the world. A definition based on observation of past practice would thus be too lengthy and cumbersome, or would necessarily be tied to one society. For the purposes of this chapter, we will define a public good in terms first suggested by Teitz (1968): a public good or public facility is one that is characterized by: (1) collective use; (2) zero short-run marginal cost; or (3) merit use.

A collective-use good or facility is one that is such a nature that its use cannot be restricted or withheld. National defence is a collective good. One resident of a country cannot, in practice, be denied the benefits of national defence if every other citizen is being provided that benefit. If this service is provided, it must be provided to everyone, with the costs shared generally. Urban open space is another example. There is no practical way that access to public open space or playgrounds can be restricted to certain users.

A zero short-run marginal cost good is one that, once established, can be used by anyone without additional cost to the provider. Public highways are an example. Short of total congestion, the cost of allowing one more tourist on the highways is negligible. Private provision of such goods is usually inefficient, and the cost of producing them and the social need for them is so great that the government must usually take up the responsibility for providing them.

A merit-use good is one whose provision is socially desirable, often because of externalities, and whose allocation through private market places would cause socially unacceptable distributions of that good, or result in the good simply not being provided at all. Schools, museums, and nature preserves are examples. Many of the debates about the proper role of government in the provision of social services focus on questions about whether particular services are truly merit goods. Health care, school lunches, higher education, day care and energy resources, are examples of goods and services whose ownership – public or private – are still debated in many countries.

Closely related to the problem of defining public goods is the classification of public goods. Classifications help define the objectives of particular goods for both planning and policy decisions. Among the simplest classifications is the suggestion by ReVelle, Marks, and Liebman (1970) that public goods be divided into ordinary goods and extraordinary, or emergency, goods. Ordinary goods include parks, public housing, highways, water supplies, and garbage disposal facilities. In contrast to these are goods, such as health care, fire protection and police protection, that are often associated with emergencies. The objectives and locational considerations of these two classes of goods are often quite different and therefore they should be planned for separately. ReVelle's classification scheme is relatively crude, however, and the distinction between ordinary and extraordinary goods is not always clear in practice.

Austin (1974) has suggested another classification that is especially relevant to locational problems. The emphasis in Austin's scheme is on the effects of the facility on the surrounding population. Each facility is one of three types:

1. Site-noxious facilities: Those facilities that are socially desirable, but whose presence is a nuisance. Garbage dumps and incinerators are typical.

2. Site-neutral facilities: Those facilities whose utility is approximately the same at all locations within the service area. High schools and universities are examples.

3. Site-preferred facilities: Those facilities whose social utility is greatest to those closest to them. The decline in social utility with distance may be rather gradual, as in the case for

public parks, or relatively steep, as in
the case of fire protection.

Generally, recreation facilities are site-preferred. In certain instances, though, the classification may be different, or at least more difficult. Playgrounds are usually desirable facilities to have near one's home, but those living adjacent to a playground might have their net social utility lowered by the noise, litter, and trespassing associated with the playground. The playground thus has qualities that place it in both site-noxious and site-preferred categories for different groups of users. In contrast, an historical reconstruction that might draw visitors from far distances, and thus generate a positive economic impact for the local community, may actually be classified as a site-neutral facility because it benefits a wide region. But in fact, the economic benefits derived from the presence of that facility are more important to local people than the vaguer social benefits, and thus on economic grounds one might consider the reconstruction a site-preferred facility.

Objectives

Objectives of public facilities are frequently difficult to specify because they are based on vague concepts such as the quality of life or a sense of social well-being. Rather than attempt to quantify such abstract ideas, researchers adopt a surrogate or substitute for them. Because the choice of a surrogate tells a lot about the underlying philosophy and concerns of the researcher, and because it can have significant implications on the locational decision made, the choice of an objective needs to be made carefully.

A frequent objective is to satisfy some unmet need. Because no one has successfully shown that people need recreation in any scientific meaning of the word 'need', one usually defines the concept comparatively. Facilities in two or more neighbourhoods are compared to each other or to some arbitrary standard. Any place that falls short is deemed to be in need. If there are too many places in need for the available budget, one can rank candidates in terms of relative deprivation and provide facilities as far as the budget allows. Gold (1973) and Wright, *et al.* (1976) discuss some of the uses and problems of this approach to locational decisions.

Because most recreational facilities are site-preferred goods, the distance between a potential user and the facility may be used as a surrogate for the utility of that facility. Distance is employed in two different ways as an objective. First, facilities might be located to minimize the maximum distance any person must travel to use one. This is often used as a supplement to the familiar standards approach for planning facilities. A maximum distance is specified from observation of past travel patterns, or on the basis of intuition, and then every facility is mapped with the maxium distance radius plotted.

Any neighbourhood falling outside the plotted service radius is then identified as being in need (Hatry, *et al.* 1977).

The second use of distance is to locate facilities to minimize the average distance that users must travel to reach them. This also minimizes the total distance travelled. Minimizing average distance minimizes the cost to users of acquiring a desired service. This strategy can have the effect of leaving some residents far removed from facilities, though.

Another surrogate for social utility is the *per capita* rate of consumption. One locates facilities to maximize consumption, and by implication, demand. Historical *per capita* rates of participation are related to selected independent variables, such as income. If income and *per capita* rates are positively related, the planner identifies the neighbourhood with the highest *per capita* income, and thus the highest potential rate of participation. This is the preferred location for the next new facility. Demand maximization (or consumption maximization) was often employed in the USA by the Bureau of Outdoor Recreation (1968). This method of allocation, however, has a serious inherent bias that will be examined later.

Different objectives can lead to different sites, and thus different objectives can be incompatible. Care must be taken to decide which objective is desired, and to ensure that the results of pursuing that objective are socially and politically acceptable. Cicchetti (1971) discussed some of the problems that each of three different objectives for locating urban recreational facilities can create.

White (1979) added a note of caution about using distance or demand measures as surrogates for social utility when he warned that these methods ignore linkages among different types of facilities. He noted, for example, drug and alcohol abuse clinics and hospitals often serve the same clientele. The location of clinics should thus be influenced by the location of hospitals as well as by the location of clients. In recreation, potential linkages among parks, schools, arenas, libraries, and other leisure and cultural facilities should be considered before final site selection.

Methods

The researcher has a choice of five basic models for public facility site selection: (1) mechanical analogues; (2) comparative need assessment; (3) demand maximization; (4) heuristic programming; and (5) intuitive modelling. Comparative need assessment and demand maximization have developed directly from certain objectives; the others are more general and may be used with any of several different objectives. Details of each are given below.

Mechanical analogues

Mechanical analogues, in the form of a Varignon frame, use gravity and mechanical forces to simulate the competing needs of different neighbourhoods for a facility. This method is useful for locating only one large facility when the need for that facility can be expressed as a single uniform, quantitative index – for example, if need is proportional to population size. Travel in the community being studied must also be equally easy in all directions. Four steps and some simple hardware are needed to identify the optimal site. Figure 7.1 illustrates this method.

1. The region is mapped on to a sheet of plastic, wood, or metal. Holes are drilled at the geographic or population centre of each neighbourhood.
2. A string is fed through each hole and all are tied together at a central point on top of the board, but left free to move over the surface of the map.
3. Weights proportional to the relative need of each neighbourhood are attached to the end of each string underneath the board.
4. The board is raised and the weights allowed to come to an equilibrium. The point underneath the knot on top of the board is the optimal location for the facility. The closest available site for development is then identified.

There are problems with this method beyond the limitation and assumptions already given. Under most circumstances the optimal location will be a point central to the various neighbourhoods. A number of neighbourhoods with relatively minor needs can overwhelm the pull of a single neighbourhood with a greater need. This may be seen as a type of compromise, but the compromise is not necessarily the socially equitable solution. Further, if the region is very irregularly shaped, the optimal location could fall outside the region. The model cannot easily be adapted to adjust for the presence of other facilities, and it is inapplicable to locating two facilities simultaneously.

Because of these problems, the primary advantage of the mechanical

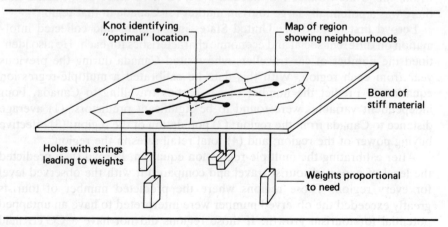

Figure 7.1 Mechanical analogue process for site selection

157

analogue is its novelty. It serves well to introduce the problem of public facility location and illustrates a simplified approach to site selection. But it has very limited usefulness for real planning. See Eilon, *et al.* (1971) and Shea (1966) for more about the applications and limitations of this method.

Comparative need

The comparative need method also balances the pull of different neighbour-hoods against each other, but this method selects the neighbourhood with the greatest relative need, rather than a compromise solution among many neigh-bourhoods. Because this method ranks different neighbourhoods, it permits the selection of sites for two or more facilities. The central issue is, of course, the measurement of need. For general recreation services, Staley (1968) sug-gested comparing the resources of a neighbourhood with its needs to estimate relative level of deprivation. He illustrated this method for the city of Los Angeles (USA). Resources and needs were measured by indices composed of several variables. Because the variables were measured in different units, Staley converted them to a type of standardized score called C-Scores (Guil-ford 1956). C-Scores allow variables originally measured in different units to be compared and combined. The resource index is the sum of the C-Scores of paid recreation staff *per capita*, number of recreation centres *per capita*, and park area *per capita*. The need index is the sum of scores for youth pop-ulation density, median income, and rate of juvenile delinquency. By sub-tracting the need index from the resource index for each neighbourhood, Staley identified relative needs and ranked all neighbourhoods in order of decreasing comparative need.

A different approach to defining need is given in Ecroyd's (1972) work for the Canadian Government Travel Bureau (CGTB), now known as the Canadian Government Office of Tourism. Ecroyd wished to identify regions within the United States that needed a CGTB field office in the sense that there was a potentially large tourism market for Canada in that region.

Ecroyd first divided the United States into regions and collected infor-mation on different social and economic characteristics for each. He also iden-tified the number of car travellers who visited Canada during the previous year from each region. With this data he calibrated a multiple-regression equation to predict the number of car parties travelling to Canada. Four independent variables were found to be significant predictors: (1) average distance to Canada from the region; (2) population of the region; (3) effective buying power of the region; and (4) total retail sales in the region.

After calibrating the multiple-regression equation, Ecroyd then predicted the level of expected tourist travel and compared it with the observed level for every region. Those regions where the predicted number of tourists greatly exceeded the observed number were interpreted to have an untapped potential for tourism growth. If those regions did not have a CGTB field office, Ecroyd named them as likely candidates for future office locations.

A disadvantage of the comparative need approach is its omission of cost consideration. The provision of identical facilities in different regions usually incurs different costs because of differences in the cost of land, labour, material, and in opportunity costs. Two calculations are used to supplement the comparative need approach: calculation of benefit–cost ratios and calculation of net benefits.

Benefit–cost analysis (BCA) is a well-established and much studied method for allocating public resources, so we will not consider it in detail here. Instead, we will examine it only in the context of public facility location. In that context, BCA has three major weaknesses. First, it tells us nothing about spatial relationships. Although it can be used to compare different projects in different locations, spatial differences, relationships, and dependencies are not directly analysed. The distribution of benefits and costs among geographical and social groups is also ignored – or to put it more accurately, the distribution of costs and benefits is assumed to be constant across all regions and groups. Finally, benefit–cost analysis was designed to analyse only monetary costs and benefits. Economists and economic geographers have developed surrogate prices for some non-monetary aspects of projects, but these have had limited success in planning projects. Social costs such as frustration and bitterness over the loss of private land for the development of a park are difficult to ever express in monetary terms. Maass (1966), Klaasen (1968), and Austin (1974) discuss benefit-cost analysis as a site-selection technique in greater detail.

An alternative to BCA is to use a cost-effectiveness ratio in which monetary benefits are replaced by some other measure of social utility, such as the number of people served. The ratio is homologous to the BCA ratio, except that it is a measure of the number of people served per unit cost rather than unit benefit per unit cost. The problem with this approach is that replacing monetary benefits with some other measure does not avoid the difficulty of trying to express different types of benefits in a common unit of measurement. Thus, instead of pound or peso, one tries to express all benefits in terms of person-units or some other notion.

The net benefit method refers to an examination of the arithmetic difference between costs and benefits, rather than their ratio. The usefulness of this method has been discussed in Chapter 5 in the context of site selection for private businesses, and has been applied by Onokerhoraye (1976) to public facility location. Onokerhoraye identified four influences on benefits that should be assessed by a planner seeking to select an optimal site for a public facility: population characteristics (number, density, birth and death rates, migration patterns); social characteristics (income, occupations, family patterns, racial mix); technological characteristics (car ownership, adequacy of communications); and some evaluation of likely citizen response to the facilities.

After the benefits from the provision of a facility at each location or neighbourhood have been assessed, one estimates the costs of the facility for

159

both capital investment and operations. The net difference between costs and benefits is then calculated for each location, and those areas with the highest net 'profit' are given priority for development.

There are substantial problems with using the net benefit approach. First, there is no direct spatial consideration built into this method. Potential sites are selected before actual analysis – arbitrarily or according to some unspecified model – thus the resulting decisions are only as good as this initial round of site selections. Further, the author did not explain different benefits converted to common units of measurement, nor how these can be compared to monetary costs. Because most social programmes and services involve a transfer of wealth from one sector of society to another, it is also necessary to estimate the opportunity costs and the distribution of income associated with each potential development. In other words, it is not enough to know what it costs to build and operate a facility, one must also know what society will have to do without in order to pay for that facility, who will be paying for it, and who will be enjoying it.

Heuristic programming

Heuristic programming is a method for searching out the solution to a problem through an incremental routine. Just what this means will become clearer when we look at an example, but one should recognize from the outset that heuristic programming is more a stategy for solving a broad class of problems than a specific technique. To illustrate this strategy, we begin with the relatively simple problem of selecting the site for a facility. Seven steps are necessary to find the solution.

1. Define the region within which the facility is to be located. Specify boundaries, linkages, nodes, neighbourhoods, and any other spatial relationships relevant to the problem.
2. Define the objective of the facility – for example minimization of total distance travelled by all users.
3. Mathematically define the objective. This is called 'specifying the objective function'. For minimizing total travel distance, the objective function would be:

$$Z_j = \sum_{i=1}^{n} P_i D_{ij} \qquad\qquad [7.1]$$

where: Z_j = the value of the objective function, and this is what is to be minimized

   P_i = the population of the ith neighbourhood to be served by the facility

   D_{ij} = distance between the ith neighbourhood and the jth point (the tentative location of the facility)

   n = total number of neighbourhoods

4. Select a reasonable tentative site for the facility by inspection.
5. Calculate Z_j for this first location.
6. Choose another point, j, a short distance away from the first point. Calculate Z_j for this point.
7. Continue to relocate j and to calculate Z_j all around the area of the original j until a minimum Z_j is found. This is the optimal location.

Obviously this procedure can become rather lengthy if one were to try it by hand; so it is almost always done by a computer with a type of program called a 'linear program'. Linear programming seeks to optimize some objective function within specified conditions such as budget constraints or a maximum number of facilities. Ward (1964) and Moore (1968) provide overviews of linear programming and its applications in heuristic programming for locational problems.

Complex as this process might seem, most locational problems require still more complicated procedures. Often several facilities must be located simultaneously. Further, a particular person is usually allocated to a facility, and before the objective function can be estimated for a tentative solution, all people must be allocated according to an additional objective allocation formula. These two tasks, allocation of users and location of facilities, give their names to a special form of site-selection problems: location–allocation problems. Some examples of location–allocation problems for public service include ReVelle and Swain (1970), ReVelle and Church (1977), Hodgson and Doyle (1978), Robertson (1978), and Goodchild and Booth (1980). We will examine the later example in more detail.

Several years ago, London, Ontario, had 11 pools serving 460 neighbourhoods. The City Council wished to add two new pools. Goodchild and Booth employed a heuristic programme to select the optimal sites for these new pools. They first conducted a poolside survey at existing pools and discovered there was.considerable overlap among the service areas of the pools. Although people did appear to consider distance before selecting a pool, variations in pool attractiveness caused some users to pass by a closer pool in favour of a more distant one. This fact complicated the development of a location–allocation model. Unlike many other facilities such as schools or fire stations where users are allocated by an authority to a particular facility to produce a series of efficient, exclusive hinterlands, recreation facility users allocate themselves.

Next, Goodchild and Booth realized that not every person had the same desire to visit a pool and thus there were different probabilities that needed to be considered before developing an allocation algorithm. On the basis of previous research, the decided age was the single most significant variable influencing rates of swimming. This meant that the population in each neighbourhood had to be disaggregated by age cohorts and a separate weight or probability applied to each age group.

With these considerations in mind, Goodchild and Booth devised a two-stage solution. They first defined an allocation formula that estimated the number of people attending a particular pool from a given neighbourhood as a function of the size of different age groups, the distance to the pool, and the pool's attractiveness. Specifically:

$$I_{ij} = \frac{(\sum_{l} a_l P_{il}) A_j / D_{ij}^b}{\sum_{k} A_k / D_{ik}^b} \qquad [7.2]$$

where: a = probability of person in age group l participating in swimming
P_{il} = population of age group l in neighbourhood i
A_j = attractiveness of pool j
D_{ij} = distance between neighbourhood i and pool j
k = set of all pools, including pool j
b = an empirically estimated parameter

Given this equation, the objective function was specified as:

Minimize $Z = \sum_i \sum_j I_{ij} D_{ij}$ [7.3]

which means they wished to find locations for the two pools that would minimize the total distance travelled by all swimmers to all pools.

Goodchild and Booth first located the two pools at likely spots and calculated Z for all pools, existing and new. They then moved each of the two pools a short distance and recalculated Z for the new pattern. This was repeated until a minimum Z was obtained.

This particular problem required several decisions that are common to many recreation location–allocation problems. First, the costs of developing pools and budget constraints must be set. In the London case, Goodchild and Booth assumed the costs were approxiamtely equal at all sites, and that the available budget would be adequate for any proposed development. If these assumptions could not be met, some form of cost constraint would have to be added to the linear programme. Another decision concerned the objective function. Because population was a component of the objective function, the researchers needed to decide the best way to define population. Their choice was to use weighted age groups. For other location–allocation problems one might use total daytime population or income group size. One also needs to decide whether to use current population figures or projections of populations. If projections are to be used, how are these to be made, and for what horizon? One should also consider the possibility of facility location influencing future population distributions through encouraging or discouraging migration into certain neighbourhoods.

Distance must also be defined. Straight-line distance is commonly used, although road network distance may also be appropriate. Hodgson and Doyle

(1978) suggested using travel times and that some consideration of different modes of travel (especially private car versus public transport) be made.

Goodchild and Booth estimated both relative attractiveness of the pools and the age cohort weights from observation. There are numerous other methods available to estimate attractiveness and attendence probabilities. One must decide which method is best, taking into consideration both the benefits to be derived from greater precision and the costs incurred by employing more powerful methods.

Demand maximization

The demand maximization method is based on the belief that facilities should go where they will generate the greatest *per capita* use. Neighbourhoods with the greatest potential use rates have, by implication, the greatest need, or at least will have the greatest appreciation of the facilities. Society as a whole, it is argued, benefits most when facilities are located so that they will be used to the greatest extent possible. The basic procedure for demand maximization consists of the following steps.

1. Identify some socio-economic variable that is reliably and strongly related to *per capita* participation rates in the activity to be provided at the facility.
2. Formalize the relationship identified in Step 1 by graphing the socio-economic variable against *per capita* participation. Figure 7.2 is a typical

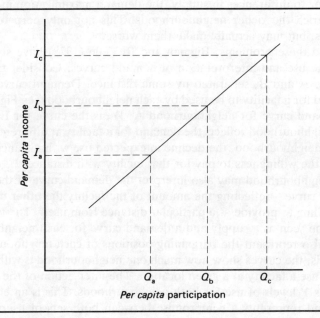

Figure 7.2 Hypothetical income–participation relationship for demand maximization method

result. In this case, *per capita* income has been identified as the predictor variable.

3. Measure the *per capita* income in each of the study neighbourhoods. Three hypothetical neighbourhoods and their associated incomes have been located on Fig. 7.2: I_a, I_b, I_c. Each income can be associated with an expected rate of *per capita* participation: Q_a, Q_b, Q_c. With the strategy of selecting maximum demand, neighbourhood C is identified as the preferred location.

Several comments about this method are in order. First, demand maximization can be used only if a reasonably stable and reliable monotonic relationship between use and some other variable can be identified. If no relationship is found, or if the curve rises for a range of values and then falls over another range, no single site can be identified as optimal. This approach is relatively crude in that it identifies only the neighbourhood in which a facility might be located. It cannot pinpoint sites within that neighbourhood. Further, the activity to be provided must be the same for all possible locations if one is to make valid comparisons. In other words, one cannot compare the demand for tennis courts in neighbourhood A with the demand for a pool in neighbourhood B or for a playground in neighbourhood C.

A more serious problem with demand maximization is the assumption that differences in *per capita* rates of participation reflect differences only in demand. If the differences are due in part to past social or economic inequalities or to differences in supply, the demand maximization method will tend to enrich the richer neighbourhoods. This not only perpetuates past inequalities, but may actually make them worse.

To avoid these problems, Bigman and ReVelle (1978) have suggested a twist on the use and interpretation of demand curves. Consider two neighbourhoods, A and B, separated by some distance. Demand curves may be constructed for a facility to be used by each neighbourhood (see Fig. 7.3). W_a is the demand curve for neighbourhood A; W_b is the curve for B. A curve for one neighbourhood reflects the demand for a facility at different distances from that neighbourhood, the decline in expected use with distance, and the decline in the willingness to pay for that facility with distance.

Each neighbourhood may also interpret the demand curve of the other as the supply curve – reflecting the amount of the facility the other neighbourhood is willing to provide at a particular distance from itself. The two curves may thus be seen as a supply and a demand curve for each neighbourhood, and they also represent the bargaining positions of each neighbourhood. In other words, the curves show how much one neighbourhood is willing to pay for and to use a facility at a given location. The intersection of the curves, at d, provides Y levels of use for both neighbourhoods. This is an equilibrium solution and represents a compromise between both sets of users. In fact, this solution is an ideal Pareto optimal solution – no other location can be chosen without hurting at least one neighbourhood.

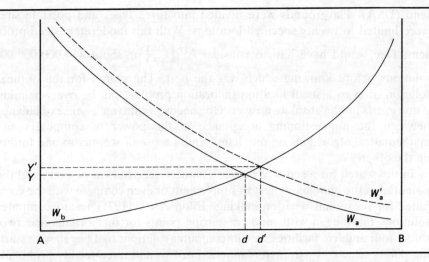

Figure 7.3 The demand–bargaining solution for site selection (after Bigman and ReVelle 1978)

Figure 7.3 is drawn with the demand curves for the A and B nearly identical. If, however, one neighbourhood is much more affluent and has a correspondingly greater demand, its demand curve will be shifted outward: residents of that neighbourhood are willing to travel farther for a given level of use. If the shifted demand curve is W_a', observe what happens to the intersection with W_b. The equilibrium location shifts *closer* to the less affluent neighbourhood, and the total quantity provided increases.

Unfortunately, this theoretical model applies to the limited case of only two neighbourhoods. Additional work might be undertaken to generalize this demand bargaining solution to more than two neighbourhoods, and to empirically apply the generalized form to an actual facility location problem.

Intuitive solutions

One step in heuristic programming was to select an initial location for consideration by inspection. The purpose of this was to assist the computer in finding the optimal location in the entire region. Because the heuristic programme proceeds through a series of small changes, examining combinations of locations and allocations, and because computer budgets are limited, one can never be sure the optimal solution is ever found, Usually one must settle for a reasonable solution, reflecting at least a local minimum in a plausible area for development rather than the absolute minimum over the entire region.

The difficulty of finding the absolute optimal solution can be best appreciated by looking at a numerical example. Dee (1970) attempted to identify the best location for seventeen playgrounds for the city of Baltimore, Maryland (USA). Playgrounds were divided into three types and possible sites were limited to twenty specified locations. With this moderately-sized problem, Dee would have had to consider $3^{17} \begin{bmatrix} 20 \\ 17 \end{bmatrix}$ or about 150,000,000,000 solutions before knowing which was the best. The search for the optimal solution of even a small location–allocation problem can be overwhelming if one insists on the absolute answer. One needs to cultivate a sense of balance between the unquestioning acceptance of the power of computers and mathematical algorithms on one hand, and a sense of scepticism and futility on the other.

In the search for a sense of balance, some researchers have examined the potential of the human intellect to supplement or even compete with the computer for locational decision-making. Eilon *et al.* (1971) tested computer solutions that began with random starting points for fifty origins and two, three, four and five facilities, versus computer solutions that began with starting points selected by trained planners. For two and three facility problems, there was no advantage to using an intuitively chosen starting point. However, for four and five facilities, the human-assisted solution was superior to that produced by the computer alone.

A more interesting test was made by Schneider (1971). He examined the problem of locating emergency health care facilities, given a pattern of probable car accidents in an urban area. After supplying his test subjects with a street map, speed limits, a distribution of accident probabilities, and instructions concerning the criteria for selecting the best location, he asked them to locate a specified number of emergency care centres to minimize travel time. The test subjects were able, on the average, to identify better sites (those with lower travel times) than the computer.

It would be needlessly cynical to dismiss heuristic programming on the basis of this one experiment, but it does suggest that the informed opinion of a trained researcher or planner can often produce an acceptable solution. Considering the relative costs of using human judgement versus the costs of developing, calibrating, and solving a complex linear algorithm, the human solution often may be preferable.

Summary

Public facility location is an important planning issue. A few methods have been developed and used, but much more work needs to be done to develop, refine, and test these tools. The site selection methods of the next generation of geographers will probably be extensions of the same methods we have examined, especially in the form of more elaborate and systematized intuitive procedures. Some of the work that might be undertaken in the near future includes the following subjects:

166

Objectives used to locate public facilities are usually quantitative surrogates for vague notions of public well-being. The usefulness and reliability of quantitative objectives is well-established, but their validity is not. The objectives chosen in the past for social services in general may not be the best for recreation services in particular. Surrogates based more directly on a philosophy of recreation or on a formal statement of the role of recreation in public life might lead to the definition of more precise and valid objectives, and ultimately to more effective recreation system.

Improved statements of objectives will also assist in the development of improved classifications of public recreation facilities. These classifications serve as guides for planning and managing facilities, and would assist in the refinement of locational models for specific types of facilities. Classification schemes should be based on the objectives of the facilities, their social and environmental effects, and on differences in form (linear facilities such as trails versus point facilities such as nature centres, or indoor facilities versus outdoor facilities).

Work done to date on developing self-allocating models is inadequate. Most allocation models assign users to the nearest facility but for recreation, users are normally free to assign themselves – and the allocation models should accommodate this. Goodchild and Booth have begun this work and it should be extended.

Because public facility planning often involves decisions about locating several facilities at different times, work is needed to add a temporal dimension to locational models. It is not enough to know where facilities should be built; one must also be able to decide the best sequencing and timing of their development.

Recreation facilities are more diverse, in total, than many other public facilities such as fire stations, schools, or police stations. Another research need, therefore, is the identification of the effects of differences among recreational facilities on the decisions about their location. Current methods have been designed to apply to nearly identical and fungible facilities. The effects of differences among facilities, including difference in scales and design on locational model validity is not known.

Finally, comparisons of the solutions of different methods for the same problem would help identify the relative costs and benefits of each method. The limited available evidence suggests that intuitive models may be the most cost-effective, but further testing of both the effectiveness and efficiency of different methods is needed.

Additional readings

Abernathy, W. J. and Hershey, J. C. (1972) 'A spatial allocation model for regional health services planning', *Operations Research*, **20**, 629–42

Church, R. and ReVelle, C. (1974) 'The maximal covering location problem', *Papers of the Regional Science Association*, **32**, 101–18

Cooper, L. (1963) 'Location–allocation problems', *Operations Research*, **4**, 331–43

Hodgson, M. J. (1978) 'Towards more realistic allocation in location–allocation models: an interaction approach', *Environment and Planning A*, **10**, 1273–86

Holmes, J., Williams, F. B., and Brown, L. A. (1972) 'Facility location under maximum travel restrictions: an example using day care facilities', *Geographical Analysis*, **4**, 258–66

Robinson, W. C. (1976) the *Utility of Retail Site Selection for the Public Library*, Occasional Paper 122, University of Illinois Graduate School of Library Science, Urbana, Illinois

Scott, A. J. (1971) 'Dynamic location–allocation systems: some basic planning strategies', *Environment and Planning*, **3**, 73–82

Wheeler, J. L. (1958) *The Effective Location of Public Library Buildings*, Occasional Paper 52, University of Illinois Graduate School of Library Science, Urbana, Illinois

CHAPTER 8

Normative research on travel

Recreational travel can produce many changes in community life. Tourists bring money and ideas; they demand to be fed, housed, and entertained. If resources are allocated to meet their demands, the availability of resources for the demands of local residents will change. Jobs are created in response to the need for tourism services, and those jobs can create social problems as easily as they create new affluence.

Research on the promotion or limitation of recreational travel is scarce in the social sciences. The paucity of work is due, in part, to the complexity of issues that must be considered before one can suggest the optimal level of tourism and travel development. The information shortage is also due to the fact that decisions about desirable levels of travel-related development must be made by civil and political leaders responding to the values and needs of society, rather than in response to a scientific analysis of travel impacts.

The purpose of this chapter is to identify and discuss some of the basic issues that should be considered as part of any decision to set a goal for, or a limit on, tourism and travel development. These are the issues that a researcher can study in order to make the decision-makers' jobs easier and their actions more informed and rational. Unlike previous chapters, details of specific methods will not be considered. Because of the wide range of issues, and the wider range of methods for analysing them, we will concern ourselves only with identifying basic and enduring topics associated with normative research into travel.

These topics are the types of effects travel may have on the regions in which it occurs. The topics can be grouped into three broad categories: (1) economic effects; (2) social effects; and (3) ecological effects. Each of these will be examined in the following sections. The chapter concludes with a review of some of the factors that influence the nature and magnitude of the effects.

169

Economic effects

Recreational travel induces growth on three levels: (1) local; (2) regional; and (3) national. The magnitude of this growth will be different among the various levels. It is necessary to consider each one separately. The changes induced by travel are at any level generally predictable. These include increases in employment and income in some sectors of the economy. Such benefits of tourism development may be partially or completely offset by various costs, including development and operational costs, as well as social and cultural problems. Studies that have looked at economic effects include the work of Gray (1970) and Peters (1969) on tourism as a force in international development and trade. Ouma (1970) in East Africa, Bond and Ladman (1972) in Latin America, and Jones and Goldsmith (1969) in Puerto Rico, considered the effects of tourism on national economies. Henderson (1975) in Greater Tayside, Scotland, and Strang (1970) in Door County, Wisconsin (USA), measured effects on local economies.

Employment

Tourists require roads, airports, hotels, fast-food outlets, gift shops, and many other facilities. These, in turn, require workers. People must be employed to plan, design, and construct them. Then other people must be hired to operate and maintain them. Facilities stimulate related service jobs such as taxi drivers, tour leaders, and interpreters. These jobs are direct results of tourism development. There are also indirect or induced increases in employment: more restaurants mean more work for people employed in agriculture and food distribution. Hotel offices require office services, financial services, and insurance. Gift shops create new jobs for artisans and manufacturers.

Income

New jobs are supported by new money, and this means new income for the people obtaining the jobs. Within a limited context, then, tourism adds wealth to an economy. On a larger scale, however, tourism merely circulates existing wealth among social groups and geographic regions. Unlike primary economic activities such as mining, or secondary activities such as manufacturing, tourism does not create truly new wealth. This effect is most clearly seen when one compares the transfer of money from one region to another as tourists travel. A gain in one region means a loss in another.

To estimate the addition of wealth to a region, it is necessary to estimate the number and expenditure of local tourists as well as those of non-local tourists. Expenditure estimates are usually expressed in terms of specialized sectors of the tourism industry such as: accommodation expenditure; food and drink sales; transportation services; and crafts sales.

For some destinations, especially islands served by cruise ships or airlines, it is also desirable to disaggregate tourists into different groups. For example, visitors to a Caribbean island will usually include: (1) tourists staying one or more nights on the island; (2) crews of visiting airplanes and ships on a stopover; and (3) tourists staying on board cruise ships. Each of these will have different effects on the local economy, based in large part on how long they stay. Local residents who patronize restaurants, shops, nightclubs, and other attractions may represent another substantial portion of the clientele for tourist businesses.

Multipliers

Money spent by tourists goes into the pocketbooks and bank accounts of local businesses. This money, in turn, is spent on salaries, supplies, insurance, and taxes. Each time a tourist makes an expenditure, a ripple of additional spending is sent through the economy. This ripple is called a multiplier. The multiplier describes the additional spending or job creation caused by a given level of tourist spending. A large multiplier means that an expenditure of one unit produces a relatively large amount of additional economic activity. If money is 'exported' through the purchase of goods from outside the region, through repayment of loans, or through taxes, the multiplier is reduced. Mathematically, the multiplier may be defined as:

$$M = \frac{\Delta I}{\Delta T} \tag{8.1}$$

where: M = tourist multiplier
ΔI = change in income resulting from a change in tourist spending
ΔT = change in tourist spending

The calculation of a multiplier first requires itemization of the expenditures between the tourist sectors of the economy and all other sectors. Some rather complicated matrix algebra is then used to convert these exchanges into a multiplier. Although multipliers are calculated from original economic data, many researchers prefer to rely on estimates based on previous research. If a multiplier has been calculated for an economy and a level of development comparable to the one being studied, the use of the original multiplier as an estimate can greatly simplify the assessment of economic effects. The danger is always present, of course, that the context in which a multiplier was first calculated is sufficiently different from the context in which one wishes to apply it as an estimate that the conclusions will not be valid. However, the potential usefulness of estimated multipliers, in the view and practice of many researchers, is sufficiently great to warrant that risk. A few examples of the use of economic multipliers include Strang (1970), Bryden (1973), the National Council of Applied Economic Research of India (1975), Archer (1976), and Hanna (1977).

171

Beyond the problems of obtaining adequate data and having the necessary methodological capabilities, several other challenges confront the researcher hoping to develop an accurate estimate of the tourist multiplier. First, income estimates that form the basis for $\triangle I$ usually include profits, wages, and interest paid to foreign nationals working in tourism industries and to foreign investors. For major developments, the ultimate investors may be difficult to identify, but they will frequently include a significant percentage of non-local entrepreneurs. Another problem with multipliers is that they are based on the assumption that opportunity costs – losses the economy incurs when money is spent on tourism rather than on other types of development – are negligible. This may be true for large, well-integrated economies in which tourism plays a minor role, but it is rarely true for developing countries. Another assumption, even riskier to make, is that demand, prices, and consumption patterns are stable. This assumption is ironic because one of the reasons for encouraging tourism growth is to promote economic change. As inflation changes prices and incomes, as spending patterns change, coefficients reflecting economic transactions will change, and the multiplier changes. If much of the new wealth goes to higher income groups, as is often the case, they can be expected to increase their consumption. Because higher income groups tend to import more than other income groups, the amount of money leaving the economy will increase and the multiplier will decrease.

The multiplier is a difficult, expensive, and unstable statistic to derive. The reason it generates so much interest is that omission of the multiplier means one necessarily misses a substantial portion of the real effects of tourism.

Other benefits

Income and job creation are the most common benefits to be derived from tourism, but under the right circumstance, other benefits may be realized. If the volume of tourist trade is large enough, the infrastructure (roads, utilities, etc.) can be expanded to a significant degree. If this expansion is large enough, economies of scale may be possible. Thus the road network, a power plant, or an airport may be built at a lower cost per unit than would have been possible without tourism. Bryden (1973) discusses this briefly in the context of Caribbean tourism development.

Externalities are sometimes created through tourism growth. For example, the demand for land for hotels and other facilities will force up the price of land. Rising prices will encourage land speculators to enter the market, causing prices to rise still more. The beneficiaries of higher property values will, of course, be those who owned and developed the land, and perhaps local governments who enjoy higher returns from property taxes. Generally, this benefit is ignored because it favours those already favoured by the economy. It is, nonetheless, a real benefit to some people. On the other hand, rising land values can force out small landowners, and can prevent private individuals from acquiring a home of their own – and this cost should not be ignored either.

Development costs

Facilities, the physical basis for tourism, cost money – usually a lot of money. Costs include land, material, and labour. Because the total bill can be substantial, development capital is often obtained through loans. One must then add the cost of the capital itself, the interest on the loan, to total costs. Some projects require foreign investment to obtain the needed capital. Foreign loans mean a leakage of capital back to the investor, and because the lender usually wishes to be paid back in his own currency, the costs of foreign exchange must be added to total costs. If the exchange rates become unfavourable (for the borrower), these costs can suddenly escalate.

Operating costs

Development costs are only the first to be paid. Once a facility is constructed and the doors open, salaries, wages, utilities, maintenance, supplies, insurance, and taxes begin to come due. These costs can be high initially, and they tend to increase with time. Employees expect higher wages as they gain experience; maintenance of facilities costs more as the facilities age; costs of supplies and services tend to increase with time.

Opportunity costs

A tourism facility does not just cost the sum of development and operations. The money spent on that facility is no longer available for other uses. The value of these missed opportunities represents a hidden but real cost of any project. As long as the chosen project returns benefits greater than the costs incurred through lost opportunities, the choice of projects was acceptable. However, if the money could have been spent on some other project that would have returned greater net benefits, the chosen project may not have been the best decision.

Opportunity costs, though, are not easy to estimate. One must first identify the missed opportunities. Then a forecast needs to be made of both the gross benefits and the gross costs for each opportunity. These are then used to estimate net benefits. The distribution of net benefits over time must then be calculated and appropriately discounted. These figures are then compared to the discounted net benefits of the chosen or tentative project to determine total opportunity costs. Vaughn (1977) discusses measurement and definitional issues associated with opportunity costs and tourism development in more detail.

Risk and uncertainty

Risk and uncertainty are costs because they lead to a higher interest rate for loans, increased collateral for loans, more insurance, more planning, or less expansion and growth. Both are conditions of ignorance that can result in actual financial loss. Risk differs from uncertainty in that risk can be expressed in terms of objective probabilities. Uncertainty has no known probability.

Tourism is especially vulnerable to these two costs. Local operators are subject to changes in whim, fashion, and taste in the travel market. Fluctuations in disposable incomes in distant countries can affect the health of resort regions. Uncertainty in fuel supplies and costs adversely affect the numbers of flights and of travellers going to distant destinations.

Foreign investors must accept a certain degree of uncertainty about local politics, running the chance their businesses may be nationalized in the future. On the other hand, local political leaders may be subject to unpredictable pressures from foreign political events and leaders and from multinational corporations. Tourism is a highly visible industry, and therefore is a popular target for labour unrest, political demonstrations, and even terrorism (see, for example, Steinecke 1979, for an analysis of tourism in the Republic of Ireland). Finally, the vagaries of weather, earthquakes, and even wild animals affect local resorts.

Social effects

The effects of tourism on social life and structure are harder to document than economic effects. Part of the reason for this is that perceptions of social change are intimately tied to values, and thus are qualitative and subjective. Even if there is general agreement that a change has occurred, it is difficult to prove that the change resulted from tourism, and even more difficult to decide whether the change was good or bad. The UNESCO (1976) report, Cohen (1972), and Jafari (1974) identify and document some of the more common social changes to be expected from tourism.

Demonstration effect

Tourists not only bring money to a region, they may bring a strong, visible 'consumer' lifestyle with them. In a large city of a wealthy country, tourists and their spending habits may not be especially noticed, but in a small or poor region, they can be both noticeable and disruptive. Consumption of food, drink, local culture, local services, souvenirs, and all the other commercial amenities tourist regions have to sell, can set an example of a higher material level of living than is traditional among local residents. This example can lead to a phenomenon known as the demonstration effect.

The demonstration effect can take any of several forms. Local wealth may not be saved or invested at the same rate as before the tourists came as local people spend more to acquire material goods. Note that if these material goods are imports, the demonstration effect can worsen the balance of payments in the host economy.

The demonstration effect may also give rise to a social hybrid called the marginal man (Press 1969; Jafari 1974). The marginal man is a resident of the host country who has accepted the values and lifestyle of tourists and tries to achieve them. Frequently he fails, but in trying is seen by his compatriots as a 'traitor' to local values. He becomes caught between two cultures and lives on their margins.

Foreign influences that create the marginal man may also create – or be perceived to create – other social problems. Establishment of, or increase in, prostitution, gambling, drinking, and drug abuse may be attributed to tourists. McPheters · and Stronge (1974) have documented a strong empirical relationship between variations in the number of tourists and variations in the incidence of murder, rape, and other violent crimes in Miami, Florida (USA).

The demonstration effect is ironic because the tourist is living a lifestyle and enjoying spending patterns he would never accept for himself back home. Yet this temporary, indulgent fantasy is seen as a model for the ideal, modern way of life. It should be noted, however, there is little firm, empirical evidence that the demonstration effect is widespread. The mechanisms that create it and cause it to operate in some cultures but not in others, are unknown. Documentation and analysis of this effect is a subject for which more research is needed. A few preliminary attempts to study it include Nurkse (1962 and 1970), Taylor (1975), and Greenwood (1976).

Social stratification and socialization

Relationships among social groups can change as a result of tourism development. In poorer countries, the addition of an active travel industry will add new occupations and wealth, increasing both the number and types of jobs and the range of wealth in each occupation group. This may, in turn, change the basis of social class from occupation to income (Greenwood 1976).

The demonstration effect and a changing social order may lead to conspicuous consumption. Rather than seeking social identity and status in family and friendship ties, or through cooperation with others in the same occupation, people may begin to compete by trying to acquire more and more material goods. Family sizes might decrease, marriages can occur at different times in life from before, and mobility may increase as people seek new jobs in new locations.

Generational conflicts can result when younger members of families adopt tourism-induced values while older members retain traditional ones. This can have the further effect of increasing neglect of the elderly as children leave home to set up new, smaller households far away. Sibling rivalry may increase as family businesses become more lucrative in the tourism-enriched economy, or as family inheritances (especially real estate) increase in value. As women find jobs outside the home, especially for the first time, home life and male–female relationships have to adjust.

The long-term desirability of these changes is a matter of personal and social values. Neither change nor understanding of change comes easily. This is true, of course, for modernization and industrialization in any setting. Tourism, though, frequently exhibits one difference compared to other industries, that exacerbates problems. In the past, for other industries, people often left rural areas more or less willingly to seek the benefits and accept the costs of progress. In the case of tourism, progress comes, invited or not, to the people. Traditional rural life may become enmeshed without warning in the intricacies of industrial development, real estate speculation, and re-definition of social responsibilities. Press (1969), McKean (1973), Greenwood (1976), and Johnson (1978) have addressed these issues.

Self-respect

Part of the appeal of foreign countries to tourists is the fact that they are 'foreign' – they offer a change from familiar places and scenes. Curious costumes and customs (to the tourist), however, are the fabric and soul of the day-to-day life of people who live there. Tourism developers, especially those who are not residents of the destination country, may fail to appreciate the significance of local traditions. Religious beliefs, traditional dress, secular celebrations, and other mores might be reduced to tourist commodities in the search for a marketable tourist product. The loss of self-respect that accompanies the commercialization of a culture and of the human spirit is more than just a regrettable by-product of tourism. It is an insult to a people, and it can trigger violence.

The scientific study and measurement of the loss of self-respect is important for tourism evaluation, but it is not easy to accomplish. A trained psychologist working in a developed country using sophisticated testing techniques on a small sample of volunteers could probably identify respect-related changes and problems. But how does one apply this clinical approach to tens of thousands of people in a culture where such probing would be alien? Assessment of the problem of dignity and the development of methods to combat or to prevent its loss, are virtually unknown in the tourism literature. A few studies that have at least recognized the importance of the issue include Sutton (1967), Anzola-Betancourt (1972), Schwinsky (1973), Johnson (1978), and Butler (1979).

Cultural re-awakening

The parade of thousands of tourists through one's homeland does not necessarily diminish one's dignity. Local residents may 'fight back' by developing or rediscovering a sense of pride in themselves and their history. Authentic crafts, literature, dance, music, drama, rituals, cuisine, and costumes may enjoy a renaissance stimulated both by the tourists' appreciation of local culture, and by the need for reasserting a local sense of identity.

Cultural re-awakening may also result in the restoration of architectural monuments, buildings, and the preservation of important landscapes. Without tourists, these may have been allowed to slowly decay without notice. With tourists, the increased use may hasten deterioration, resulting in quicker recognition of the problem and a strong response to rectify it.

Xenophobia

Xenophobia, the fear of strangers, can result from any social change created by the presence of tourists that the individual finds hard to accept. In addition to the types of changes we have discussed earlier, several other conditions can contribute to the development of xenophobia. Crowding is one of the most common. Congestion in markets, on roadways, in shops, and at recreational facilities can slowly and steadily increase the level of frustration among local residents. Some facilities, such as beaches, may eventually be marked off-limits to anyone but the patrons of exclusive resorts. Exclusion from formerly public open space may further aggravate long-time residents.

More generally, xenophobia can result from a sense of loss of control over one's destiny. Changes in family structure, in relationships with other residents, in the pace of life, and even in the ease of physical movement, are sharp reminders that the resident is no longer as 'free' or as 'important' as he once thought he was. Local bureaucrats may grow in number in response to the need for more planning and zoning, to control land sales and industrial expansion, and to take advantage of the new taxable income with the inevitable result of a loss of personal freedom that is associated with bigger government.

A sense of helplessness can also come about from the strings attached to foreign investment. These strings may include the requirement to import certain quantities of goods from the investing country to be sold through local shops, and the requirement that key management jobs may require favourable trade terms for exports to the investing country. The investing country may also attempt to influence local leaders to create an environment more favourable for further foreign investment, regardless of the effects on local residents. In the extreme, this can result in reprisals in the form of civil unrest and government take-over of foreign-owned businesses. Sutton (1967), Anzola-Betancourt (1972), Schwinsky (1973), Jafari (1974), and Butler (1978) elaborate on aspects of xenophobia.

Ecological effects

Methods for assessing the environmental effects of any form of development are well established, so we will not go into the details of impact assessment here. Some useful sources for further reading include the International Union for the Conservation of Nature (IUCN 1967), Lloyd (1970), Satchell and Marren (1976), Lopez de Sebastian (1976), and Wall and Wright (1977). Tourism development affects five different components of the natural environment: (1) soils; (2) flora; (3) fauna; (4) water; (5) noise levels. As with economic and social effects, environmental effects may be good, bad, or mixed.

Soils

Increased use of an area frequently results in greater soil compaction. This, in turn, leads to a change in ground vegetation and to increased run-off of rain and snow-melt. Most compaction is usually associated with human feet, although vehicular traffic is a serious problem, too. The pressure on soil structure from human tread and from vehicular tread differ. Humans tend to exert less pressure per unit area than most vehicles, unless the person is wearing shoes with thin high-heels. The human foot adds a twisting action to the vertical pressure that can dislodge the soil surface. Vehicles cause a lateral pushing resulting in ruts, a backward longitudinal force usually showing up as a spray of dust and stones behind moving vehicles, and a forward longitudinal pressure that causes a series of semi-permanent ripples to form on asphalt as well as on soil.

Soil composition is also altered by the presence of humans. Pollution and littering add chemicals to the soil by leaching of superficial materials, spillage of liquids, and physical incorporation of material into the soil. In areas frequented by dogs, horses, and other animals there may be an increase in organic matter and nutrients in the soil. This modest benefit is offset by the killing of grass caused by decomposition, aesthetic degradation associated with the sight and smell of animal waste, and the danger of disease and parasite infestation.

Increased run-off can cause increased erosion. This may undermine roads and building foundations and remove valuable topsoil. Erosion also results in increased silt loads in surface water-bodies with a resulting decline in water quality and possible loss of aquatic life.

Flora

Heavy human use of any open space will have adverse effects on the diversity, total biomass, and health of plant species. Trampling directly kills plants; soil compaction alters the micro-climate and water balance and thus kills plants. These initial changes in the local biotic community can lead to the eventual

178

loss of other species and their replacement by hardier and often less desirable species.

Plants may be lost by the picking of wild flowers or their removal for transplanting by collectors. Of lesser concern, but still of potentially great impact, is the importation of foreign plants by landscapers. A plant brought in has the potential for spreading naturally and for displacing local species through competition. Most ornamentals used by landscapers, however, are so temperamental that few could survive, much less compete, in the wild.

Fauna

Most wildlife species are adversely affected by the proximity of human beings. When possible, they will move on to avoid human contact. If this is not possible, they must either adapt to the presence of man, or die. Loss of ground cover, changes in water quality, dredging and filling of wetlands, and increased noise levels also have effects. In addition to the physical loss of animals, human pressure increases the incidence of disease, alters feeding habits, and disrupts mating behaviour. Harvesting of wildlife can also mean serious trouble for local populations if it is not controlled. Over-harvesting of fish and shellfish for restaurants is a special problem in waters off resort communities.

As with flora, animal species can be introduced into a locality. This most often occurs with some game animals and fish, and for zoos and aquaria, but it is also done for aesthetic reasons in vacation home developments. In a few cases pets are released or escape and, under favourable conditions, become established.

Water

Water is as essential to the life of the tourism industry as it is to the life of a human being. Concern for the environmental effects of tourism frequently emphasize water quality and quantity over all other aspects of the environment. Swimming pools, air conditioning, washing, bathing, drinking, sewage treatment, and all other uses of water, increase as the number of tourists increases. For most purposes, water must be fresh. Thus a desert resort or a resort on a small island may experience water shortages created by persistent and heavy tourist demands, despite the possible presence of quantities of salt water.

Any form of development produces waste. If treatment facilities are not adequate, some of this waste will end up in the water. Soaps and kitchen sewage add nutrients to water bodies, promoting algae blooms, aquatic plant growth, and may kill off some desirable fish species. Human sewage also increases nutrient levels and creates health hazards such as the possibility of typhoid and diphtheria.

Garbage dumps, land fills, and fuel spills from outboard motor boats and tankers add toxic chemicals to water-bodies. Lead compounds are a common component in fuels and other industrial chemicals, and as these accumulate in bottom sediments they become long-term health hazards.

Dissolved oxygen is frequently used as a measure of water quality. It is influenced by the number of photosynthetic organisms releasing oxygen, the rate of oxygen absorption from the atmosphere, the mixing of oxygen-deficient bottom water with oxygen-rich surface water, and the demand for dissolved oxygen from respiring organisms. Oil spills and nutrient pollution tend to lower dissolved oxygen, which can spell trouble for desirable fish species.

Finally, water temperature affects both the quantity and quality of plant and animal life in water-bodies. Temperatures are raised by warm water discharged from air-conditioning units and power-generating plants. These are not tourism-specific activities, of course, but tourism increases their prevalence. Higher water temperatures, within a limited range, may be beneficial. Heated water can be used for supplemental heating of accommodation or facilities, and may promote fish life (except for species such as trout and salmon).

Noise

One of the newest, least-studied, and most annoying environmental effects of development is noise. Noise comes from many sources – vehicular traffic, nightclubs and restaurants, amusement parks, airports, and construction equipment. The increase in noise levels from tourist-related sources can hardly be denied, but few baseline studies have been completed to monitor actual changes, or the effects of these changes on human well-being. Most studies that have been completed on noise tend to focus on the physiological effects of intense noise in industrial settings, but a few other projects have examined the effects of recreational vehicle noise on the riders (Bess and Poynor 1972; Chaney and McClain 1971).

Context of change

Which of many potential changes will occur and whether change is beneficial or detrimental depends on many variables. These variables provide a context in which potential and actual changes are evaluated and in which forecasts and policies should be made.

One important variable is the strength of the local economy and culture. Established economies and cultures can accommodate change and even guide it to the advantage of the local residents more successfully than a society that is impoverished, politically inexperienced, or without a strong sense of destiny. The availability of a skilled labour force that provides employees and

180

managers for tourism industries also influences how successfully the community can exploit the benefits of tourism development. If few local residents can get involved directly in the tourism industry as workers, planners, or managers, change will either pass them by or it will be imposed on them according to someone else's values.

The degree of difference between residents and tourists influences the amount of potential disruption caused by tourists. Obvious differences in skin colour, dress, or language as well as less obvious differences in values, manners, religious practices, and social customs, also create friction.

The number of tourists compared to the number of residents, their length of stay, and the spatial integration (physical proximity) of tourists with residents has an effect on their acceptance by the local population. In general, the greater the number, the longer the stay, the more spatial interaction with local residents, the greater the effects. However, with longer stays and with more complete spatial and social integration, tourists may become acculturated into local society and may cause fewer disruptions or resentments than those who are more transient and insensitive.

Tourists' activities are another potential source of problems. If these activities are limited to light shopping, occasional trips to quiet museums, and some sunbathing on private beaches, the effect on the local population may be minor. If large, noisy tour groups suddenly descend into crowded marketplaces for browsing, if they wander through churches and temples during religious services, if they interrupt local workers and craftsmen by taking pictures, if they compete with local residents for scarce seats on public transportation, other effects will become more noticeable and the tensions between host and guest will inevitably increase.

Some cultural groups may be pre-occupied by a history of colonial exploitation and slavery. Any attempt at tourism development from the outside may be interpreted as an attempt to re-establish oppressive social conditions and will be strongly resisted.

The social, economic, and cultural policies of host governments also have an influence on potential change. The form and effects of tourism development will vary greatly in response to the hopes and fears of different governments and their economic and social policies, be they capitalist, socialist, or communist. National policies reflecting beliefs about the potential benefits or dangers associated with encouraging foreign visitors to come, or in allowing nationals to visit other countries, will also have effects. A region where the government is indifferent towards tourism will have a different experience from a region where the government is strongly in favour of tourism promotion, and both will have different experiences from areas where governments see and treat tourists as enemies. Attitudes toward nature conservation and parks will have other implications for how tourism is promoted and how the resources of the host country are managed and allocated.

Foreign laws and international treaties play their role, too. Laws governing income tax deduction for attending conventions in foreign countries can have a significant effect on the economy of some countries that might otherwise host international conferences. For example, restrictive American legislation in the late 1970s and early 1980s that eliminated convention costs as a tax deductible expense when the convention was outside the United States (domestic conventions were unaffected), cost Canada an estimated $100,000,000 per year in tourist revenues.

Other legislation that can affect in important ways the numbers, attitudes, and spending habits of foreign visitors include: laws governing visas and passports; the amount of money a national or visitor may take out of a country; restrictions on modes of travel; restrictions on tourists' access to certain regions of the country or to the general public; prohibitions on travel to certain countries or refusals to accept visitors that would arrive from certain countries; and customs policies. International conventions that affect the location of events such as the Olympics and world fairs also have implications for tourism promotion at the national level.

There is never a single, right answer about the desirable level of tourism development or the capacity of a destination region to host tourists. Answers concerning limits and capacities are best obtained by a series of evaluations and policy reviews while development is allowed to proceed slowly and incrementally. Only through cautious, deliberate evaluation of on-going development and policy applications can intelligent decisions be made regarding what is best for host and guest. Getz (1977) has expanded on this point and suggested a research programme for implementing tourism evaluation procedures for all the subjects considered in this chapter. New methods and new applications of existing methods are needed. New concepts and theories are needed. 'Progress' through tourism continues apace and geographers seeking to understand and guide that progress have reason to be busy.

Chapter 9

Conclusions

Geographic inquiry into recreation dates from the earliest years of this century and has involved researchers on every inhabited continent. Yet recreation geography remains only an emerging specialization. Some have suggested the reason for this is the fact that recreation is perceived as trivial, not fit for 'serious' researchers (e.g., Wolfe 1964). There may be some truth in this explanation. It is plausible that some geographers have mistaken the subjective experience of recreation with the objective study of recreation. Or it may be that the qualities of recreation, as perceived by academic geographers, place it beyond their intellectual grasp. This, too, is a plausible explanation. Many of the transcendent emotions – joy, hope, pathos, grief, and jollity – have been ignored by psychologists until recent years because these feelings were beyond the reach of traditional psychological research tools. It would be no surprise to learn that the study of human pleasure (recreation) would seem foreign to a person interested in spatial relationships. Finally, the apparent lack of substantive progress may be explained by the fact that, contrary to 'popular opinion', current research is quite adequate to meet current needs, or at least answers the questions geographers care about. There has been no overwhelming need to produce a systematic body of knowledge about recreation.

Whatever the reasons, things are changing. New intellectual concepts and new research methodologies are allowing the study of phenomena formerly inaccessible. Recreation also has become a way of making big profits; it has become respectable. A growing number of young geographers do care deeply about the current status of recreation geography and are eager to move it into new frontiers. This chapter reviews the history and philosophy of recreation geography as revealed through the work discussed in the first eight chapters and makes some comments about future endeavours.

Philosophy and practice

Any field of inquiry begins by describing, defining, and classifying selected phenomena. It is not insignificant that the first tasks God gave to the first human was to name the animals He had created. This process of observing and naming is of fundamental importance to all work that follows. Only when a name can be given to something to preserve its existence in our minds and to distinguish it from all other things does that thing begin to truly exist for us. Observing, naming, and describing is thus the first type of research. It might be more formally called naïve phenomenology because it is a simple, uncritical, and unsophisticated interest in observing things around us. Much recreation geography is still at this level; descriptions, inventories, and classifications are active topics of research. Definitions also involve the attention of many researchers and scholars in recreation. Part of the shared experience of students in recreation and leisure studies departments in universities is exposure to a seemingly endless debate about proper definitions of recreation.

Naïve phenomenology soon leads into another, slightly more complex form of research. As more and more phenomena are defined and classified, researchers begin to develop preferences for studying certain types. They begin to specialize. Further, recreation has direct bearing on many social and political issues. Government and planning agencies have long encouraged recreation research or have directly participated in research. Their concerns, of course, go beyond naming and counting. They desire tools that will help them achieve political or social ends. The result of these two conditions, specialization and the desire for application, gives rise to the next stage of research, naïve induction.

Naïve induction is the conceptually unsophisticated search for tools and for applications of existing knowledge. Note that it is the concepts that are relatively simple; the methods, usually statistical techniques, can be quite complex. This distinction is most clearly seen in the development and refinement of elaborate models to forecast trends in recreational travel. The methods require understanding of advanced mathematics and computers, but the basic concept and issue – taking a trip – is almost childishly simple.

Both naïve phenomenology and naïve induction exist at the same time. They are complementary, and they constitute the foundation for subsequent progress in most disciplines. Recreation geography is still at the stage of naïve phenomenology and induction, but pressure is growing for the field to break beyond the limits of these.

The desire for a breakthrough is expressed in two forms. First, it is argued that we need to develop clearer statements of research needs and priorities. Only through the development of some type of agenda for research will geographers be able to get a sense of direction that will allow the field to make substantive progress. This viewpoint is especially prevalent in the United States. A few examples of statements made over many years that urge the production of research agenda include Dana (1957), the Outdoor Recreation Resources Review Commission (1962), the National Academy of Sciences (1969), the Outdoor Recreation Research Needs Workshop (Bureau of Outdoor Recreation 1974), and a 1980 unpublished survey by the US Department of the Interior asking American researchers to suggest high priority research topics.

Alternatively, development of theory is cited as the single greatest need of the field. From this perspective, the call for research priority lists is essentially a continuation of past practice. Research efforts done under the guidance of a national agenda may be better coordinated, but they are not likely to lead to a cumulative body of scientific knowledge. Brown, Dyer, and Whaley (1973) and Smith (1975) have argued the importance of theory as a guiding spirit in all research – theoretical and applied. Other geographers and social scientists have gone further and suggested specific ideas that might provide a nucleus for the formation of theory. Cheek and Burdge (1974) for example, observed that much recreation is done in social groups, but that researchers seem to assume that it is always done by individuals. They suggested that greater theoretical understanding of recreation could be achieved if attention were directed to examining the types of groups that form the basis for recreation, the reasons for these groups, and their interactions.

Mitchell (1969) opined that too little attention had been given to the problems of cities by recreation geographers. Not only do cities have serious problems, in Mitchell's view, but they are the source of most of the demand for recreation. He concluded that recreation research should be organized around a search for the development of urban recreation theory. The same suggestion has also been made by Stansfield (1971).

Campbell (1966) also observed that cities had been largely ignored by recreation geographers, but felt that travel within cities, and between cities, and between cities and their hinterlands provided the best organizing nucleus for theory development. Wolfe (1964) has made an especially articulate case for the use of mobility as the core of recreation geography. Yefremov (1975) has asserted that the proper focus for Soviet geographers interested in recreation was on tourism, broadly defined, and especially on the phenomenon of travel.

None of these suggestions, despite their value and interest, have produced the breakthrough their authors were seeking. They desired, to use a term proposed by Kuhn (1971), a 'scientific revolution'. We are still in a 'pre-paradigm' state in which there is little agreement among geographers as to proper definitions, questions, methods, and phenomena when one studies recreation. In a mature discipline, Kuhn noted, such agreement has been reached – they have a paradigm.

How can recreation geographers achieve a paradigm? To answer that question, we need to examine another debate in geography that has implications for both the type of paradigm that might be developed, and even for whether such a paradigm can be developed. The debate is between two schools of scientific philosophy: logical positivism and phenomenology.

Logical positivism and phenomenology represent types of paradigms. They are mature perspectives that go beyond the concerns of naïve induction and naïve phenomenology. Those who belong to one or the other are no longer content to see their job as one of description only or to provide tools for practitioners. Their highest priority is to understand the world through a search for laws and patterns; they have this in common. Their conception of understanding and of legitimate methods for acquiring understanding, however, differ profoundly.

Although generalizations are difficult and dangerous, logical positivism may be thought of as the objective search for the truth, while phenomenology is the subjective search for a truth. Logical positivism is a doctrine that allows only verifiable tools and testable data and hypotheses to be used. The method of this philosophy are often described as the 'scientific method'. Ackerman (1963) summarized these as:

1. Observe and describe selected phenomena.
2. Construct hypotheses to explain observations.
3. Test hypotheses through experiment or further observation.
4. Replicate and verify experiments and observations.
5. Build a theory from verified hypotheses.
6. Base new observations and hypotheses on theory.

The emphasis on the objective and testable is both a strength and a weakness. Statements made as the result of positivist research can often be trusted to be valid and reliable, as far as they go. The problem is that totally objective tests and data miss much of the world as experienced by human beings.

Phenomenology is a reaction to the limitations of positivism. Among its supporters are Relph (1970), Tuan (1971a, 1971b), and Billinge (1977). The basis of the phenomenological approach is the view that a person cannot directly know any one part of the world without subjecting it to some form of human perception and that one cannot isolate one aspect of the world from the larger context of human values and experiences in which it occurs. The methods employed by phenomenologists will vary with the topic being studied and among different researchers. They share, however, the belief that one must understand something of humanity before one can understand something of the world.

This understanding of the importance of human perception and values, at the most general level, and the role of the observer in interpreting the observed, is phenomenology's great strength. It is also its great weakness. The methods employed by phenomenologists are often beyond replication or verification. Phenomenology tends to create many idiographic and non-cumulative studies.

The debate between advocates of positivism and phenomenology is a heated one, and it is difficult, perhaps impossible, to resolve it rationally. Yet it must be resolved in practice by each researcher. Personal resolution is usually made on the basis of training and preferences for styles of scholarship. In the longer run, it is likely that a synthesis of the two positions will occur: some sort of positivist phenomenology or phenomenological positivism. This synthesis, because it will be a form of compromise, will necessarily be a tolerant style of research. The compromise may allow researchers to study experiences, perceptions, and values, but only after these have been made as neutral and precise as possible for research topics. This compromise, if it is achieved, may be analogous in form to the construction of a church. The beliefs of the faithful determine the form of the structure and of its interior design. Beliefs influence whether the focus is on a pulpit or an altar. If it is on an altar, belief influences whether it is hidden or visible, whether it faces the people or faces away from them. Belief says whether there is a spire and whether icons are present. These issues are analogous to the issues addressed by phenomenology. They can be understood only by reference to values and experiences. However, all of these issues, the design features of a church, must be built literally on a strong foundation.

There are definite physical laws that affect the construction of a church building. Walls constructed of a particular material, using a particular technique, will have certain limits to their load-bearing capacity. The span between supports that hold up the roof is determined also by material and design. Different materials have different resistances to weathering, wear, and strain. The proper material needs to be chosen for each part of the church for it to function properly. The church will stand only if physical laws are not broken. These laws are the object of logical positivism. Whether a church stands or falls thus depends on positivist laws; whether the religion stands or falls depends on phenomenological 'laws'. Both building and faith co-exist; each depends on the other for meaning and expression.

Our discussion so far has been largely abstract. What does all this mean for the practice of research? The abstraction may become more real if we consider the evolution of the field in terms of the topics examined throughout the book.

As suggested before, research develops from simpler forms into more specialized forms, and then into greater sophistication. And when we look at the history of research in recreation geography, this is exactly the pattern we observe. A useful way of summarizing that pattern may be to visualize the subject as a tree. The tree draws its strength from roots that go deeply into other disciplines, and it produces new branches and adds strength to existing branches over the years. Figure 9.1 is an illustration of a possible 'tree of recreation geography'.

Two limbs representing the major themes of recreation geography split off from the main trunk: travel-based studies and resource-based studies. Travel-based studies evolved from simple concerns for describing recreational travel. Research on travel has become increasingly specialized and developed to the point where it now includes evaluations of the effects of travel, analyses of the relationships between different variables and travel habits, and forecast of travel. Forecasting is an especially active area of research. Much of the current work on the subject is now a series of refinements of existing models, comparisons of different model formulations, and variations on different methods for calibrating models. Other branches have not progressed as far. More attention needs to be given to them to keep growth in a healthy balance.

An interesting off-shoot of travel research is the emergence of hodography. Hodography, the writing about and study of backroads, and by implication, the human experience of travel, is actually a continuation of an older tradition of travelogues and travel diaries. Hodography is a phenomenological reaction to the seeming excesses of quantitative travel research, especially as exhibited by the work in travel forecasting. Whether hodography will remain only an interesting intellectual reaction to another line of work, or whether it will eventually make major contributions by itself is debatable. In any event, it does keep recreation geography in touch with an old and deep humanistic tradition.

Resource-based studies have evolved from the description and inventory of resources and users. These now extend to the development of models for site selection, the use of various evaluative techniques for resource and landscape studies, and the analysis of trends in resource uses. The breadth of work on resources is as diverse as the resources themselves. There are, however, few concepts and less theory to guide the long-term growth of this work. As noted earlier, the need for theory in this research is a strongly felt need.

The ideas and methods of much work in recreation geography come from many sources: other specializations in geography as well as from other disciplines. Although virtually any field may provide something of use to a recreation geographer (for example, physics provided the gravity model), only a small number of disciplines provide the majority of ideas. Ecology and physical geography have provided insights from the natural sciences. Civil engineering has made contributions in traffic studies and in remote-sensing methods. Quantitative geography has provided better understanding of statistical methods, and economic geography has been especially productive for both methods and concepts. Sociology, psychology, and anthropology have added to the understanding of individual and group behaviour.

Prospects

So much for the shape of things past and present. What about the shape of things to come? What about the paradigm we discussed earlier? It appears that in our future there may be a form of intellectual revolution. If we look at disciplines that have made their own breakthroughs, we see they share one thing in common. Each has a number of great questions – issues of ultimate concern. These are questions that sooner or later puzzle every thoughtful person in his life. Eventually, these puzzles give rise to disciplines devoted

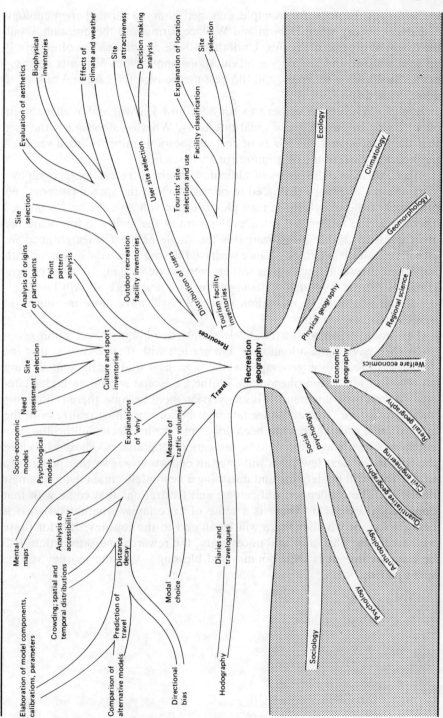

Figure 9.1 The tree of recreation geography

to their study. Biology, for example, emerged from the naïve phenomenology of natural history when Darwin and Wallace formalized the question about the origin of life and of species. Until then, these questions were often mixed up with simpler and less important questions about types of plants and animals, classification schemes, and the best method for the care and raising of domesticated species.

It is not relevant to us here to consider how Darwin and Wallace went about trying to answer these great questions. What is important is the fact that they recognized the power of certain questions in providing a sense of purpose and direction...of a future for their science.

What, then, are the issues of ultimate concern to recreation geography? What are the questions that need to be asked about the spatial patterns and processes of the search for human pleasure that will give the field a future? There are none recognized yet. Development of the ability to formulate the great question in our specialization is the single greatest research need we face in recreation geography. Once we have this, more specific questions with important practical applications will emerge. Better-organized research programmes can be formulated; stronger theories and methods will be developed; and education in recreation geography will have more meaning and purpose than ever before.

This book began with a relatively simple definition of recreation geography. We have come a long way, and are left with the conclusion that the definition of recreation geography as the organized study of the patterns and processes of recreation phenomena on the landscape is both an understatement and an overstatement. It is an overstatement because there is little formal organization. It is an understatement because we now realize both the great volume of work that has been done, and the intellectual difficulties facing those who are attempting to be recreation geographers. Those who enter the field in the next few years will have an opportunity few other people can share. They will be defining and nurturing a new intellectual creation, a new discipline. The challenges, difficulties, and frustrations that come with that opportunity are great. There is a sense of uncertainty whether progress is being made, or whether there will be an end to the journey. But for those who accept the challenge and uncertainty, the rewards and satisfactions will be even greater. It is their doom – and blessing – that the journey will be spent playing.

References

Ackerman, E. A. (1963) 'Where is a research frontier?', *Annals of the Association of American Geographers*, **53**, 429–40

Ackroyd, P. (1970) *Sports Pavilions*, The National Playing Fields Association, London

Adams, J. S. (1969) 'Directional bias in intra-urban migration,' *Economic Geography*, **45**, 302–23

Adams, R. L. A. (1973) 'Uncertainty in nature, cognitive dissonance, and the perceptual distortion of environmental information: weather forecasts and New England beach trip decisions', *Economic Geography*, **49**, 287–97

Adie, D. W. (1975) *Marinas: A Working Guide to Their Development and Design*, Architectural Press, London, and Cahners Books, Boston, Massachusetts

Aldini, C. L. (1977) 'An analysis of the factors contributing to the successful location of major league baseball franchises', unpublished PhD dissertation, Department of Resources Development, Michigan State University, East Lansing, Michigan

Aldskogius, H. (1967) 'Vacation home settlement in the Siljan region', *Geografiska Annaler*, **49B**, 69–95

Anonymous (1974a) *Trends in UK Visitors to Destinations Outside Europe*, Tourism Planning and Research Ltd, London

Anonymous (1974b) *Trends in West German Visitors to Destinations Outside Europe*, Tourism Planning and Research Ltd, London

Anzola-Betancourt, R. (1972) 'An architectural approach to tourism in the Caribbean', *Proceedings of the First Special Inter-American Travel Congress*, OEA/SER K/III, **2**, Turismo 5, 13–23

Applebaum, W. (1968) 'Store characteristics and operating performance', in Kornblau, C. (ed.) *Guide to Store Location Research*, 48–51, Addison-Wesley, Reading, Massachusetts

Arbel, A. and Pizam, A. (1977) 'Some determinants of urban hotel location: the tourists' inclinations', *Journal of Travel Research*, **15**, 18–22

Archer, B. H. (1976) 'The uses and abuses of multipliers', in Gearing, C. E., Swart, W. W., and Var, T. (eds.) *Planning for Tourism Development*, 115–32, Praeger, New York

Atlas de Provence (1976) *Atlas de Provence--Cote d'Azur*, Le Paradou: ACTES.

Austin, M. G. (1974) 'The evaluation of urban public facility location: an alternative to benefit–cost analysis', *Geographical Analysis*, **6**, 135–46

References

Bambiger, M. S. and Vandersypen, H. L. (1969) *Major Commercial Airport Location*, The Transportation Center, Northwestern University, Evanston, Illinois

Beaman, J. G., Cheung, H. K. and Knetsch, J. L. (1977) 'Obtaining efficient estimates of park use and testing for the structural adequacy of models', *The Canadian Journal of Statistics, Section C*, **5–6**, 75–92

Beaman, J. G. and Smith, S. L. J. (1976a) 'The definition and evaluation of a class of alternative-site functions', in *Canadian Outdoor Recreation Demand Study, Volume II: The Technical Notes*, 333–48, Parks Canada, Ottawa

Beaman, J. G. and Smith, S. L. J. (1976b) 'A scheme for decomposing park attendance loading curves and related analysis methodologies', in *Canadian Outdoor Recreation Demand Study, Volume II: The Technical Notes*, 504–20 Parks Canada, Ottawa

Bentley, G. A., Bruce, A. and Jones, D. R. (1977) 'Intra-urban journeys and activity packages', *Socio-Economic Planning Sciences*, **11**, 213–20

Beresford, M. W. (1971) *History on the Ground*, Methuen, London

Berry, B. J. L. (1967) *Geography of Market Centers and Retail Distribution*, Prentice-Hall, Englewood Cliffs, New Jersey

Berry, B. J. L. and Baker, A. M. (1968) 'Geographic sampling', in Berry, B. J. L. and Marble, D. F. (eds.) *Spatial Analysis*, 91–100, Prentice-Hall, Englewood Cliffs, New Jersey

Bess, F. H. and Poynor, R. E. (1972) 'Snowmobile engine noise and hearing', *Archives of Otolaryngology*, **95**, 164–68

Bevins, M. I., Brown, T. L., Cole, G. L., Hock, K. J. and LaPage, W. F. (1974) *Analysis of the Campground Market in the Northeast*, USDA Forest Service Bulletin 679, University of Vermont Agricultural Experiment Station, Burlington, Vermont

Bigman, D. and ReVelle, C. (1978) 'The theory of welfare considerations in public facility location problems', *Geographical Analysis*, **10**, 229–40

Billinge, M. (1977) 'In search of negativism: phenomenology and historical geography', *Journal of Historical Geography*, **3**, 55–67

Bloombaum, M. (1970) 'Doing smallest space analysis', *Journal of Conflict Resolution*, **14**, 409–16

Blouet, B. W. and Lawson, M. P. (eds.) (1975) *Images of the Plains: The Role of Human Nature in Settlement*, University of Nebraska Press, Lincoln, Nebraska

Bond, M. E. and Ladman, J. R. (1972) 'International tourism and economic development: a special case for Latin America', *Mississippi Valley Journal*, **8**, 43–55

Borejko, W. (1968) 'Study on the effectiveness of migrations', *Geographica Polonica*, **14**, 305–12

Boyer, M. (1962) 'La géographie des vacances de français', *Revue de Géographie Alpine*, **50**, 485–518

Brancher, D. M. (1968) 'The English country lane and its future', *Traffic Quarterly*, **22**, 19–28

Brehm, J. W. and Cohen, A. R. (1962) *Explorations in Cognitive Dissonance*, John Wiley and Sons, New York

Brick, J. C. (1978) 'Gasoline service station appraisal', in Friedman, E. (ed.) *Encyclopedia of Real Estate Appraising*, 3rd ed, 949–82, Prentice-Hall, Englewood Cliffs, New Jersey

Britton, R. A. (1979) 'The image of the Third World in tourism marketing', *Annals of Tourism Research*, **6**, 318–29

192

Brown, L. A. and Moore, E. G. (1970) 'The intra-urban migration process: a perspective', *Geografiska Annaler*, **52B**, 1–13

Brown, P. J., Dyer, A. and Whaley, R. S. (1973) 'Recreation research – so what?', *Journal of Leisure Research*, **5**, 16–24

Brown, W. G., Singh, A. and Castle, E. N. (1965) 'Net economic value of the Oregon salmon-steelhead sport fisheries', *Journal of Wildlife Management*, **29**, 266–79

Brownell, G. G. (1975) *Travel Agency Management*, Southern University Press, Birmingham, Alabama

Bryden, J. M. (1973) *Tourism and Development: A Case Study of the Commonwealth Caribbean*, Cambridge University Press

Buchanan, J. M. (1965) 'An economic theory of clubs', *Economica*, **32**, 1–14

Burby, R. J., Donnelly, T. G. and Weiss, S. F. (1972) 'Vacation home location: a model for simulating the residential development of rural recreation areas', *Regional Studies*, **6**, 421–39

Bureau of Outdoor Recreation (1968) 'Recreation and aesthetics – appendix 1', in *Report for Development of Water Resources in Appalachia*, US Department of the Interior, Washington, DC

Bureau of Outdoor Recreation (1974) *Proceedings of the Outdoor Recreation Research Needs Workshop*, US Department of the Interior, Washington, DC

Burkart, A. J. and Medlik, S. (1974) *Tourism: Past, Present, and Future*, Heinemann Educational, London

Burton, R. C. J. (1974) *The Recreational Carrying Capacity of the Countryside*, Occasional Publication #11, Keele University Library, Keele, England

Butler, R. W. (1972) *Recreation Opportunity as an Indicator of the Quality of Life*, Science Council of Canada, Ottawa

Butler, R. W. (1978) 'The impact of recreation on life styles of rural communities: a case study of Sleat, Isle of Skye', in *Studies in the Geography of Tourism and Recreation, Volume 1*, 187–201, Verlag Ferdinand Hirt, Wien

Butler, R. W. (1979) 'The implication of potential tourism development in the Canadian Arctic for the Inuit', in *Studies in the Geography of Tourism and Recreation, Volume 2*, 67– 72, Verlag Ferdinand Hirt, Wien

Campbell, C. K. (1966) 'An approach to research in recreational geography', in *BC Geographical Series No. 7*, 85–90, Department of Geography, University of British Columbia, Vancouver

Campbell, C. K. (1967) 'An urban skiing hinterland', unpublished PhD dissertation, Department of Geography, University of British Columbia, Vancouver

Campbell, R. D., LeBlanc, K. L. and Mason, M. A. (1962) *Shoreline Recreation Resources of the United States*, Outdoor Recreation Resources Review Commission Study Report 4, US Government Printing Office, Washington, DC

Canadian Government Office of Tourism (1978) *Planning Canadian Campgrounds*, Department of Industry, Trade, and Commerce, Ottawa

Canoyer, H. G. (1946) *Selecting a Store Location*, Department of Commerce, Economic Series No. 56, US Department of Commerce, Washington, DC

Cantor, L. M. and Hatherly, J. (1979) 'The medieval parks of England', *Geography*, **64**, Part 2, 71–85

Carlson, A. S. (1938) 'Recreation industry of New Hampshire', *Economic Geography*, **14**, 255–70

Carrothers, G. A. P. (1956) 'An historical review of the gravity and potential concepts of human interaction', *Journal of the American Institute of Planners*, **22**, 94–102

Carter, M. R. (1971) 'A method of analysing patterns of tourist activity in a large rural area: the Highlands and Islands of Scotland', *Regional Studies*, **5**, 29–37

Cesario, F. J. (1976) 'Estimating park attractiveness, population centre emissiveness, and the effect of distance in outdoor recreation travel', in *Canadian Outdoor Recreation Demand Study, Volume II: The Technical Notes*, 99–133, Parks Canada, Ottawa

Cesario, F. J. (1978) 'A new method for analyzing outdoor recreation trip data: a reply', *Journal of Leisure Research*, **10**, 153–55

Cesario F. J. and Knetsch, J. L. (1976) 'A recreation site demand and benefit estimation model', *Regional Studies*, **10**, 97–104

Chaney, R. B. and McClain, S. C. (1971) 'Auditory temporary threshold shift in snow-mobile users', in Crocker, M. J. (ed.) *Noise and Vibration Control Engineering*, 277–78, Purdue Noise Control Conference, Purdue University, West Lafayette, Indiana

Chanter, D. O. and Owen, D. F. (1976) 'Nature reserves: a customer satisfaction index', *Oikos Acta Oecologica Scandinavica*, **27**, 165–67

Chapin, F. S. and Weiss, S. F. (1968) 'A probabilistic model for residential growth', *Transportation Research*, **2**, 375–90

Cheek, N. H. and Burdge, R. J. (1974) *Outdoor Recreation and Planning: A Sociological Overview*, Department of Sociology, Iowa State University, Ames, Iowa

Cheek, N. H., Field, D. R. and Burdge, R. J. (1976) *Leisure and Recreation Places*, Ann Arbor Science Publications, Ann Arbor, Michigan

Cheung, H. K. (1972) 'A day-use visitation model', *Journal of Leisure Research*, **4**, 139–56

Christaller, W. (1933) *Die Zentralen Orte in Süddeutschland*, Jena

Christaller, W. (1964) 'Some considerations of tourism location in Europe: the peripheral regions – underdeveloped countries – recreation areas', *Papers of the Regional Science Association*, **12**, 95–105

Chubb, M. and Bauman, E. H. (1977) 'Assessing the recreation potential of rivers', *Journal of Soil and Water Conservation*, **32**, 97–102

Cicchetti, C. J. (1971) 'Some economic issues in planning urban recreation facilities', *Land Economics*, **47**, 14–23

Clark, C. and Peters, G. H. (1965) 'The "intervening opportunities" method of traffic analysis', *Traffic Quarterly*, **19**, 101–19

Clark, P. J. and Evans, F. C. (1955) 'On some aspects of spatial patterns is biological populations', *Science*, **121**, 397–98

Claus, R. J. and Hardwick, W. G. (1972) *The Mobile Consumer*, Collier-Macmillan Canada, Don Mills, Ontario

Clout, H. D. (1969) 'Second homes in France', *Journal of the Town Planning Institute*, **55**, 440–43

Cohen, E. (1972) 'Toward a sociology of international tourism', *Social Research*, **39**,164–82

Colenutt, R. J. (1969) 'Modelling travel patterns of day visitors to the countryside', *Area*, **3**, 43–47

Colgan, R. T. (1972) *A Financial Feasibility Study and Management Plan for the Proposed Lake Dunlap Recreation Area, Guadelupe County, Texas*, Technical Report 4, Department of Recreation and Parks, Texas A & M University, College Station, Texas

Cook, W. L. and Holland, R. (1967) *Public Golf Courses*, National Recreation and Park Association Management Aids Bulletin 18, Washington, DC

Coppock, J. T., Duffield, B. and Sewell, D. (1974) 'Classification and analysis of recreation resources', in Lavery, P. (ed.) *Recreational Geography*, 231–58, David and Charles, London

Cordell, J. K., James, G. A. and Griffith, R. F. (1970) *Estimating Recreation Use at Visitor Information Centers*, USDA Forest Service Research Paper SE-69, South-eastern Forest Experiment Station, Asheville, North Carolina

Corsi, T. M. and Harvey, M. E. (1980) 'Travel trends and energy', in *Proceedings of the 1980 National Outdoor Recreation Trends Symposium*, 59–70, General Technical Report, NE-57, Northeast Forest Experiment Station, USDA Forest Service, Broomall, Pennsylvania

Cracknell, B. (1967) 'Accessibility to the countryside as a factor in planning for leisure', *Regional Studies*, 1, 147–61.

Crawford, O. G. S. (1960) *Archaeology in the Field*, Phoenix House, London

Cribier, F. (1969) *La Grande Migration d'Eté des Citadins en France*, CNRS Memoires et Documents no. hors série, Paris

Crompton, J. L. and Van Doren, C. S. (1976) 'Amusement parks, theme parks, and municipal leisure services: contrasts in adaptation to cultural change', *Leisure Today*, in *Journal of Physical Education and Recreation*, 47, 18–22

Crowe, R. B. (1970) *A Climatic Classification of the Northwest Territories for Recreation and Tourism*, Department of Transport and the Canadian Meteorological Service, Ottawa

Crowe, R. B., McKay, G. A. and Baker, W. M. (1977) *The Tourism and Outdoor Recreation Climate of Ontario*, three volumes, Atmospheric Environment Canada, Toronto

Crumpacker, D. W., Zei, G., Moroni, A. and Cavalli-Sforza, L. L. (1976) 'Air distance versus road distance as a geographical measure for studies in human population structure', *Geographical Analysis*, 8, 215–23

Dacey, M. F. (1967) 'Some properties of order distance for random point distributions', *Geografiska Annaler*, 49B, 25–32

Dacey, M. F. and Tung, T. (1962) 'The identification of randomness in point patterns', *Journal of Regional Science*, 4, 83–96

Dalrymple, D. J. and Thompson, D. L. (1969) *Retailing: An Economic View*, Collier-Macmillan, London, and Free Press, New York

Dana, S. T. (1957) *Problem Analysis Research in Forest Recreation*, USDA Forest Service, Washington, DC

Danilova, N. A. (1973) 'Klimat pribaltiki i prodolzhitelnost' perioda, blagopriyatnogo dlya turizma', in Kovalev, S. A. (ed.) *Geograpfiya i Turizm, Geografii*, 93, Izdatel stor Mysl, Moscow

Dearinger, J. A. and Woolwine, G. M. (1971) *Measuring the Intangible Values of Natural Streams, Part I: Applications of the Uniqueness Concept*, Research Report 40, Water Resources Institute, University of Kentucky, Lexington, Kentucky

Deasy, G. F. (1949) 'The tourist industry in a "north woods" county', *Economic Geography*, 25, 240–59

Deasy, G. F. and Griess, P. R. (1966) 'Impact of a tourist facility on its hinterland', *Annals of the Association of American Geographers*, 56, 29–306.

Dee, N. (1970) 'Urban playgrounds: an optimal location model', unpublished PhD dissertation, The Johns Hopkins University, Baltimore, Maryland

References

Dee, N. and Leibman, J. C. (1970) 'A statistical study of attendance at urban playgrounds', *Journal of Leisure Research*, **2**, 145–59

Defert, P. (1960) 'Introduction à une géographie touristique et thermale de l 'Europe', *Acta Geographica*, **36**, 4–11

Dent, O. (1974) 'Human spatial mobility: the case of recreational travel', *Australian Geographical Studies*, **12**, 230–48

Dison, D. W. and Hale, C. W. (1977) 'Gravity versus intervening opportunity models in explanation of spatial trade flows', *Growth and Change*, **8**, 15–22

Dorney, R. S. (1976) 'Biophysical and cultural–historic land classification and mapping for Canadian urban and urbanizing land', in *Proceedings of the Workshop on Ecological Classification in Urban Areas*, Toronto

Drury, N. B. (1957) from a presentation to the National Conference on National Parks, quoted by Ellis, J. B. and Van Doren, C. S. (1966) in 'A comparative evaluation of gravity and system theory models for statewide recreational traffic flows', *Journal of Regional Science*, **6**, 57–70

Dubaniewicz, H. (1976) 'An appraisal of the natural environment of the Łódź Region for the needs of economic development and recreation', *Geographica Polonica*, **34**, 265–71

Duffell, J. R. and Goodall, G. R. (1969) 'Worcestershire and Staffordshire recreational survey', *Journal of the Town Planning Institute*, **55**, 16–23

Duffey, E. (1974) *Nature Reserves and Wildlife*, Heinemann Educational, London

Dulaney, D. E. (1968) 'Awareness, rules, and propositional control: a confrontation with s-r behavior theory', in Dixon, T. R. and Horton, D. L. (eds.) *Verbal Behavior and General Behavior Theory*, 340–87, Prentice-Hall, Englewood Cliffs, New Jersey

Dwyer, J. F., Kelly, J. R. and Bowes, M. D. (1977) *Improved Procedures for Valuation of the Contribution of Recreation to National Economic Development*, Water Resources Center, Research Report 128, University of Illinois, Urbana, Illinois

Earp, J. H., Hall, R. D. and McDonald, M. (1976) 'Modal choice behavior and the value of travel time', in Heggie, I. G. (ed.) *Modal Choice and the Value of Travel Time*, 45–85, Clarendon Press, Oxford

Ecroyd, L. G. (1972) 'A stochastic analysis of USA tourism markets for location policy of Canadian government field offices', unpublished Master's thesis, College of Business and Public Administration, Florida Atlantic University, Boca Raton, Florida

Edwards, S. L. and Dennis, S. J. (1976) 'Long distance day tripping in Great Britain', *Journal of Transport Economics and Policy*, **10**, 237–56

Eilon, S., Watson-Gandy, C. D. T. and Christofides, N. (1971) *Distribution Management: Mathematical Modelling and Practical Analysis*, Griffin Press, London

Ellis, J. B. and Van Doren, C. S. (1966) 'A comparative evaluation of gravity and system theory models for statewide recreational traffic flows', *Journal of Regional Science*, **6** , 57–70

Elsner, G. H. (1976) 'Quantifying landscape dimensions for land-use planning', in *Proceedings of the XVI IUFRO World Congress*, Oslo

Elson, M. J. (1976) 'Activity space and recreational spatial behaviour', *Town Planning Review*, **47**, 241–55

Ewing, G. O. and Kulka, T. (1979) 'Revealed and stated preference analysis of ski resort attractiveness', *Leisure Sciences*, **2**, 249–75

Fabos, J. (1971) 'An analysis of environmental quality ranking systems', in *Recreation*

Symposium Proceedings, 40–55 USDA Forest Service Northeast Experiment Station, Upper Darby, Pennsylvania

Farrar, D. E. and Glauber, R. R. (1967) 'Multicollinearity in regression analysis: the problem revisited', *Review of Economics and Statistics*, **49**, 92–107

Festinger, L. (1964) *Conflict, Decision, and Dissonance*, Stanford University Press, Stanford, California

Filippovich, L. S. (1979) 'Mapping of recreational development around a large city', *Soviet Geography*, **20**, 361–69

Fines, K. D. (1968) 'Landscape evaluation: a research project in East Sussex', *Regional Studies*, **2**, 41–55

Fishbein, M. (1963) 'An investigation of the relationships between beliefs about an object and the attitude toward that object', *Human Relations*, **16**, 232–40

Fishbein, M. (1967) 'Attitude and the prediction of behaviour', in Fishbein, M. (ed.) *Readings in Attitude Theory and Measurement*, 477–92, John Wiley and Sons, New York

Fisher, W. F. (1962) 'Methods of evaluating lands for recreational use', in *Recreation in Wild-Land Management*, University of California Agricultural Experiment Station, David, California

Fortin, P. A., Ritchie, J. R. B. and Arsenault, J. (1978) *A Study of the Decision Process of North American Associations Concerning the Choice of a Convention Site*, Conseil de planification et de developement du Québec, Laval, Québec

Foster, J. H. (1964) 'Measuring the productivity of land used for outdoor recreation', *Land Economics*, **40**, 224–27

Gearing, C. E., Swart, W. W. and Var, T. (1974) 'Establishing a measure of touristic attractiveness', *Journal of Travel Research*, **12**, 1–8

Getz, D. (1977) 'The impact of tourism on host communities: a research approach', in Duffield, B. S. (ed.) *Tourism: A Tool for Regional Development*, 9.1–9.13, Tourism and Recreation Research Unit, University of Edinburgh, Edinburgh

Gilbert, G., Peterson, G. L. and Schafer, J. L. (1972) 'Markov renewal model of linked trip travel behaviour', *Transportation Engineering Journal*, **97**, 691–704

Gilg, A. W. (1974) 'A critique of Linton's method of assessing scenery as a natural resource', *Scottish Geographical Magazine*, **90**, 125–29

Gilg, A. W. (1976) 'Assessing scenery as a natural resource: causes of variation in Linton's method', *Scottish Geographical Magazine*, **92**, 41–49

Gimbarzevsky, P., Lopovkhine, N and Addison, P. (1978) *Biophysical Resources of Pukaskwa National Park*, Information Report FMR-X-106, Forest Management Institute, Environment Canada, Ottawa

Gimmy, A. E. (1978) *Tennis and Racquet Sport Projects: A Guide to Appraisal, Market Analysis, Development, and Financing*, American Institute of Real Estate Appraisers, Washington, DC

Glushkova, V. G. and Shepelev, N. P. (1977) 'Problems in the spatial management of weekend recreation outside large cities', *Soviet Geography*, **18**, 100–07

Gold, S. M. (1973) *Urban Recreation Planning* (Chap. 5, especially), Lea and Febiger, Philadelphia, Pennsylvania

Goldfeld, S. M. and Quandt, R. E. (1965) 'Some tests of homoscedasticity', *Journal of the American Statistical Association*, **60**, 539–47

Goldsmith, O. F. R. (1973) 'Dunedin's vacation hinterland 1971/72', unpublished MA thesis, Department of Geography, University of Otago, Dunedin, New Zealand

References

Golledge, R. (1970) *Process Approaches to the Analysis of Human Spatial Behaviour*, Discussion Paper 16, Department of Geography, The Ohio State University, Columbus, Ohio

Goodchild, M. F. and Booth, P. J. (1980) 'Location and allocation of recreation facilities: public swimming pools in London, Ontario', *Ontario Geographer*, **15**, 35–51

Goodchild, M. F. and Ross, J. H. C. (1971) *Methodological Explorations Within the Preference Model of Consumer Spatial Behaviour*, Geographical Papers No. 12, Department of Geography, University of Western Ontario, London, Ontario

Goodey, B. (1970) *Perception of the Environment*, Occasional Paper 17, Centre for Urban and Regional Studies, University of Birmingham, Birmingham. England

Goodman, L. A. (1963) 'Statistical methods for the preliminary analysis of transaction flows', *Econometrica*, **31**, 197–208

Goodrich, J. N. (1978) 'The relationship between preferences for and perceptions of vacation destinations: applications of a choice model', *Journal of Travel Research*, **17**, 8–13

Gould, P. and White, R. (1974) *Mental Maps*, Penguin Books, Harmondsworth, Middlesex

Gray, H. P. (1970) *International Travel – International Trade*, Heath Lexington Books, Lexington, Massachusetts

Green, P. E. and Carmone, F. J. (1970) *Multi-dimensional Scaling and Related Techniques in Marketing Analysis*, Allyn and Bacon, Boston, Massachusetts

Green, P. E. and Tull, P. S. (1975) *Research for Marketing Decisions*, 3rd ed., Prentice-Hall, Englewood Cliffs, New Jersey

Greenhut, M. L. (1956) *Plant Location in Theory and Practice*, University of North Carolina Press, Chapel Hill, North Carolina

Greenwood, D. J. (1976) 'Tourism as an agent of change: a Spanish Basque case', *Annals of Tourism Research*, **3**, 128–42

Grieg-Smith, P. (1964) *Quantitative Plant Ecology*, 2nd ed., Butterworth's Scientific Publications, London

Grinstein, A. (1955) 'Vacations: a psycho-analytic study', *International Journal of Psycho-Analysis*, **36**, 177–86

Grubb, H. and Goodwin, J. (1968) *Economic Evaluation of Water-Oriented Recreation*, Report 84, Texas Water Development Board, Austin, Texas

Gruen, C. and Gruen, N. J. (1966) *Store Location and Customer Behavior*, Technical Bulletin 56, Urban Land Institute, Washington, DC

Guilford, J. P. (1956) *Fundamental Statistics in Psychology and Education*, 2nd ed., 501–03, McGraw-Hill, New York

Gunn, C. A. (1972) *Vacationscape*, University of Texas Press, Austin, Texas

Gunn, C. A. Hanna, J. W., Parenzin, A. J. and Blumberg, F. M. (1974) *Development of Criteria for Evaluating Urban River Settings for Tourism-Recreation Use*, Texas Water Resources Institute, Texas A & M University, College Station, Texas.

Guttman, L. (1968) 'A general non-metric technique for finding the smallest coordinate space for a configuration of points', *Psychometrika*, **33**, 469–507

Haggett, P. (1966) *Locational Analysis in Human Geography*, Edward Arnold, London, and St Martin's Press, New York

Haley, A. J. (1979) 'Municipal recreation and park standards in the United States: central cities and suburbs', *Leisure Sciences*, **2**, 277–91

Hamill, L. (1974) 'Statistical tests of Leopold's system for quantifying aesthetic factors among rivers', *Water Resources Research*, **10**, 395–401

Hamill, L. (1975) 'Analysis of Leopold's quantitative comparisons of landscape aesthetics', *Journal of Leisure Research*, **7**, 16–28

Hanna, M. (1977) 'Regional tourism multiplier studies – their findings and uses', in Duffield, B. S. (ed.) *Tourism: A Tool for Regional Development*, 6.1–6.11, Tourism and Recreation Research Unit, University of Edinburgh, Edinburgh, Scotland

Hanson, P. (1977) 'The activity patterns of elderly households', *Geografiska Annaler*, **59B**, 109–24

Hatry, H. P., Blair, L. H., Fisk, D. M., Greiner, J. M., Hall, J. R. and Schaeman, P. S. (1977) *How Effective Are Your Community Services?*, The Urban Institute and the International City Management Association, Washington, DC

Hecock, R. D. (1970) 'Recreation behavior pattern as related to site characteristics of beaches', *Journal of Leisure Research*, **2**, 237–50

Hemmens, G. C. (1966) *The Structure of Urban Activity Systems*, Center for Urban and Regional Studies, Chapel Hill, North Carolina

Hemmens, G. C. (1970) 'Analysis and simulation of urban activity patterns', *Socio-Economic Planning Sciences*, **4**, 53–66

Hendee, J. C., Clark, R. N., Hogans, M. L., Wood, D. and Koch, R. W. (1976) *Code-A-Site: A System for Inventory of Dispersed Recreational Sites in Roaded Areas, Back-Country, and Wilderness*, USDA Forest Service Research Paper PNW-209, Pacific Northwest Forest and Range Experiment Station, Portland, Oregon

Henderson, D. M. (1975) *The Economic Impact of Tourism: A Case Study in Greater Tayside*, Report 13, Tourism and Recreation Research Unit, University of Edinburgh, Scotland

Heurtier, R. (1968) 'Essai de climatologie touristique synoptique, de l 'Europe Occidentale et Méditeraneén pendant la saison d' eté, *La Meteorologie*, **11**, 71–103 and 519–66

Hill, G. A. (1974) 'Central New York snow-mobilers and patterns of vehicle use', *Journal of Leisure Research*, **6**, 280–92

Hodgson, J. N. (1973) 'The feasibility study: determining the investment potential of a new hotel', *The Cornell Hotel and Restaurant Administration Quarterly*, **14**, 13–31

Hodgson, M. J. and Doyle, P. (1978) 'The location of public services considering the mode of travel', *Socio-Economic Planning Sciences*, **12**, 49–54

Hoover, E. M. (1948) *The Location of Economic Activity*, McGraw-Hill, New York

Horton, F. E. and Reynolds, D. R. (1971) 'Effects of urban spatial structure on individual behaviour', *Economic Geography*, **47**, 37–48

Hoskins, W. G. (1965) *The Making of the English Landscape,* Hodder and Stoughton, London

Hotelling, H. H. (1929) 'Stability in competition', *Economic Journal*, **39**, 41–57

Huff, D. L. (1963) *Probabilistic Analysis of Consumer Spatial Behaviour*, Graduate School of Business Administration, University of California, Berkeley, California

Huff, D. L. (1966) 'A programmed solution for approximating an optimum retail location', *Land Economics*, **42**, 293–303

Hunt, J. D. (1974) 'Image as a factor in tourism development, a paper presented at a workshop on Planning a Tourist Recreation Region for the Age of Leisure', Appalachian State University, Boone, North Carolina

Isachenko, A. G. (1973) 'On the method of applied landscape research', *Soviet Geography*, **14**, 229–43

References

Isard, W. (1956) *Location and Space Economy*, Massachusetts Institute of Technology Press, Cambridge, Massachusetts

IUCN (1967) *Ecological Impact of Recreation and Tourism upon Temperate Environments*, IUCN New Series 7, Morges, Switzerland

Jafari, J. (1974) 'The socioeconomic costs of tourism to developing countries', *Annals of Tourism Research*, **1**, 227–62

James, G. A. and Henley, R. K. (1968) *Sampling Procedures for Estimating Mass and Dispersed Types of Recreation Use in Large Areas*, USDA Forest Service Research Paper SE-31, Southeastern Forest Experiment Station, Asheville, North Carolina

James, G. A. and Quinkert, A. K. (1972) *Estimating Recreational Use of Developed Observation Sites*, USDA Forest Service Research Paper SE-97, SouthEastern Forest Experiment Station, Asheville, North Carolina

James, G. A. and Schreuder, H. T. (1972) *Estimating Dispersed Recreation Use Along Trails and in General Undeveloped Areas with Electric Eye Counters: Some Preliminary Results*, USDA Forest Service Research Note SE-181, Southeastern Forest Experiment Station, Asheville, North Carolina

James, G. A., Wingle, H. P., and Griggs, J. D. (1971) *Estimating Recreation Use on Large Bodies of Water*, USDA Forest Service Research Paper SE-97, Southeastern Forest Experiment Station, Asheville, North Carolina

Janelle, D. G. (1968) 'Central place development in a time-space framework', *The Professional Geographer*, **20**, 5–10

Johnson, R. B. (1978) 'The role of tourism in Tongan culture', in Zamora, M. D., Sutlive, V. H., and Altshuler, N. (eds.) *Tourism and Behavior*, Studies in Third World Societies Number 5, 55–68, Department of Anthropology, College of William and Mary, Williamsburg, Virginia

Johnston, R. J. (1971) 'Mental maps of the city: suburban preference patterns', *Environment and Planning*, **3**, 63–72

Jones, B. G. and Goldsmith, W. W. (1969) *Industrial Sectors as Agents of Social and Economic Change: The Tourism and Travel Industry in Puerto Rico*, Center for Housing and Environmental Studies, Cornell University, Ithaca, New York

Jones, P. M. (1974) 'An alternative approach to person trip modelling', *Proceedings of the PTRC Summer Annual Meeting*, Planning and Transport Research and Computation Ltd, London

Jones, R. L. and Rando, G. L. (1974) *Golf Course Development*, The Urban Land Institute, Washington, DC

Kamp, B. D., Crompton, J. L. and Hensarling, D. M. (1979) 'The reactions of travelers to gasoline rationing and increases in gasoline prices', *Journal of Travel Research*, **18**, 37–41

Killion, G. L. (1969) 'An exploratory investigation into tourist research techniques with application to the North Coast tourist industry', in *Research Series in Applied Geography*, 88–108, Department of Geography, University of New England, Armidale, New South Wales

Klaassen, L. H. (1968) *Social Amenities in Area Economic Growth: An Analysis of Methods for Determining Local Social Amenities*, Organization for Economic Cooperation and Development, Paris

Klausner, S. Z. (1969) 'Recreation as social action, Appendix A', 61–73 in *A Prog-*

200

ram for Outdoor Recreation Research, National Academy of Sciences, Washington, DC

Kotas, R. (ed.) (1975) *Market Orientation in the Hotel and Catering Industry*, Surrey University Press, London

Kuhn, T. S. (1971) *The Structure of Scientific Revolutions*, 2nd ed., University of Chicago Press, Chicago, Illinois

Lansing, J. B. and Blood, D. M. (1964) *The Changing Travel Market*, 41–58 especially, Survey Research Center, Ann Arbor, Michigan

LaPage, W. F. and Cormier, P. L. (1977) 'Images of camping – barriers to participation', *Journal of Travel Research*, **15**, 21–25

Law, S. (1967) 'Planning for outdoor recreation', *Journal of the Town Planning Institute*, **53**, 383–86

Lentnek, B., Van Doren, C. S. and Trail, J. R. (1969) 'Spatial behavior in recreational boating', *Journal of Leisure Research*, **1**, 103–24

Leopold, L. B. (1969) 'Landscape esthetics', *Natural History*, **78**, 36–45

Lewin, K. (1963) *Field Theory in Social Science*, Tavistock, London

Lewis, P. (1967) 'The highway corridor as a concept in design and planning', *Highway Research Record*, **166**

Lime, D. W. and Lorence, G. A. (1974) *Improving Estimates of Wilderness Use from Mandatory Travel Permits*, USDA Forest Service Research Paper NC-101, North Central Forest Experiment Station, St Paul, Minnesota

Lineberry, R. L. (1975) 'Equality, public policy, and public services: the underclass hypothesis and the limits to equality', paper delivered at the annual meeting of the American Political Science Association

Linton, D. L. (1968) 'The assessment of scenery as a natural resource', *Scottish Geographical Magazine*, **4**, 219–38

Litton, R. B. (1968) *Forest Landscape Description and Inventories*, USDA Forest Service Research Paper PSW-49, Pacific Southwest Forest and Range Experiment Station, Berkeley, California

Litton, R. B. (1973) *Landscape Control Points: A Procedure for Predicting and Monitoring Impacts*, USDA Forest Service Research Paper PSW-91, Pacific Southwest Forest and Range Experiment Station, Berkeley, California

Lloyd, R. J. (1970) *Countryside Recreation: The Ecological Implications*, Lindsey County Council, Lincoln, England

Lopez de Sebastian, J. (1976) 'Nature conservation and skiing resorts: problems of social evaluation in Spain', *Landscape Planning*, **3**, 89–100

Lösch, A. (1944) *Die Raümliche Ordnung der Wirtschaft*, Gustav Fischer, Jena.

Lovingood, P. E. and Mitchell, L. S. (1978) 'The structure of public and private recreational systems: Columbia, South Carolina', *Journal of Leisure Research*, **10**, 21–36

Lucas, W. J. (1969) *Planning Considerations for Winter Sports Resort Development*, USDA Forest Service, Denver, Colorado

Luce, R. D. (1959) *Individual Choice Behavior*, John Wiley and Sons, New York

Lundberg, D. E. (1970) *The Hotel and Restaurant Business*, Institutions Magazine, Chicago, Illinois

Lundberg, D. E. (1972) *The Tourist Business*, Institutions/Volume Feeding Management Magazine, Chicago, Illinois

Maass, A. (1966) 'Benefit–cost analysis: its relevance to public investment decisions',

References

Quarterly Journal of Economics, **80**, 208–26

McKean, P. F. (1973) 'Tourism, culture change, and culture conservation in Bali', paper presented at the IXth International Congress of Anthropological and Ethnological Science, Chicago, Illinois

McPheters, L. R. and Stronge, W. B. (1974) 'Crime as an environmental externality of tourism: Miami, Florida', *Land Economics*, **50**, 288–92

Malinvaud, E. (1970) *Statistical Methods of Econometrics*, 2nd rev. ed., translated by A. Silvey, pp. 554–569, North Holland Publishing Company, Amsterdam, and Amsterdam Elsevier Publishing, New York

Marble, D. F. (1967) *A Theoretical Exploration of Individual Travel Behaviour*, Studies in Geography No. 13, Department of Geography, Northwestern University, Evanston, Illinois

Mariot, P. (1969) 'Priestorové aspekty cestovného rucho a otázky gravitacného zázemia náusterných miest', *Geografický Casopis*, **21**, 287–312

Matley, I. (1976) *The Geography of International Tourism*, Resource Paper 76–1, Association of American Geographers, Washington, DC

Maw, R. (1969) 'Construction of a leisure model', *Official Architecture and Planning*, 32: 924–35

Mayo, E. (1975) 'Tourism and the national parks: a psychographic and attitudinal study', *Journal of Travel Research*, **14**, 14–18

Mercer, D. C. (1970) 'Urban recreational hinterlands: a review and example', *The Professional Geographer*, **22**, 74–78

Mercer, D. C. (1971a) 'Discretionary travel behaviour and the urban mental map', *Australian Geographical Studies*, **9**, 133–43

Mercer, D. C. (1971b) 'The demand for recreation at the urban fringe: the example of Ferntree Gully National Park', *The Australian Geographer*, **11**, 504–07

Mercer, D. C. (1972) 'Beach usage in the Melbourne Region', *The Australian Geographer*, **12**, 123–39

Mills, J. D. (1977) *Site Selection Guidelines*, Marketing Guidelines, Tulsa, Oklahoma

Miossec, J. M. (1977) 'Un modéle de l'espace touristique', *L'Espace Géographique*, **6**, 41–48

Mitchell, L. S. (1969) 'Toward a theory of public urban recreation', *Proceedings of the Association of American Geographers*, **1**, 103–08

Mitchell, L. S. and Lovingood, P. E. (1976) 'Public urban recreation: an investigation of spatial relationships', *Journal of Leisure Research*, **8**, 6–20

Mladenka, K. R. and Hill, K. Q. (1977) 'The distribution of benefits in an urban environment: parks and libraries in Houston', *Urban Affairs Quarterly*, **3**, 73–94

Moeller, G. H. and Beazley, R. I. (no date) *A Simple Computer Approach to Regional Identification with an Outdoor Recreation Planning Example*, Occasional Papers in Geography 3, Department of Geography, Southern Illinois University, Carbondale, Illinois

Moore, P. G. (1968) *Basic Operational Research*, Pitman, London

Morisita, M. (1957) 'A new method for the estimation of density by the spacing method applicable to non-randomly distributed populations', *Seiro-Seitai*, **7**, 134–44

Murphy, P. A. (1977) 'Second homes in New South Wales', *The Australian Geographer*, **13**, 310–17

Murphy, P. E. and Rosenblood, L. (1974) 'Tourism: an exercise in spatial search', *The Canadian Geographer*, **18**, 201–10

National Academy of Sciences (1969) *A Program for Outdoor Recreation Research*,

National Academy of Sciences for the Bureau of Outdoor Recreation, Washington, DC

National Council of Applied Economic Research (1975) *Cost Benefit Study of Tourism*, NCAER, New Delhi

National League of Cities (1968) *Recreation in the Nation's Cities: Problems and Approaches*, Bureau of Outdoor Recreation, Washington, DC

Neal, J. E. and Trocke, J. K. (1971) *A Guide for a Feasibility Study of Recreation Enterprises*, Extension Bulletin 705, Natural Resources Series, Michigan State University, East Lansing, Michigan

Nefedova, V. B., Smirnova, Ye. D. and Shvidchenko, L. G. (1974) 'Techniques for the recreation evaluation of an area', *Soviet Geography*, **15**, 507–12

Nelson, R. L. (1958) *The Selection of Retail Locations*, F. W. Dodge Corporation, New York

Niewiarowski, W. (1976) 'Some problems in the evaluation of the natural environment for the demands of tourism and recreation: a case study of the Bydogszcz Region', *Geographica Polonica*, **34**, 241–54

Nolan, S. D. (1976) 'Tourists' use and evaluation of travel information sources', *Journal of Travel Research*, **14**, 6–8

Nulsen, D. R. and Nulsen, R. H. (1971) *Management and Investment Potential of Mobile Homes and Recreational Vehicle Parks*, Trail-R-Club of America, Beverly Hills, California

Nurkse, R. (1962) *Problems of Capital Formation in Under-Developed Countries*, Oxford University Press

Nurkse, R. (1970) 'Some international aspects of the problem of economic development', in Nurkse, R. (ed.) *The Economics of Underdevelopment*, 266–88, Oxford University Press

Ohlin, B. (1935) *Inter-regional and International Trade*, Harvard University Press, Cambridge, Massachusetts

Okabe, A. (1976) 'A theoretical comparison of the opportunity and gravity models', *Regional Science and Urban Economics*, **6**, 381–97

Onokerhoraye, A. G. (1976) 'A conceptual framework for the location of public facilities in the urban areas of developing countries: the Nigerian case', *Socio-Economic Planning Sciences*, **10**, 237–40

Ontario Ministry of Culture and Recreation (1979) *Feasibility Studies for Recreation Facilities*, OMCR, Toronto

Ouma, J. P. B. M. (1970) *Evolution of Tourism in East Africa: 1900–2000*, East African Literature Bureau, Nairobi

Outdoor Recreation Resources Review Commission (1962) *Study Reports*, nos. 1, 3, 4, 5, 6, 8, 11, 13, 19, 20, 22, 24, 26, 27, US Department of the Interior, Washington, DC

Parks Canada (1974) *A Wild Rivers Proposal*, Department of Indian and Northern Affairs, Ottawa

Parks Canada (1976) *Canadian Outdoor Recreation Demand Study, Volume II: The Technical Notes*, Chs. 2 and 4, Department of Indian and Northern Affairs, Ottawa

Patmore, J. A. (1971) 'Routeways and recreation patterns', in Lavery, P. (ed.) *Recreational Geography*, 70–96, David and Charles, London

Pearce, D. (1979) 'Towards a geography of tourism', *Annals of Tourism Research*, **6**, 245–72

Perry, A. H. (1972) 'Weather, climate, and tourism', *Weather*, **27**, 199–203

References

Peters, M. (1969) *International Tourism: The Economics and Development of the International Tourist Trade*, Hutchinson, London

Pielo, E. C. (1959) 'The use of point-to-point distances in the study of patterns of plant populations', *Journal of Ecology*, **47**, 607–12

Pignataro, L. J. (1973) *Traffic Engineering: Theory and Practice*, Prentice-Hall, Englewood Cliffs, New Jersey

Pigram, J. J. J. and Hobbs, J. E. (1975) 'The weather, outdoor recreation, and tourism', *Journal of Physical Education and Recreation*, **46**, 12–13

Pinder, D., Shimada, I. and Gregory, D. (1979) 'The nearest-neighbor statistic: archaeological application and new developments', *American Antiquity*, **44**, 430–45

Piperoglou, J. (1966) 'Identification and definition of regions in Greek tourist planning', *Papers of the Regional Science Association*, **18**, 169–76

Podd, G. O. and Lesure, J. D. (1964) *Planning and Operating Motels and Motor Hotels*, Hayden Book Company, Rochelle Park, New Jersey

Press, I. (1969) 'Ambiguity and innovation: implications for the genesis of the culture broker', *American Anthropologist*, **71**, 205–17

Ragatz, R. L. (1969) *Vacation Homes: An Analysis of the Market of a Seasonal Recreational Housing Development*, Department of Housing and Design, Cornell University, Ithaca, New York

Rajotte, F. (1977) 'Evaluating the cultural and environmental impact of Pacific tourism', *Pacific Perspective*, **6**, 41–8

Department of Geography, Trent University, Peterborough, Ontario

Rajotte, F. (1977) Evaluating the cultural and environmental impact of Pacific tourism, *Pacific Perspective*, **6**, 41–8

Recreation Resources Center (1975) *A Regional Study of Recreation Travel Behavior and Participation Patterns*, University of Wisconsin Extension, and Department of Agricultural Economics, University of Wisconsin, Madison, Wisconsin

Reilly, W. J. (1931) *The Law of Retail Gravitation*, Putnam Press, New York

Relph, E. (1970) 'An inquiry into relations between phenomenology and geography', *The Canadian Geographer*, **14**, 193–201

ReVelle, C. and Church, R. (1977) 'A spatial model for the location construct of Teitz', *Papers of the Regional Science Association*, **39**, 129–35

ReVelle, C., Marks, D. and Leibman, J. C. (1970) 'An analysis of private and public sector location models', *Management Science*, **16**, 692–707

ReVelle, C. and Swain, R. W. (1970) 'Central facilities location', *Geographical Analysis*, **2**, 30–42

Ritchie, W. and Mather, A. S. (1976) 'The recreational use of beach complexes of the Highlands and Islands: a note', *Scottish Geographical Magazine*, **92**, 61–63

Ritter, W. (1975) 'Recreation and tourism in Islamic countries', *Ekistics,* **40**, 56–69

Robertson, I. M. L. (1978) 'Planning and location of recreation centres in an urban area: a case study of Glasgow', *Regional Studies*, **12**, 419–27

Rolfe, E. (1964) 'Analysis of a spatial distribution of neighborhood parks in Lansing: 1920–1960', *Papers of the Michigan Academy of Science, Arts, and Letters*, **50**, 479–91

Rooney, J. F. (1974) *A Geography of American Sport*, Addison-Wesley, Reading, Massachusetts

Rosenberg, M. J. (1956) 'Cognitive structure and attitudinal affect', *Journal of Abnormal and Social Psychology*, **53**, 367–72

Ross, J. H. C. (1973) *A Measure of Site Attraction*, Lands Directorate, Occasional Paper 2, Environment Canada, Ottawa

Ross, J. H. C. and Ewing, G. O. (1976) 'Potential function in evaluating the need for recreation facilities', in *Canadian Outdoor Recreation Demand Study, Volume II: The Technical Notes*, 654–62, Parks Canada, Ottawa

Satchell, J. E. and Marren, P. R. (1976) *The Effects of Recreation on the Ecology of Natural Landscapes*, Council of Europe, Strasbourg

Schewe, C. D. and Calantone, R. J. (1978) 'Psychographic segmentation of tourists', *Journal of Travel Research*, **16**, 14–20

Schneider, J. B. (1971) 'Solving urban location problems: human intuition versus the computer', *Journal of the American Institute of Planners*, **37**, 95–99

Scholz, W. (1975) *Profitable Hotel/Motel Management*, Prentice-Hall, Englewood Cliffs, New Jersey

Schwind, P. (1971) *Migration and Regional Development in the United States: 1950–1960*, Research Paper 133, Department of Geography, University of Chicago, Chicago, Illinois

Schwinsky, R. (1973) *Dir Sozio-Ekonomischen Faktoren des Fremdenverkehrs in Entwicklungslandern: der Fall Guatemala*, St Gallen Beitrage zum Fremdenverkehrs und zur Verkehrwirtschaft, Berne

Scott, D. R., Schewe, C. D. and Frederick, D. G. (1978) 'A multi-brand/multi-attribute model of tourist state choice', *Journal of Travel Research*, **17**, 23–29

Sealy, K. R. (1976) *Airport Strategy and Planning*, Oxford University Press

Seckler, D. W. (1966) 'On the uses and abuses of economic science in evaluating public outdoor recreation', *Land Economics*, **42**, 485–94

Selke, A. C. (1936) 'Geographic aspects of the German tourist trade', *Economic Geography*, **12**, 205–16

Shafer, E. L., Hamilton, J. F. and Schmidt, E. (1969) 'Natural landscape preferences: a predictive model', *Journal of Leisure Research*, **1**, 1–19

Shafer, E. L. and Meitz, J. (1970) *It Seems Possible to Quantify Scenic Beauty in Photographs* USDA Forest Service Research Paper NE-162, Northeastern Forest Experiment Station, Upper Darby Pennsylvania

Shea, A. (1966) 'Determination of the optimal location of depots', *Proceedings of the 4th International Conference of Operations Research*, Boston, Massachusetts

Shivji, I. G. (ed.) (1973) *Tourism and Socialist Development*, Tanzania Publishing House, Dar es Salaam

Sidaway, R. (1972) 'Assessing day visitors and camping use in the New Forest', paper presented to Recreation Economics Symposium, Department of the Environment, London

Simpson, E. H. (1949) 'Measurement of diversity', *Nature*, **163**, 688

Smith, C. J. and Smith, C. A. (1979) 'Hodography: a plea for the backroads', *Leisure Sciences*, **1**, 411–26

Smith, S. L. J. (1975) 'Toward meta-recreation research', *Journal of Leisure Research*, **7**, 235–39

Smith, S. L. J. (1978) 'The take of the track: the future of the *parimutuel* racing industry in Ontario', paper presented at the Second Canadian Congress on Leisure Research, Toronto

Smith, S. L. J. (1981) 'Intervening opportunities and travel to urban recreation centres', *Journal of Leisure Research*, **12**, 296–308

References

Smith, S. L. J. and Brown, B. A. (1981) 'Directional bias in vacation travel', *Annals of Tourism Research*, forthcoming

Smith, S. L. J. and Smale, B. J. A. (1980) 'Classification of visitors to agreements for recreation and conservation sites, National Parks, and related sites', *Contact*, **12**, 35–55

Solomon, P. J. and George, W. R. (1976) 'An empirical investigation of the effects of the energy crisis on tourism', *Journal of Travel Research*, **14**, 9–13

Sonquist, J. A. and Morgan, J. N. (1970) *The Detection of Interaction Effects*, Monograph 35, Survey Research Center, Ann Arbor, Michigan

Spatafora, V. (1973) 'A historical economic analysis of the distribution of winery-owned stores in Ontario: 1927–1971', unpublished BA thesis, Department of Geography, Waterloo Lutheran University, Waterloo, Ontario

Staley, E. J. (1968) *An Instrument for Determining Comparative Priority of Need for Neighborhood Recreation Services in the City of Los Angeles*, Recreation and Youth Services Planning Council, Los Angeles, California

Stansfield, C. A. (1971) 'The geography of resorts: problems and potentials', *The Professional Geographer*, **23**, 164–66

Stansfield, C. A. and Rickert, J. E. (1970) 'The recreational business district', *Journal of Leisure Research*, **2**, 213–25

State of New York (1970) *Statewide Comprehensive Outdoor Recreation Plan Technical paper 1: Recreation Supply Inventory* and *Technical Paper 6: Potential Recreation and Open Space Areas*, Office of Parks and Recreation, Albany, New York

Stea, D. (1968) 'On the measurement of mental maps: an experimental model for studying spatial and geographical orientation', a paper presented at the Annual Meeting of the Association of American Geographers, Washington, DC

Steinecke, A. (1979) 'An analysis of differences between the travel attitudes and demand patterns of diverse visitor groups and the reaction to political-military conflicts: the Republic of Ireland as a case study', in *Studies in the Geography of Tourism and Recreation, Volume 2*, 115– 31, Verlag Ferdinand Hirt, Wien

Stewart, J. Q. (1948) 'Demographic gravitation: evidence and applications', *Sociometry*, **11**, 31–58

Stouffer, S. A. (1940) 'Intervening opportunities: a theory relating mobility and distance', *American Sociological Review*, **5**, 845–67

Strahler, A. N. (1969) *Physical Geography*, 3rd ed., John Wiley and Sons, New York

Strang, W. A. (1970) *Recreation and the Local Economy*, Sea Grant Technical Report 4, University of Wisconsin, Madison, Wisconsin

Stuart, D. G. (1968) 'Freeways, parks, and parkways', *Traffic Quarterly*, **22**, 129–36

Stynes, D. J. (1978) 'The peaking problem in outdoor recreation: measurement and analysis', a paper presented at the Annual Meeting of the National Recreation and Parks Association, Miami, Florida

Sutton, W. A. (1967) 'Travel and understanding: notes on the special structure of touring', *International Journal of Comparative Sociology*, **8**, 218–23

Symanski, R. (1974) 'Prostitution in Nevada', *Annals of the Association of American Geographers*, **64**, 357–78

Tanner, J. C. (1957) *Relations between Population, Distance, and Traffic – Some Theoretical Considerations*, Research Note RN-2921, Road Research Laboratory, Harmondsworth, England

Tapia, L. L. (1967) 'A study of tourists' motivations', in Cuervo, R. (ed.) *Tourism as a Medium of Human Communications*, 80–183, Mexican Government Tourism Department, Mexico City

Taylor, F. (1975) *Jamaica – The Welcoming Society: Myths and Reality*, Working Paper 8, Institute of Social and Economic Research, University of the West Indies, Jamaica

Taylor, G. D. (1965) 'An approach to the inventory of recreational lands', *The Canadian Geographer*, **9**, 84–91

Taylor, G. D. and Thompson, C. W. (1966) 'Proposed methodology for an inventory and classification of land for recreational use', *Forestry Chronicle*, **42**, 153–59

Taylor, V. (1975) 'The recreation business district: a component of the East London urban morphology', *South African Geographer*, **5**, 139–44

Teitz, M. (1968) 'Toward a theory of urban public facility location', *Papers of the Regional Science Association*, **21**, 35–51

Thompson, P. T. (1971) *The Use of Mountain Recreational Resources: A Comparison of Recreation and Tourism in the Colorado Rockies and the Swiss Alps*, Graduate School of Business, University of Colorado, Boulder, Colorado

Tobler, W. (1967/77) 'Spatial interaction patterns', *Journal of Environmental Systems*, **6**, 271–301

Tombaugh, L. W. (1970) 'Factors influencing vacation home location', *Journal of Leisure Research*, **2**, 54–63

Toyne, P. (1974) *Recreation and Environment*, Macmillan Education, London

Tuan, Yi-Fu (1971a) 'Geography, phenomenology, and the study of human nature', *The Canadian Geographer*, **15**, 181–92

Tuan, Yi-Fu (1971b) *Man and Nature*, Resource Paper 10, Association of American Geographers, Washington, DC

Turner, L. (1974) 'Tourism and social science – from Blackpool to Beridorn and Bali', *Annals of Tourism Research*, **1**, 180–205

Turner, L. (1976) 'The international division of leisure: tourism and the Third World', *Annals of Tourism Research*, **4**, 12–24

Ullman, E. L. and Volk, D. J. (1962) 'An operational model for predicting reservoir attendance and benefits: implications of a location approach to water recreation', *Papers of the Michigan Academy of Science, Arts, and Letters*, **47**, 473–84

UNESCO (1976) 'The effects of tourism on socio-economic values', *Annals of Tourism Research*, **4**, 74–105

United States Army Corps of Engineers (June 1974) *Plan Formulation and Evaluation Studies – Recreation*, Vol. II, Appendix A, *Estimating Initial Reservoir Recreation Use – Project Data*, IWR Research Report 74–R1 by the USAE Institute for Water Resources, Kingman Building, Fort Belvoir, Virginia 22060

Van Doren, C. S. (1967) 'A recreational travel model for predicting campers at Michigan State Parks', unpublished PhD dissertation, Department of Geography, Michigan State University, East Lansing, Michigan

Van Doren, C. S. (1975) 'Spatiality and planning for recreation', in van der Smissen, B. (compiler) *Indicators of Change in the Recreation Environment*, 335–58, Penn State HPER Series 6, Department of Health, Physical Education, and Recreation, The Pennsylvania State University, College Park, Pennsylvania

Van Lier, H. N. (1973) *Determination of Planning Capacity and Layout Criteria of Outdoor Recreation Projects*, Centre for Agricultural Publishing and Documentation, Wageningen, The Netherlands

References

Van Lier, H. N. (1978) 'Comments on the article of F. J. Cesario: a new method for analyzing outdoor recreation trip data', *Journal of Leisure Research*, **10**, 150–52

Var T., Beck, R. A. D. and Loftus, P. (1977) 'Determination of touristic attractiveness of the touristic areas in British Columbia', *Journal of Travel Research*, **5**, 23–29

Vaughn, R. (1977) 'Opportunity cost and the assessment and development of regional tourism', in Duffield, B. S. (ed.) *Tourism: A Tool for Regional Development*, 8.1–8.9, Tourism and Recreation Research Unit, University of Edinburgh, Edinburgh

Veal, A. J. (1974) *Environmental Perception and Recreation*, Research Memorandum 39, Centre for Urban and Regional Studies, University of Birmingham, Birmingham, England

Vickerman, R. W. (1975) 'The leisure sector in urban areas', in *The Economics of Leisure and Recreation*, Ch. 8, Macmillan, London

Volk, D. J. (1965) 'Factors affecting recreational use of national parks', paper presented at the Annual Meeting of the Association of American Geographers, Columbus, Ohio

Von Thünen, J. H. (1875) *Der Isolierte Staat in Beziehung auf Landwirtschaft und Nationalökonomie*, 3rd ed., Schumacher-Zarchlin, Berlin

Wall, G. (1971) 'Car owners and holiday activities', in Lavery, P. (ed.) *Recreational Geography*. 97–111, David and Charles, London

Wall, G. and Greer, T. (1980) 'Recreational hinterlands: a theoretical and empirical analysis', in *Contemporary Leisure Research, Proceedings of the Second Canadian Congress on Leisure Research*, 110–19 Ontario Research Council on Leisure, Toronto

Wall, G. and Wright, C. (1977) *The Environmental Impact of Outdoor Recreation*, Publication Number 11, Department of Geography, University of Waterloo, Waterloo, Ontario

Walters, A. A. (1968) *An Introduction to Econometrics*, 125–28, Macmillan, London

Ward, R. A. (1964) *Operational Research in Local Government*, Allen and Unwin, London

Warntz, W. and Neft, D. S. (1960) 'Contributions to statistical methodology for areal distributions', *Journal of Regional Science*, **2**, 47–66

Watson, P. L. (1974) *The Value of Time: Behavioral Models of Modal Choice*, Lexington Books, Lexington, Massachusetts

Weber, A. (1909) *Über den Standort der Industrien, Part I*, Reine Theorie des Standarts, Tübingen

Weber, A. (1911) 'Die standortslehre und die handelspolitik', *Archive für Sozialwissenschaft und Sozialpolitik*, **32**, 667–88

Wehrwein, G. S. and Parson, K. H. (1932) *Recreation as a Land Use*, Bulletin 422, University of Wisconsin Agricultural Experiment Station, Madison, Wisconsin

Wells, W. D. (1975) 'Psychographics: a critical review', *Journal of Marketing Research*, **12**, 196–213

Wennergren, E. B. and Nielsen, D. B. (1968) *A Probabilistic Approach to Estimating Demand for Outdoor Recreation*, Bulletin 478, Utah Agricultural Experiment Station, Logan, Utah

Whetten, N. L. and Rapport, V. A. (1934) *The Recreational Uses of Land in Connecticut*, Bulletin 194, Connecticut Experiment Station, Connecticut State College, Storrs, Connecticut

White, A. N. (1979) 'Accessibility and public facility location', *Economic Geography*, **55**,18–35

White, P., Wall, G. and Priddle, G. (1978) 'Anti-social behavior in Ontario Provincial Parks', *Recreation Research Review*, **6**, 13–23

Whitehead, J. I. (1965) 'Road traffic growth and capacity in a holiday district (Dorset)', *Proceedings of the Institution of Civil Engineers*, **30**, 589–608

Williams, A. V. and Zelinsky, W. (1970) 'On some patterns of international tourist flows', *Economic Geography*, **46**, 549–67

Wolfe, R. I. (1964) 'Perspective on outdoor recreation: a bibliographic survey', *The Geographical Review*, **54**, 203–38

Wolfe, R. I. (1966) *Parameters of Recreational Travel in Ontario*, DHO Report RB111, Department of Highways of Ontario, Downsview, Ontario

Wolfe, R. I. (1967) *A Theory of Recreational Highway Traffic*, DHO Report RR129, Department of Highways of Ontario, Downsview, Ontario

Wolfe, R. I. (1972) 'The inertia model', *Journal of Leisure Research*, **4**, 73–76

Wolfe, R. I. (1978) 'Vacation homes as social indicators: observations from Canadian census data', *Leisure Sciences*, **1**, 327–43

Wolfe, R. I. (1980) 'Pattern of recreational highway traffic in time of energy scarcity', in *Contemporary Leisure Research, Proceedings of the Second Canadian Congress on Leisure Research*, 503–07, Ontario Research Council on Leisure, Toronto

Woodside, A. G. and Etzel, M. J. (1980) 'Impact of physical and mental handicaps on vacation travel behaviour', *Journal of Travel Research*, **18**, 9–11

Woodside, A. S. and Clokey, J. D. (1974) 'Multi-attribute/multi-brand models', *Journal of Advertising Research*, **14**, 33–40

Wright, J. R., Braithwaite, W. M. and Forster, R. R. (1976) *Planning for Urban Recreation Open Space: Toward Community Specific Standards*, Centre for Resources Development, University of Guelph, Guelph, Ontario

Wyckoff, D. D. and Sasser, W. E. (1978) *The Chain-Restaurant Industry*, Lexington Books, Lexington, Massachusetts

Yefremov, Yu. K. (1975) 'Geography of tourism', *Soviet Geography*, **16**, 205–17

Yokeno, N. (1974) 'The general equilibrium system of "space-economies" for tourism', *Reports for the Japan Academic Society of Tourism*, **8**, 38–44

Young, C. W. and Smith, R. V. (1979) 'Aggregated and disaggregated outdoor recreation participation models', *Leisure Sciences*, **2**, 143–54

Zaring, J. (1977) 'The romantic face of Wales', *Annals of the Association of American Geographers*, **67**, 397–418

Zentilli, B. (1975) 'Determining national park boundaries', *Parks*, **1**,7–10

Zipf, G. K. (1946) 'The P_1P_2/D hypothesis: on inter-city movement of persons', *American Sociological Review*, **11**, 677–86

Author Index

210

Author index

Author index

Place index

Austria 150
Australia 27
  Canberra 76, 113
  Fern Tree Gully National Park 94
  Melbourne 87, 95
  New South Wales 64
    Newcastle 64
  North Coast 6–7
    Kingscliffe 7

Bahamas 88
Barbados 88

Canada 8–12, 15, 27, 33, 36, 42–3, 45, 60,
    80, 84, 124, 147, 150, 158, 181–2
  British Columbia 42, 66
    Vancouver Island 95
  Ontario 6, 28–9, 32, 70
    Elmira 150
    London 161–2
    Niagara Falls 69
    Point Pelee National Park 55
    Pukaskwa National Park 14
    Stratford 67
    Toronto 1, 95
    Trent–Severn Waterway 36
  Quebec
    Quebec City 40, 113
  Rocky Mountains 1
  Saskatchewan 133, 144
Caribbean 19, 63, 171, 172
Chile
  Rapa Nui National Park 55
Cuba 63
Czechoslovakia 79

Denmark
  Jutland 63
  Tivoli 83

East Africa 4, 170
East Germany 148
Egypt
  Sinai 59
Eire 149–50

France 62, 79
  Aix-en-Provence 150
  Brittany 150
  Cannes 58, 67
  Paris 3
  Provence 3
  Riviera 150

Germany 82
Great Britain 19, 47, 48, 124, 125
  England 55, 141
    Birmingham 95
    Brighton 3
    Cannock Chase 6
    Dorset 135
    East Sussex 19–20
      Lewes 96–7
    Exeter 68
    Forest of Dean 36, 94, 141
    Isle of Wight 93
    London 94, 142–3
    Watford 78
  Northern Ireland 149, 174
  Scotland 20–1
    Cuillin 19
    Greater Tayside 170

Place index

Subject index

Subject index

Recreation geography

THEMES IN RESOURCE MANAGEMENT
Edited by Professor Bruce Mitchell, University of Waterloo

STEPHEN SMITH

Recreation geography

Longman
London and New York

Longman Group Limited
Longman House
Burnt Mill, Harlow, Essex
CM20 2JE, England
and Associated Companies throughout the World.

*Published in the United States of America
by Longman Inc., New York*

First published 1983

British Library Cataloguing in Publication Data
Smith, Stephen
    Recreation geography. – (Themes in resource management)
    1. Recreation areas
    I. Title   II. Series
    333.7'8   GV182

    ISBN 0-582-30050-9

Library of Congress Cataloguing in Publication Data
Smith, Stephen, 1946–
    Recreation geography.
    (Themes in resource management)
    Bibliography: p.
    Includes index.
    1. Recreation – Research.   2. Recreation areas – Research.
    I. Title.   II. Series.
    GV14.5.S546   1983   790'.072   81-20749
    ISBN 0-582-30050-9   AACR2

Printed in Hong Kong by Astros Printing Ltd